Maxine McKew is a Vice Chancellor's Fellow at the University of Melbourne. She also works as an advisor on education to the not-for-profit group Social Ventures Australia and is a member of the board of Per Capita.

At the 2007 federal election Maxine McKew wrote herself into Australian political history as only the second candidate ever to beat a prime minister in his own seat. She was immediately elevated to the executive and served as Parliamentary Secretary for Early Childhood, and later as Parliamentary Secretary for Infrastructure and Regional Development.

Before making the switch to politics, Maxine had a thirty-year career as a broadcast and print journalist. As host of *Lateline* and part-time anchor of *7.30 Report* she earned a reputation as one of the country's most authoritative interviewers. Her television reporting has been recognised by her peers with both Logie and Walkley awards for broadcast excellence, while her work for *The Bulletin* saw her secure the Magazine Publishers' Award for Columnist of the Year.

A sought-after speaker and facilitator, Maxine is represented by Claxton Communications and is involved in a range of voluntary activities.

Tales from the POLITICAL TRENCHES

MAXINE McKEW

MELBOURNE
UNIVERSITY
PRESS

MELBOURNE UNIVERSITY PRESS
An imprint of Melbourne University Publishing Limited
187 Grattan Street, Carlton, Victoria 3053, Australia
mup-info@unimelb.edu.au
www.mup.com.au

First published 2012
Reprinted (three times), 2012
Text © Maxine McKew, 2012
Design and typography © Melbourne University Publishing Limited, 2012

Cover design by Philip Campbell Design
Typeset in Bembo 12.5/15.5pt by Cannon Typesetting
Printed by Griffin Press, South Australia

National Library of Australia Cataloguing-in-Publication entry

McKew, Maxine.

Tales from the political trenches / Maxine McKew.

9780522862218 (pbk.)
9780522862225 (ebook)

McKew, Maxine.

Australian Labor Party—Biography.
Women politicians—Australia—Biography.
Politicians—Australia—Biography.
Women—Political activity—Australia.
Journalists—Australia—Biography.
Women journalists—Australia—Biography.
Australia—Politics and government—Biography.

324.2092

CONTENTS

ACKNOWLEDGMENTS

I WOULD LIKE to thank the following people for their assistance and wisdom: Trish Drum, Erin Dale, Sue Pike, Trish Hurley, Lucienne Joy and Kathleen O'Hare. Thanks as well to Max Walsh and Tom Hogg for helping me with specialist advice. To the wonderful team at Melbourne University Publishing—Louise Adler, Sally Heath, Cathy Smith, Terri King and Anouska Jones—you have my deep gratitude for your belief in and patience with a first-time author. Thanks as well to Don Watson for constant encouragement and help, and for teaching me the power of a short sentence. To the many ministers, MPs, public servants and staffers, I thank you for your time and candour. I am also particularly grateful to Professor Glyn Davis, Vice-Chancellor at the University of Melbourne, for the provision of a fellowship that allowed me the time and space to write this book. And finally, to my partner Bob, I hope you think this book captures the mad, the bad and the glorious.

IT'S A CONTEST OF IDEAS

'PAUL HERE, MAXINE. Paul Keating.'

Well of course it is. There is no mistaking the voice. It's low, distinctive and full of either threat or promise. Sometimes both. He is calling, as many are, to be part of the thrill of it, and to acknowledge the sheer chutzpah of what turned out to be one of the most audacious of political campaigns: the successful quest to unseat John Howard in his own seat of Bennelong.

'Well done, love. You've sent the little fella packing.'

Keating had followed the 2007 campaign for months and with growing conviction that Kevin Rudd would triumph over his old rival. But Bennelong? Could the Prime Minister, John Howard, be cut down in his own constituency, an area that had kept returning him to office for thirty-three years?

That's exactly what happened. And when the end came, it was an unsentimental despatch. The attitude seemed to be 'enjoy your retirement'. John Howard's parliamentary career ended when the final two-party preferred vote came in at 51.4–48.6 in my favour.

For those of us on the Labor side, in those blissful days straight after the election, everything seemed so clear and straightforward. Howard was history and, as members of Kevin Rudd's new Labor government, we were all set to go for it. We would re-fashion the country. End the culture wars. No more them and us politics. No more Indian doctors like Mohamed Haneef being locked up because of dodgy AFP work.[1] We would build the future, and redefine the 'light on the hill' for a new generation of activists. Creative. Challenging. Positive. That's what I wanted from the new Labor government. That's why I went out and beat Howard.

Far from being cynical about politics, I thought it a grand undertaking. That sentiment was in large part fired by politicians like Keating.

As a younger journalist, fresh from a posting in North America and newly installed as a member of the Canberra press gallery, I was in the room at the National Press Club on the night of 7 December 1990 when Paul Keating delivered his famous Placido Domingo speech. I barely remember the references to the Spanish tenor but the brilliance of the speech was in the generational call to arms. Keating, at that stage still thwarted in his ambition to take over from Bob Hawke as Prime Minister, did something that few ever attempt. He told us why politics matters. He talked about leadership and why it matters. *Politicians change the world.* That's what Paul Keating said that night in what was both a homage to the imagination and fighting spirit of the American presidential greats in willing their nation into being and a rebuke to the mediocrity of much of Australian leadership. As a job application it was in a class of its own. It was equal parts offensive and thrilling.

What I remember most vividly from that night was the final exhortation.

'There are two types in this world—voyeurs and players.' Keating paused and I swear he looked straight at me as he issued his challenge. 'And who wants to be a voyeur?'

I've never forgotten it. I took a long time to make the switch to politics from journalism but by 2007 I'd had enough of asking questions. I had the awards, the kudos, a lot of editorial autonomy, an action-packed CV and more invitations than I could accept. Life was good. Life was too easy. It was certainly too easy playing that familiar party animal, the dinnertime political critic. Although in my household, and with my circle of friends—many of them journalists and political operatives—it was more a case of being the breakfast, lunch and dinner critic.

I didn't want to sit out another election as observer, analyst and scourge. I decided to test myself and be fully engaged in the business of politics. I didn't want to die wondering.

I took the biggest risk of my life and signed up as a player at the beginning of 2007 in the belief that Kevin Rudd, the party's new leader, would have the opportunity to re-imagine the modern Labor story in a government that would chart a new course for a smart, engaged Australia.

As it turned out, my time in politics was intense but brief. As was Rudd's as Prime Minister. While it lasted, I found political life to be intoxicating, joyous, humbling; but also brutish, backstabbing and marked by the kinds of betrayals and dishonesty that I consider to be unforgivable. And self-defeating. Five years on from the historic win against John Howard, when Kevin Rudd delivered his party not just victory but one of the biggest swings in forty years, the Australian Labor Party is fighting for its relevance. According to demographer and former Labor Senator John Black, by the middle of 2012, with most polls showing Labor's primary vote stuck at 30 per cent, Julia Gillard had cost her party two million votes.[2] Rudd had won 5.4 million primary votes at the 2007 federal election with an appeal so broad-based that it shattered John Howard's hold on his own seat of Bennelong.

In 2007 Bennelong voted for change, not for drama and disaffection. And not for the decapitation of a first-term Prime Minister. That should never have happened. But it did happen and it was because the self-interest of a few opportunists trumped the wider interest. The ambition of an impatient deputy has ended up destroying the hopes of those of us who worked hard to bury the Howard years. The massive miscalculation by Gillard and those who supported her move against Rudd in June 2010 has produced, for Labor supporters, the worst of scenarios: the likely triumph of the conservative forces at the next election.

It could have been different and for a while it was.

During that exquisite summer at the end of the year-long campaign and as we entered the 2008 political year, Rudd's first year as Australia's twenty-sixth Prime Minister, there was every reason to believe that we were set for a period of decisive, bold government. We would lead with a sure touch and clarity of purpose.

As I saw it, as the new MP for Bennelong I was about to join a group of savvy, energetic, committed people who wanted what I wanted: a progressive, modern, self-confident Australia that embraced change and saw limitless opportunities in our fortuitous placement as a developed economy in a region that would define the twenty-first century.

Labor MPs, party members and political progressives across the country had all waited a long time for this. Paul Keating, especially, had waited a long time.

After 1996, his own party tried to lock him in a cupboard. Didn't want to know him. 'A massive, massive mistake' is how NSW Senator John Faulkner described to me the attempt by Labor in the opposition years from 1996 on to carve Keating out of the modern Labor story.

It must have cut deep. Being on the outer in a small pond like Australia is a lonely place to be.

But Keating has always been sustained by a genuine inner confidence and an absolute conviction that *his* story would prevail. As a journalist I'd listened to this story first-hand on multiple occasions, at press conferences, at dinners and at the back of the press plane. He got no thanks for it at the time but Keating correctly predicted that Australia was set to soar as we headed into the new century; that if we combined economic vibrancy with a sophisticated and heartfelt reconciliation and regional engagement agenda, then we would be able to confidently claim ownership of what the former PM calls 'a unique socio-economic model'.

I always found this optimistic view of Australia to be both compelling and obvious. It was a story that suited my temperament and beliefs, so during the 2007 campaign I developed my own variation on this theme.

The discipline and clarity of Rudd's key messages—*fairness for working families* and *action on climate change*—were absolutely critical to the success of the national campaign. They were central to mine as well but I had the added complexity of trying to convince a conservative electorate that Labor understood the subtle and interesting ways the area was changing. Wherever I looked across Bennelong—at the research-driven companies clustered around the Macquarie University campus; the small businesses started by newly arrived Chinese and Korean immigrants; or the interesting start-ups, often run by professional women who had fled the family-unfriendly corporate world—it all added up to a community that was smart, ambitious and innovative. So that's how I talked about Bennelong. I talked the area *up* and tried to reflect back to constituents their achievements, as well as pointing to the possibilities ahead under a Labor government.

This rhetorical addition turned out to be a bit too much for one of the lesser media boyos on the national campaign team, who decided I was off the reservation. With no authority from anyone he took it upon himself to make a special trip out to my office in Eastwood. It was towards the end of the campaign, with only weeks to go before the election on 24 November. There were no opening pleasantries.

'Don't fuck with the message, Max-INE!' was the inelegant but economic missive. It was a malicious and unsettling intrusion by someone who was a complete non-entity as far as Rudd and National Campaign Director Tim Gartrell were concerned. When I complained, Gartrell pulled him into line, but if ever there was an early warning sign of the reductionist poison that would crimp our efforts in government, this was it.

I stuck to my guns. Right through the long months of campaigning in 2007, I could see how people were responding to what was a positive, creative and distinctive campaign. Where Howard looked and sounded desperate, I was fearless. I had nothing to lose. Howard's entire career was on the line.

I think this is what Keating liked. The sheer breathtaking front of a local campaign where we went for broke.

And now, a few days after a victory that gave hope to millions across the nation, Keating was on the phone with some advice.

'Remember this. When you get to Canberra, it's a contest of ideas. You got that? It's a contest of ideas. This is the stuff that matters.'

He was right, of course, and I think that most of the class of 2007 believed it. Not all, but most. You can hear it in the language of our first speeches in Parliament—the optimism, the belief, the desire for something better.

On 14 February 2008, at around 1.30 p.m., the new Speaker, Harry Jenkins, gave me the call and I got to my feet for the formal start of my parliamentary career. I had spent a couple of weekends refining what I wanted to say, so with mates, supporters and my stepmother Mary all watching from the public gallery, this is part of what I said:

> I come to this place with the firm conviction that the contest of ideas matters, that belief matters, and knowledge matters. While it is true that the great ideological struggles of the twentieth century are behind us, the ground has shifted in this new decade and in this new century. The sheer complexity of modern life bewilders many, but the new century is also a rich one and there is much to appreciate. The seat of Bennelong, which I am proud to represent, provides a near perfect snapshot of how the country is changing. Join the throng on the weekend in the Eastwood Mall and you find that Rowe Street is a modern day Babel and a dynamic part of cosmopolitan Sydney. There is a younger generation entirely at ease with who we are and what we are becoming. They will be citizens of the world, trained here but orbiting around the world and working and playing in those places that will enrich them.

They will still call Australia home, but when they are in Delhi, Hong Kong or London what story will they be telling about home? How do we want the Australian story to look for the coming generation? I think it needs to be a big story and that it is time to revive some big ambitions about how we build sustainable cities, how we restore our rivers, how we re-create a first-rate education system that elevates excellence for all and how we treat everyone with dignity and equality, regardless of physical ability, race or sexual preference.

I wanted to capture the way the modern Australian story comes together in Bennelong with the well-trained, ethnically diverse and ambitious individuals who live and work in the north-west of Sydney. These are people who are progressive, competitive and outward looking. Howard had always talked about 'the aspirationals' but this was never the right description for the constituents of Bennelong. How could it be? If you live in a $900,000 house in Ryde or Gladesville, then you have well and truly arrived. You may well have a huge mortgage and be as concerned about interest rates as voters in less affluent areas, but you are also politically attuned to a range of higher order issues: climate change action, clever investment in universities and research, intelligent design of city infrastructure and the like. Over and above that, I couldn't fail to notice that Bennelong contained a very high proportion of female working professionals, and many of them had long since tired of Howard's one-foot-in-the-future, one-foot-in-the-past approach.

They are by no means natural Labor voters, but nor can they be accurately described as dyed-in-the-wool conservatives. What I divined, and what Rudd effectively played to nationally throughout 2007, is that you can appeal to these individuals if you have a credible message about the complexities of the modern economy and about smart investment for the future.

The mistaken view of the 2007 Bennelong campaign is that I aggressively chased the Asian vote, but it was always much more broad-based than that. As I told Margot Saville when she was writing her book, *The Battle for Bennelong*, I went after the Liberal vote and that is why Labor secured strong swings in places like Epping and Denistone and Carlingford, affluent Sydney suburbs where Labor's vote had always been weak. By the end of the long Howard years, many Liberals were appalled at the way their Prime Minister and local member was playing fast and loose with the system. There was the casual disregard for the rights of refugees and the long stubborness surrounding the repatriation to Australia of the Guantanamo-detained David Hicks; or, closer to the interests of many, the fundamental breach of basic industrial rights through WorkChoices. No matter how well-off, everyone seemed to have a story of a family member, usually a younger person, who was having difficulty negotiating on their own behalf in Howard's new IR world. Others had had enough of the culture wars. They thought it tedious and were ready for something better.

I thought the new government would put an end to the rancour and bitterness. And that is why I made this plea in my first speech in the Parliament:

> What people want now is an intelligent national conversation. The prevailing orthodoxy to this point has been that, because we are enjoying such bounty, we are indifferent to the bigger societal questions. I happen to think that the 2007 campaign demolished that idea. Most of the commentators missed the mood shift. But it is there. All sorts of people know that politics and policymaking matter. Our national spirit matters. The lesson for me from the past year is that there is a great reservoir of goodwill that lies untapped beneath the surface of our national life, and smart governments will find ways to liberate and direct it.

Looking back on these words five years later, and still dealing with the disappointment of not retaining Bennelong at the 2010 election, I am left asking the obvious questions.

How did we squander the opportunity? How did we manage to execute a strategic and timely intervention during the global financial crisis only to have a majority of Australians write us off as inferior economic managers? Why did we buckle so early on a market mechanism for dealing with climate change? And above all, having got rid of John Howard—from the prime ministership and from his own seat—how the hell have we managed to ensure that it is the Howard legacy, and not a reformist Labor legacy, that is still central to the national narrative?

It is a bitter fact for my side of politics that the Howard years are still with us. Consider the rhetoric concerning refugees. It's still fearful, not welcoming. And just like Howard, the Gillard government chooses to play divide and rule. Instead of the embrace of a grand coalition, the Prime Minister indulges her Treasurer Wayne Swan as he takes irrelevant swipes at a couple of the country's billionaires.[3] Gillard herself favours a geographic divide: the North Shore versus the rest. And where Howard traded on a certain societal nostalgia for the world of Don Bradman and stay-at-home mums, Labor in office has flirted with economic nostalgia: for protectionism and industry handouts.

One of the deepest points of distress for Labor supporters, and the reason we have lost significant votes to the left and the right, is our comprehensive failure to articulate and act on our core beliefs and, in doing so, to change the tone of the country. It's no longer a simple case of battlers versus elites. Now everyone is yelling from their own corner. Debate today is more shrill than sane. What passes for public discourse is extreme and vacuous sloganeering.

Above all, Paul Keating's dictum that 'the contest of ideas matters' seems like something from another era. It's been replaced by a bitter contest of personalities.

In any job I've had, I've always gravitated to where the intellectual energy is, but that was difficult to locate by the time I arrived in Canberra. As a new government we seemed consumed with busyness, announcements, doorstops, photo opportunities, facile point-scoring on Sky News every morning and of course the ubiquitous 'talking points'—a set of notes churned out daily by the media masters in the Prime Minister's office that was nothing more than a childish summary of the government's message. It had little to do with communication but everything to do with control. It turned out that the attitude of 'don't fuck with the message' was not an aberration but a guiding star.

The infuriating thing for many ministers is that a mountain of good policy work was undertaken from the start, but it was as if we didn't believe in it enough to take the time to explain the complexity. Either that or we had such a low opinion of the electorate that we thought they wouldn't be able to digest it. I recall one minister who had a fondness for referring to the electorate as 'bogans'. Why bother to lift the tone if your attitudes form a snug fit with a Chris Lilley caricature?

It's hard not to conclude that at some point in the last decade the political class gave up on the contest of ideas and the only thing that is left is a shouting contest. The media love the theatrics, and who can blame them if the political class doesn't take itself seriously?

Labor has paid a very big price for underestimating the electorate, for talking down to people. The rage reflected in Labor's abysmal polling ever since the disastrous election result of August 2010 is the voice of voters screaming back at the government, 'We're not ten-year-olds!'

It could have been so different. There *is* a confident, sophisticated Labor story to tell about our present and our future and it needs to be based on our capacity for innovation, the creativity of our workforce and our openness to others.

Instead, we have sounded punitive and scolding. Rather than lift the nation with some inspiring words, Julia Gillard's first message as Prime Minister was to tell Australians that they should 'set their alarm clocks early'.[4]

Is this the best that modern Labor can do? It is certainly a long way from the party of Chifley and Whitlam and Hawke and Keating—the great enlargers who weren't afraid of power and who used the authority of office to bully and charm the nation into being better than it thought it was.

The trade-offs involved in minority government have meant there is no longer any political capital to draw on. But even when there was, after Rudd's extraordinary win in 2007, we failed to use it properly. I think it's because we lacked an updated and relevant analysis of the world in which we were operating. And I don't just mean the big strategic regional shifts, but the societal shifts: the different ways we live and work. A world where there is increasingly less distinction between home space and work space. This is the iPad generation, one that is constantly 'on'. They don't use alarm clocks. It's a world where education, training and work are no longer distinct entities, where a different conception of these activities is producing a new kind of creative worker. A world where a good idea that's hatched in North Ryde can source capital in South-East Asia and use social media for everything from hiring to marketing.

And see over there the 24-year-old knowledge worker perched precariously on the kite ski off St Kilda beach? She's off to Shanghai next week and she may not be back for quite a while.

And over here, the tall thin kid up the front of the class? He's an Afghan refugee who is learning English in record time at Marsden High School in Sydney's north-west. Look out for him because he already has three jobs, is whip-smart, self-reliant and bloody grateful to be here.

Paul Keating calls these individuals the 'new wealth workers' and it was Labor governments throughout the 1980s and '90s that built the economic and social incubator that enabled their emergence.

This was the inheritance. So what happened?

When we roared back into office at the end of 2007 we had many of the right ideas and policy approaches to appeal to these people, but we lacked a coherent intellectual foundation. There was no broad agreement across the leadership group and across the ministry of the key principles that should guide the moulding of modern Australia. The long years in opposition had not been put to good use to develop that framework.

Keating refers to this period, from the loss of government in 1996 to 2007, as 'Labor's lost years'. You can argue this is self-serving but it's hard to deny when you consider the history.

From 1996 on, Labor was fixated on finding the next messiah, changing leaders five times—Kim Beazley to Simon Crean to Mark Latham, back to Beazley and finally Kevin Rudd. With all the intrigue and effort that went into this, it left too little time for the work that would arm the leader with some integrated policy firepower.

Labor needed to craft the 21st-century version of the economic reform agenda inherited from Hawke and Keating. Had the party done so, the Rudd government would have been better placed to turn the deftly managed global financial crisis into a massive opportunity. Instead, from 1996 on, there was deep ambivalence about the inheritance. Many in the party wanted to run from the record.

As Annabel Crabb has documented in *Losing It*, the die was cast early in 1997 when Beazley as Labor opposition leader staged a retreat from parts of this agenda:

> Labor, he promised, would freeze tariffs in the car and textile industries and re-regulate the workplace, giving workers greater certainty about their livelihoods. His tone was one of apology for the discomfort occasioned by the former Labor government's activities and he acknowledged that Keating had blocked his ears to voters' concerns.[5]

There aren't too many leaders who don't attempt to re-badge themselves and break, to some extent, from the record of their predecessors. With a figure as controversial as Keating, Beazley's approach was, in part, understandable. But the result was policy confusion on the broader economic strategy and it lasted for years. It was a failure of nerve. A failure of belief.

The contradictions mounted as Beazley spent months pursuing Howard over the details of his consumption tax, the GST; he was utterly convinced he was on the path to victory in

2001 with his 'rollback' policy. Ahead of the election, Beazley promised a staged removal of the tax from some key household expenditures.

But there was no unity on this one. NSW party secretary John Della Bosca could see that in a modern economy there was no sense in denying an obvious source of revenue to the government and that Howard was set to snooker Beazley. In an interview that I secured for *The Bulletin* magazine in July 2000, Della Bosca advised Beazley to forget about 'rollback' because the constant negative carping was a vote loser for Labor.

Della Bosca realised, as Beazley did not, that Howard was set to reap the reward from the Keating era: voters were actually open to the idea of economic change if they could see that it was in the national interest. Instead of viewing the 1998 election as a near miss and a dress rehearsal for an inevitable victory next time round, Della Bosca thought it was a cack-handed effort that walked away from the successes of the past:

> If you do a micro-analysis of the seats that people whinged about us not winning, not just in Sydney, but in Brisbane and Melbourne, you can identify booths where overwhelmingly, the tertiary educated 35–50 year olds voted against us. And these were people who even stayed with us in Keating's last election. But we actually offended these people. Howard has made them his people. But they're our people. Many have been with us since university days. But we turned them off by some of the bland things we had Kim say.[6]

There was a media firestorm when this was published and the price for this burst of political honesty was that Della Bosca lost his chance to become party president. I was tagged as some kind of political Jezebel for cruelling the chances of an important powerbroker, but my only act of sabotage had been to turn on a tape recorder.

Della Bosca, to his great credit, took it in his stride and a few months later made sure to send me a Christmas card. We both knew the interview represented a rare break from the policy timidity that seemed to have a grip on Labor.

While the party was embroiled in these internal arguments, the rest of the country was just getting on with it. We escaped the Asian financial crisis and the post 9/11 downturn in the United States.

In 2006 George Megalogenis pointed out in *The Longest Decade* that: 'History has validated Paul Keating in an unexpected way. The decade that followed his recession has run over time, into what the calendar said was the new millennium, because we kept growing when the rest of the world shrank in 2001.'[7]

Six years after Megalogenis wrote this, we are in very different territory: a post-GFC world of bewildering complexity, mass unemployment in the Northern Hemisphere, widespread insecurity, and with little in the way of decisive leadership coming out of either North America or Europe.

But it has been a very different story at the bottom of the Pacific.

In the wake of the collapse of the US financial services firm Lehman Brothers in September 2008, the event that triggered the GFC, Rudd's Labor government kept Australia working through one of the greatest financial convulsions since the Depression. Our banks remained profitable because the government provided a guarantee so that they could keep borrowing, and our major institutions, in particular the Australian Prudential Regulation Authority, did the job they were set up to do. Our housing market was not hit with anything like the price reversals that have been a feature in the United States. Fiscal stimulus, through two major government packages, boosted domestic demand and growth in employment, while exports grew due to demand from China.

It's been an exceptional achievement. The disgrace is that we limped into the election in August 2010 and manifestly failed to even mention this triumph. On election night, as we tracked Labor's collapse and the loss of the hard-won majority of the 2007 poll, with Bennelong one of the early casualties, I pointed out the obvious in an interview with ABC Television's election night host Kerry O'Brien: that our campaigning was woeful because we never claimed the success that we'd engineered. We had allowed our political rivals to define us by our failures.

It's been downhill ever since, with Labor driven by the agendas of others. As the party has staggered from one mishap to another, and been handicapped by its minority status since the 2010 election, it has suffered the further ignominy of being seen by a majority of Australians as substandard economic managers. This is in stark contrast to the multiple endorsements of the superiority of the Australian economic model that continue to come from pre-eminent international bodies, such as the IMF and the OECD. So what explains this massive disconnect?

When I started to write this book at the end of 2011, I kept thinking back to what Paul Keating had said to me after Labor's win at the end of 2007, that politics is a contest of ideas.

When he published his book *After Words* in November 2011, I read through it looking for some of the answers to Labor's contemporary problems. And there are many. Keating says that the Australian Labor Party, Australia's oldest political party, having survived since 1891, is 'a very hard outfit to manage at the best of times'.

Of the Hawke–Keating years, he writes:

> The achievement of the last Labor government was to know and understand the party's innate altruism and to take the time to guide it towards the world Australia had to belong to. To include it in the deliberations of government. To bring its constituent unions into the policy milieu. To give it a sense of mission. To convince it that Labor had power at an utterly critical juncture in Australia's history and that although the party had faced all sorts of challenges in the past, including war and depression, we had never had to change by root and branch—to fundamentally remake—a peacetime economy. This was hard work. But it was done willingly, cheerfully, and persuasively by a Cabinet with an amazing degree of policy unity and purpose.[8]

It's sixteen years since Keating lost to Howard and the country hasn't always been kind to him. One of his closest political friends, Bill Kelty, has told me of the numerous gratuitous and hostile insults Keating copped after the 1996 election.

Keating played a hard game, a ferocious game, and suffered significant payback. But he's survived all that and now there's been a shift in sentiment. It's as if Australians have forgotten why they were grumpy with Keating. When he speaks at public events, they now turn up in large numbers to enjoy the wit and the one-liners, and to get a bit wistful about the way we were.

When we meet up again in Sydney, in late November 2011, it's a fine spring day and in the streets that surround Keating's office in Potts Point you can feel the hard charge of life in Australia's biggest city. But inside Keating's domain, the visitor enters an extraordinary space—a large, elegant room decorated in the Directoire style of post-Revolutionary France. It seems pedestrian to call it 'an office'. It's more like a salon. The lighting is low rather than harsh, and Keating works, writes and thinks from a large round desk in the middle of the room. Every feature speaks to Keating's particular aesthetic: the interest in and inspiration he takes from the best of the neoclassical period at the end of the eighteenth century, when furniture, design and architecture reflected the new ideas of liberation and enlightenment.

'It all starts back there, love,' he tells me. 'The beginning of modern politics.'

But I'm here to talk about the more recent past. What about the state of the Labor Party now? Can it regain its reforming heart and a broadbased appeal? Keating is in a mood to talk. For a warm-up he takes aim at the current political class.

'Too many of them pop the bland tablet every morning. Either that or they fear the forces they will unleash if they change the template. Or perhaps it is because they have no source of inner renewal other than the latest late-night TV show, or the latest polling figures, or the latest briefing note. This is not enough.'

He goes on to lambast 'the factional tintookies' in the federal Labor caucus: 'We have them to thank for the fact that Rudd blinked on the CPRS.' In targeting the factional chiefs and party bosses, among them Mark Arbib and Karl Bitar, who worked from the end of 2009 on undermining a core government mechanism for tackling climate change—the proposed Carbon Pollution Reduction Scheme—Keating knows his party has drifted a long way from the sense of 'innate altruism' that in an earlier era made room for the negotiation of complex policy.

Keating is contemptuous of these modern operatives: 'In my day they wouldn't have got near the door. I regard all these people as lesser mortals. They don't get the message. They don't have the vocation, and high political art is a vocation.' Keating points to the 600-page tome, *After Words*, on the desk in front of him: 'It's all in there.'

After Words is an impressive compilation of Keating's ideas and speeches. When I bought a copy at my local bookshop the young woman who served me said she had been reading parts of it, in particular Keating's revealing introduction, which owes more to philosophy than to political theory. 'I didn't know we had politicians who thought like this.' Did I detect a girlish swoon?

I've seen this before. People meet Keating, men and women, and the effortless seduction begins. Some go weak at the knees. Keating without the armour is a very attractive individual. He spoke at a community event in Bennelong for me in 2008 and was such a hit I finished the event by telling the crowd that 'every woman in the room wanted to take him home and do him slowly'.

But today it's Keating the analyst who is making some emphatic points: 'The problem for Labor in recent years is that we have not had the main story out there. We needed to say that Labor is the party of transitions. Chifley did the transition from the war to the peacetime economy. Hawke and Keating did the transition from the old Australian model to the open competitive model we have today. This has seen major societal shifts. We are in transition again and now we have a much stronger economic base from which to work. But the transition now has to be a strategic and cultural transition. Everything the government does should be in this context.'

Keating does give huge credit to Rudd for managing the GFC and says it gave the government 'a new focus and sense of purpose'. In political terms, it was a gift, one of those turning points where an unexpected crisis can be used to create new opportunities.

But from the time it was obvious that the billion-dollar stimulus packages were working, when the growth and employment figures held throughout 2009, Keating reckons the government lost sight of the main point. 'We got through the GFC, but we treated it as a cameo event. We missed the opportunity to capitalise on the achievement by contextualising it.'

Gesturing out to the busy scene beyond his office, Keating talks with frustration about the current crop of Labor politicians who seem to want to run away from the remarkable story that is contemporary Australia: 'Look out there. That's the service economy. We created that. We now have a higher proportion of self-employed people. More individuals with a higher net wealth. For our traditional constituents we have had a 30 per cent increase in real wages since 1990, where wages have stayed flat in America. We have a superannuation system and universal coverage in health.' He poses the rhetorical question: 'Is it beyond the wit of the Labor party to represent that?'

Keating knows it is more complex than this, that in the post-GFC world where a financial seizure has now turned into a sovereign debt crisis, leaders the world over are struggling on multiple fronts. All the more reason, he argues, for 'centre-left parties to stand their ground and articulate what they stand for'.

He's impatient with arguments that suggest a historic shift of votes to the Greens or elsewhere. He comes back to his main point. Get the story right and give it everything you've got. 'Look, nothing will ever substitute for political dexterity, belief and energy. Nothing.'

On any reasonable analysis none of these things were on display during the 2010 election campaign. Perhaps the worst capitulation was the rejection of Rudd's earlier embrace of a big Australia.

Gillard wanted to shore up votes in monocultural Lindsay, the outer-western Sydney seat, but it turned out to be a disaster. In other seats, with large concentrations of voters from different ethnic backgrounds, Gillard's strategy seemed clear enough. She was substituting policy for a dog-whistle slogan: 'Where will we all fit?' It came across as a personal insult. Labor had nearly always been the first party of choice for newly arrived immigrants, yet here was a federal Labor government offloading the blame for the wider problems of poor planning and urban congestion. That's how it was read, and in every migrant-dominated seat in Sydney, Labor's vote went backwards. Where the margins were slim in a seat like Bennelong, it was lost to Labor and I was a goner.

The electoral cost is one thing. We are now at a point where Labor's attitudes to immigration and the confusion and lack of perspective we've developed about unauthorised boat arrivals are costing us in multiple ways.

'There is a miserableness about it and it came from Howard,' says Keating. 'It is noted in the region. As a result we look intolerant and unreasonable and unkind.'

The Labor government turned itself inside out in the wake of the 2011 High Court decision that comprehensively rejected the notion that refugees could be traded and transported across the seas to Malaysia.

Keating and I talk about this a lot. And the conversation comes back to Keating's nemesis, John Howard, who dramatically recast the debate on refugees and their treatment. So much so that eleven years after the Norwegian freighter the MV *Tampa*, with its boatload of 438 rescued Afghans, was refused permission by John Howard's government to enter Australian waters, the Tories still scream, 'Stop the boats!' Could it have been different? Was there any point at which Labor could have regained the moral high ground and altered the national conversation?

'Look,' says Keating with exasperation, 'it's the job of leaders to protect the country from its prejudice.'

Instead Labor in government has reframed *parts* of Howard's policy approach and has ended up with the kind of contortions that divide new arrivals into good and bad. Legal and illegal. Authorised and unauthorised. ASIO-approved or not.

Keating sees no point in this: 'Here we are with a continent of our own. Twenty-odd million of us and we try to pretend that the great human community outside of Australia has no right to be here and we will send them back if they try. Howard started it and it's like a virus. And the great mistake that Labor made was to effectively join with the Tories in making the phony distinctions between the civic community and the human community. Who is in and who is out? It's an issue Labor can never win on and why would you want to? In the meantime Tony Abbott is hugely negative and in many respects disgraceful, but he has currency because no one is going for him.'

It's an issue that smacks of our historic insecurity, of fear of the other, and puts at risk our 'unique socio-economic model'. Keating has no doubt where this leads.

'We end up as a country with a kind of spiritless contentment. No longer infused by truth and goodness. And whenever a country is not infused by truth and goodness it's on a path to nowhere. It's a malaise and we lose our essence.'

If, in a *Sliding Doors* moment, Keating could have been matched against John Howard in the *Tampa* election of 2001, he may not have won with language like this, but he would certainly have put some zest and moral fervour into the contest. It would have been a battle of ideas. He would at least have brought a sense of proportion to the debate and quite possibly saved his party ten years of prevarication as he argued a simple and inescapable proposition: there is no future in being suspicious of foreigners. It's a really bad look.

*

Throughout 2012, Labor MPs have told me that they face the cold contempt of voters as they move around their electorates. The euphoria and great expectations of the 2007 win have vanished. Kevin Rudd was the people's choice to replace John Howard but his untimely and brutal removal only two-and-a-half years into his prime ministership has never been accepted by Australian voters. Labor's collapse in public support and credibility can be dated from that moment. When she cut down Rudd, Julia Gillard said she would 'move forward', but she moved her party and the government to the precipice. She substituted deal-making for leadership but voters were not fooled; they saw the deals as either mediocre or tawdry. It has made it just about impossible to see the good policy work that has been done—in education, in housing, in disability care, in reform of entitlements and much else. I feel for the ministers, the staffers and the thousands of supporters for whom the Labor cause is a way of life. What sense of accomplishment will they feel after the long, grinding days and nights of effort? Will there be a substantial legacy from his period? For the most part, Labor people love to honour the past, both the wins and the noble failures, but in years to come, when we look back on this period, will there be any joy in the story we tell of the time we beat John Howard and attempted a fresh start in government? I'm not sure about that.

I very much doubt that any of us will be able to write about our time in government in the way that Paul Keating describes a time, not so long ago, when the Labor effort was all that it could be:

> … it never felt like anything less than an adventure. It felt like a big story then, and it feels like it now. It felt like we were making of Australia what it could be and should be. That we'd been granted this fantastic opportunity and privilege. In those thirteen years Australia was refashioned—not in every detail, and not always to the point of completion. No such point exists in my experience … but it was an unprecedented

period of deliberate and often brave reform in which the government and the people strived to make Australia a first-rate country—a place with a powerful economic engine and a soul to match. Sprawling and strange to outside eyes—but savvy and subtle and worldly. Sometimes you could feel the charge of energy that came from this sense of common purpose. It was palpable.[9]

Chapter 2
IT'S ALL POLITICAL ...

I CAN'T REMEMBER a time when I wasn't interested in politics. I was certainly intensely aware from a very young age that the powerful get to make decisions that determine the fate of the less powerful.

I was five when my world changed. I have a family photo, a small black-and-white one, dated July 1958. I look at it now, at the four of us—my father Brian with a protective hand on my shoulder, my mother Elaine holding my baby sister Margo, only five months old, newly christened—and everything appears as it should. We're just back from Sunday mass and standing against the big old mango tree in the backyard of the post-war Brisbane house that Dad built himself at Moorooka on the south side of Brisbane. There is pride in this photo. You can see it in the way my mother has us dressed: hats and coats, de rigueur for the times. And there is something else. Solidness and certainty. It's an image that says, 'We are a family, we are Catholic, we work for what we have, and we believe that tomorrow will be better than today.'

They say pictures don't lie but my fading photo tells a false story.

In August 1958, a month after we'd all posed in front of the mango tree, Elaine was buried from St Brendan's Catholic Church in Moorooka. Dead at thirty-three from cancer. There will be no more photos of this family. My first lesson in life? There are no certainties.

In the 1950s dads did not look after children so we were split up. My sister was cared for by a close friend, and I went to live with my grandparents, Joe and Eileen Truda, who lived an hour-and-a-half north of Brisbane at Scarborough. It was a big change. It was Joe who took me to my first day at school and Nan who took me to mass and bought the white frock and veil for my First Communion. I adored them. They were spirited people, but their hearts never healed from the loss of their only daughter. Instead, they took me in, a small sad girl, and put me at the centre of their lives.

All these arrangements changed again three years later when Dad remarried. Thank god he did because when he met Mary Rickards, a young schoolteacher, it gave him another chance: a chance to reunite his family and bring everyone back under the one roof at Moorooka. Mary would be our new mother.

It all made perfect sense. Except that we were all strangers. For three years Dad and Margo, a growing toddler, were weekly visitors, not a daily presence in my life. I didn't like the idea of another disruption. Second life lesson? Grown-ups make the decisions.

Living with my grandparents at Scarborough had been a great adventure. Surrounded on all sides by the calm waters of Deception Bay, Scarborough was a bit of a sleepy hollow, a place for pensioners and old diggers with time on their hands and stories to tell. Most of them ended up every other day in my grandparents' general store at the top of Jeays Street. When I wasn't wandering around the bayside jetties, the 'shop' was my playground, both after school and on weekends. No one told me to get lost and play outside so I hung around and listened to the adults. They mostly talked about themselves, and the world of tides and trawlers that governed life around the Bay. There was some lingering anti-Japanese sentiment from the war years, but when a local student scored honours in Japanese language studies, it was a point of community pride.

Joe's constant admonition was, 'In business you don't talk about politics or religion'—but, happily, the wider world intruded and this rule was breached daily. So I started to hear about Menzies, or 'pig-iron Bob' as he was to Eileen, my Irish grandmother. There was always a strong anti-British streak with my nan so Menzies' deference towards 'perfidious Albion' inspired constant scorn. Joe's heritage was Italian, and although born in Brisbane, he had an anti-occupier sentiment about him that was straight out of the Mezzogiorno.

Irish and Italian. It was a combustible mix. But it worked and above all I remember my grandparents constantly talking and laughing and encouraging the same in me. They didn't know the meaning of being standoffish. They were engaged and engaging and half of Scarborough seemed to gather around Nan's table for Sunday lunch.

It was from them that I first heard about the Great War and the Depression, and how they'd lost their house and so much more. Life was pinched for a long time during the 1930s but then the Americans arrived and helped to 'save' Australia in World War II. As my grandparents saw it, it was pretty straightforward. Labor's wartime Prime Minister, John Curtin, had done the right thing in looking to America, and the subsequent arrival of General Douglas MacArthur in Brisbane as Supreme Commander of Allied Forces in the South-West Pacific Area was a turning point in the fortunes of the nation. It was also something of an economic salvation for my grandparents. By the time war broke out, they'd managed to lease a shop and café at Newstead Wharf at Breakfast Creek, the entry point to the city's heart. As thousands of American servicemen poured into Brisbane, plenty of them found their way to Truda's café. Joe took the orders and Nan fed the fleet. The Battle of Brisbane, two nights of brawling and rioting by American and Australian servicemen, was waged south of the river but the only fights that Nan recalled were over who would get the last batch of her steak and kidney pies.

At the end of the 1940s they moved to Scarborough, but those intense war years always remained vivid to them. As a child I would pour over the groaning albums full of black-and-white photographs of young lean soldiers, Aussies and Yanks, all in together, some on home leave, some waiting to be shipped out. They all look so young and unspoiled by life. In some of them you glimpse an eighteen-year-old Elaine, tall and lithe and with her life ahead of her. By war's end, my grandparents were as jubilant as everyone else but mainly about one thing: their daughter hadn't ended up on a troopship bound for life on the other side of the Pacific as a war bride.

As with many families, for years after, letters would be exchanged between American and Australian families, and photos of smart American bungalows and new babies would be sent, as friendships forged in adversity were maintained.

Hearing all this in such a lively way from Nan and Joe is the reason I never grew up with any of the anti-American prejudice common to so many of my generation. My grandparents didn't live long enough to see me take up a post in the mid-1980s as foreign correspondent for the ABC based in North America, but I know they would have liked the way I gathered my own stories and made my own cross-Pacific friendships.

I loved telling American pals about how Australian Catholics had helped John Kennedy get elected to the White House in 1960. I was seven at the time and the nuns had us on our increasingly sore and scuffed knees praying for the election of the very first Catholic American President. We also had to send up daily missives to the Virgin Mary to hurry up and see to the conversion of Russia. For a bunch of schoolkids in the back-waters of Scarborough and Brisbane, we were running a crowded geopolitical agenda!

And people in Nan and Joe's shop never did manage to avoid politics. They argued the rights and wrongs of the Queensland ALP split and Vince Gair's expulsion from the party while still Premier of the state. Little noticed was the rise and rise of Johannes

Bjelke-Petersen, a farmer and Sunday school teacher and soon-to-be Cabinet minister in the Nicklin Country Party government.

So in this entirely unconscious and unstructured way, I developed a political consciousness. I was curious about the world. I asked a lot of questions. I looked beyond the front fence. I relished discussion about big things and developed a distrust of repression.

I was clueless about the way political parties worked and about the machinery of government. Even the idea of communicating with a politician wouldn't have occurred to me. Direct action for me was nothing more daring than the drafting and sending of a letter to the editor of *The Courier-Mail* to protest the censorship of an Athol Fugard play. One of my teachers told me the correspondence was the act of a show-off. But for boldness, it hardly compares with Paul Keating joining the ALP at fifteen; or Kevin Rudd, at the same age, seeking and receiving advice from the then Leader of Her Majesty's Opposition, Gough Whitlam, about how to pursue a future diplomatic career.

By the 1960s I was back living at Moorooka with Dad, Mary and Margo. We were all negotiating the politics of our new family arrangements. I chafed at the decisions others made on my behalf. They were never malign but they weren't *my* decisions. I was learning about power.

I also discovered I wanted a whole lot more than what Brisbane was offering in the 1960s. The writer David Malouf captures perfectly in many of his earlier novels the humid languor and deep provincialism of a subtropical town that seemed to be so far from the centre of things. Unimagined in those days was the café society that Brisbane is now home to, with the glitter of Southbank and buildings such as the Gallery of Modern Art as great metropolitan landmarks.

I felt starved. Of what? For a long time I didn't know. I just sensed there was a wider world out there and I wanted to know about it. *The Courier-Mail*, dropped on our lawn every morning, wasn't much help, so on weekends I would walk to the local shops and buy a copy of the Saturday *Australian* newspaper. Rupert

Murdoch began publishing the country's first national newspaper in 1964 and for me it was a window to a wider world.

It was just the right supplement to the kind of education I was receiving in my high school years at All Hallows' School, which was situated right in the centre of the city. A Sisters of Mercy Catholic school, All Hallows' was founded by Mother Vincent Whitty in 1861 and provided the first secondary schooling for girls in Queensland. It's a legendary institution and over the years has had exceptional stewardship. My stepmother Mary was educated there in the 1930s. Remarkably for the times, given that so few Queenslanders received anything like twelve years of schooling, Mary completed her Senior Examinations just as war broke out in the Pacific and then went to study at teachers' college.

Twenty years after Mary's graduation in 1940, when Margo and I were there, many of the same women who had taught during the 1930s were still teaching and the best of them did what all good teachers do: they took their charges on a daily journey of intellectual discovery and fired the imaginations of their students. Most exercised the authority they had with a light touch. Only the deeply insecure and barely competent (and there were a few) increased their blood pressure over minor rule infringements. The older I get the more I appreciate that I was taught by women, by lay and religious staff, who seemed to me to know what was worth knowing. In a geographic sense, the sisters lived tiny lives in the pre–Vatican II era, rarely venturing beyond the confines of the convent. Perhaps a short trip outside to St Stephen's Cathedral, but that was it. Yet my memory is of a group of women who, for the most part, were not bound by borders or prejudice. They were independent minded, a match for any bishop and, strange as it might sound, worldly in their outlook. So much of what I value—beauty, friendship and the life of the mind—was nurtured at All Hallows'.

There were plenty of debates and arguments at school, including about the Democratic Labor Party and whether Gough Whitlam could break the stranglehold of conservative rule in Canberra.

Vietnam was a slow-burn issue through the 1960s but by the end of the decade it was acutely personal as we all knew boys who were dreading 'the call-up' through national conscription. Whitlam promised to end the absurdity of an arrangement that could send you off to war at age twenty, yet consider you ineligible to vote until the age of twenty-one. *That* got our attention.

There was no political epiphany for me. I was a school prefect but didn't display any overt leadership skills. I wasn't much of a joiner, but a classic 'me, myself, I' product of the '60s. No one ever wrote on my report card: 'This girl is destined to beat a Prime Minister in his own seat.' Instead there was this all too prescient comment: 'Maxine is quite bright but has an inability to concentrate for any length of time.' Little wonder that I ended up working to the tight deadlines and instant amnesia of the mass media!

By the time I finished school in 1970 I had worked out that I wanted to play in a big pond. My one ambition was to escape Brisbane. Straight from school I headed off to the state's only university, the University of Queensland in Brisbane's riverside St Lucia and enrolled in an Arts degree. It was a mistake. I had no focus and dwindling interest in my chosen subjects, and was shocked to discover that the contemporary equivalents of Jean-Paul Sartre and Simone de Beauvoir were apparently on sabbatical. My Left Bank lay elsewhere.

I decided that I could reconnect with academic study later. I cancelled my courses and hatched a plan to get out of town. I worked three jobs at one point, saved enough for an air ticket and, just after my twentieth birthday, headed off to London.

My exit was within a few months of Gough Whitlam's victory for Labor at the 1972 election, and a lot of expatriate Australians were making the reverse journey. No matter. I'd tell the Londoners about the new Antipodes, about the intellectual energy and lustre that Whitlam had brought to high office and the way his reformist activism was transforming Australia.

After backpacking through Europe, I ended up with a job in the perfect place for me: the BBC's External Services Newsroom at Bush House in The Strand in London. Surrounded by people from all over the world—South Africans, New Zealanders, East Europeans, Canadians—it was a United Nations of journalism and the beginning of my real tertiary education.

My talents were so deeply appreciated by the most prestigious public broadcasting organisation in the world that I was plonked in front of an aged Olivetti, and paid (sort of) to type out copy that could be read and heard as far away as Moorooka if anyone cared to find the bandwidth. I remember only one point of tutelage: 'We put the "u" in Labour here, dear, where it properly belongs.'

What a job. British work practices being what they were in the 1970s, an eight-hour shift could be finished in a third of the time, so I got down to my real work: reading the newspapers—dozens and dozens of them from everywhere. And there were plenty of people who wanted to talk about the world of power and politics. Would US President Richard Nixon be impeached? What chance of another war between Israel and her neighbours? There was the oil shock. What did this mean?

In Britain, the protracted coal strike had brought about the three-day work week for industry and forced a change of government. A genuine change in the way unions operated would take another decade and would see a historic showdown between Margaret Thatcher and Arthur Scargill, but the dress rehearsal took place in the 1970s and for a time Britain seemed a bleak and hostile place.

But not inside the world of Bush House, where conversation was never dull. No talk of tides and trawlers here. I learned some important things at Bush House. Chief among them was that when it comes to jobs it's not the entry point or the title that matters, but the people who surround you and how willing they are to share what they know.

I've met thousands of whingers and misery warts and naysayers in my time—the people who will constantly block you and tell you why you *can't* do something—but fortunately their names elude me. It was at Bush House that I developed a knack for heading towards the most interesting group of people in the room. I still do. Go where the energy is and see what happens. That was the approach I developed as a twenty-something and it hasn't been a bad guide.

I worked at the BBC for just over six months, but that was enough to help me secure a cadetship not long after at the ABC in Brisbane in 1974. It led to a happy and productive thirty-year career as a broadcast and print journalist, principally with ABC Television and, in the late 1990s, with *The Bulletin* magazine. I never really planned any of it but it turned out to be the perfect marriage of my talents with my interests. I made a living out of being curious, doing my homework and taking the time to *listen* to what influential people were saying.

It helped that I was a bit of a gypsy, prepared to up stakes and go where the promotions seemed to take me. Courtesy of the ABC, I worked in most of the country's capitals. My rise through the ranks was incremental rather than spectacular.

Nonetheless, my eyes were always firmly on the prize. In the same way that Paul Keating would become the pin-up boy for a whole generation of political junkies, his journalistic equivalent in the 1970s and '80s was Richard Carleton. Working for the ABC and then later for *60 Minutes*, he was an arresting television presence. You were not distracted when he was on the screen. Carleton was stylish, commanding, distinctive, iconoclastic. His work didn't necessarily break news, but his singular skill was in capturing the high drama and the thrill of politics.

I wanted to be him. A lot of us did.

Then, as now, the opportunities at the top were limited. I will be forever grateful to the executive producer who, quite early in my career, helpfully suggested that I readjust my ambition and forget about being a current affairs interviewer–presenter: 'Maxine, some have it, some don't. You don't make the cut.'

What a gift this was. To this point I'd been captive to a lot of fears and doubts. Everyone else seemed smarter and better connected. But all that vanished in an instant as I looked at the dishevelled television executive in front of me—shirt hanging out over a well-lunched gut—who was telling me, in no uncertain terms, to get back in my box.

The iron entered my soul and I never looked back.

Like the country, the ABC was changing. David Hill's leadership of the ABC was critical, and throughout the 1980s he took the organisation by the throat and gave it the shake-up it badly needed. It produced a greater level of professionalism and an added layer of seriousness in tackling complex issues.

It meant, for instance, that someone like Max Walsh, with almost no television experience but a vast background in the reporting of economics and national politics as the former editor of *The Australian Financial Review*, was one of the more interesting lateral recruitments into the ABC in the 1980s. Walsh seemed to me then the sort of person who read everything, knew everyone and had an infinite number of stories to share. He had a talent for recognition—of social trends, historical shifts and the talents of individuals. He was the sort of bloke who made big calls and stood his ground. Compared with Walsh, I was a complete neophyte but we hit it off straight away when we shared adjacent office space at the old ABC site at Gore Hill. As plans were realised for a new mid-evening Canberra–Sydney news program that would focus exclusively on politics and business, Walsh told the higher-ups that he wanted me on his team.

In the middle of 1985, *The Carleton–Walsh Report* was launched with a straightforward format. Carleton covered the action-packed reform agenda of then Prime Minister Bob Hawke and Treasurer Paul Keating, while Walsh deconstructed the high-stakes corporate plays of BHP and the like. The 1980s were a wild ride for Australia and it was a Labor government that forced a style and pace of modernisation that changed everything.

My role was as news anchor and reporter. It gave me the opportunity to build a national profile for the first time. I was where I wanted to be, working with interesting people, discussing issues of consequence and on a program that had tremendous cachet.

Apart from the key players in the government, a frequent guest on the show was then leader of the opposition John Howard. No matter the time, the location or personal inconvenience, Howard would be there on the set arguing his case. The 1980s were Howard's baptism-of-fire years, lonely years. He seemed the man *least likely*. He neither looked nor sounded like a leader but those who underestimated him didn't see the constancy and the conviction. Above all, John Howard knew what it took to play a long game.

As satisfying as my role was, I was hungry for promotion and restless, once again, for foreign parts. By 1986 I had secured a posting to Washington. From Hawke's Australia to Ronald Reagan's America. My farewell gift from Walsh was a copy of Barbara Tuchman's *The Proud Tower*. The inscription read: *Never be afraid to aim high*. What was he on about? What could possibly top Washington?

I loved the nearly three years I spent in the United States. I was in my mid-thirties and had enough confidence and experience to get the best out of the posting. Washington is a great town for players whose core business is the daily trade in information.

In the second half of 1986, during Reagan's second term, it was the events generated by covert US activity in Central America that galvanised the American capital. The Iran–Contra congressional hearings absorbed my early months of reporting as they unearthed the almost unbelievable actions of Oliver North, a National Security Council staffer who diverted funds from arms sales to Iran to help finance the anti-Sandinista and anti-communist rebels in Nicaragua. All done in complete violation of the will of Congress.

It was a whopper of a story and shocking in its implications. I also remember being impressed by the accountability that the American system eventually delivered: the detail and the openness with which officials were prepared to examine the deep fissures in America's inter-governmental machinery.

I also found, joy of joys, open doors and a decision-making class that felt obligated to take the time to talk policy and politics, even to a foreign correspondent from the bottom of the Pacific.

There was another serendipitous discovery. After the rough sexism of Australia, Washington seemed to be gender blind. The bar you had to leap over was a professional one. That was it. There were plenty of women in the White House press corps and a healthy number at the senior level. The TV networks even paid their top female correspondents and anchors appropriately—that is, at the same competitive rate as the boys. What an idea!

By the late 1980s the competition, certainly among TV networks, was hotting up at home. In the great media swap of the decade, Westfield boss Frank Lowy bought the Ten Network and started a raid on the ABC's current affairs talent bank. A lot of the big names defected one after the other—Chris Masters and Kerry O'Brien among them.

The promise of a generously resourced, big-budget current affairs unit covering stories from around the world and aimed at a large commercial audience was a huge draw and, like the rest, I didn't hesitate when the call came to ask if I would join the network's new program, *Page One.*

The network moved me to New York from Washington and I met Frank Lowy in his Trump Tower Fifth Avenue apartment. He seemed a different kind of corporate titan: urbane, more interested in letting others shine than in talking himself, and just a little bemused by his new acquisition and what it meant.

How could he help, he asked me. With the Democrats Convention coming up in Atlanta, perhaps our connections on the East Coast could secure an interview with Ted Kenndy?

The senior senator from Massachusetts wasn't on the ticket in the run for the White House in 1988, but hell, who's going to argue when a story on the coming political contest between

George H.W. Bush and Michael Dukakis could be enhanced by an interview with a member of America's most famous political dynasty and an esteemed Senate legislator?

Lowy kept his word. A few months after our meeting, I interviewed Senator Ted Kennedy in Atlanta. He wore a cream, light-weight linen suit, the better to try and stay cool in the brain-numbing heat of Atlanta in July, and bravely, but not that convincingly, talked up the chances of the Democrats taking the White House back in November.

Twenty years later Kennedy chose to endorse Barack Obama over Hillary Clinton as his party's nominee for the 2008 presidential contest against Republican John McCain. He died six months after the inauguration of America's first African-American President, and in the last months of his life Kennedy was still advocating the liberal progressive causes such as healthcare reform that had been a feature of his long political career. Despite the controversies that dogged him, Kennedy had made his time count.

By the end of the 1980s I was starting to think about heading home and Kerry O'Brien provided the opportunity. O'Brien, still at that stage with the Ten Network and working across news and current affairs, was on his way to becoming *the* pre-eminent interviewer on Australian television, so I was flattered when he called me in New York one night and offered me a spot in the news bureau working with him in Canberra.

It was an awkward and disorienting transition. I left the deep chill of North America in January 1989 having filed my final story on George H.W. Bush's presidential inauguration and was catapulted back into summer in Australia's bush capital. I was ready for work but where was everybody else? Accustomed to the crowded streets of Manhattan, I remember the almost out-of-body weirdness as the taxi took me across Kings Avenue Bridge over Lake Burley Griffin on a Monday morning and I saw not a single person on the streets or in the parks. Had they dropped the neutron bomb—the one that left the buildings intact but flattened everyone?

It took me a while to appreciate Canberra's planned urbanity. What I didn't recognise at the time was that the simple act of saying 'yes' to Kerry O'Brien was life-changing. It would be eighteen years before my own inauguration as a parliamentary member of a new and different Labor government, but it was during that first year in Canberra that I met the people who would have a direct bearing on my later decision to become a political player myself.

At first Canberra intimidated me in a way that Washington never had. Parliament House, the vast new complex opened in 1988, was hard to negotiate and more clubbish than collegiate. There was only one remedy: get out there and mix it.

Australia was a different place from the one I'd left, and the debate in Canberra reflected that. Hawke, still Prime Minister, and Keating, as Treasurer, were dealing with the hangover from the '80s spending spree. The economic liberalisation they had engineered led to a massive expansion of the finance industry and the kind of injudicious lending that resulted in a boom in speculative corporate takeover activity. All headline-grabbing stuff while it lasted but soon there were tears and recriminations.

As we reported the bankruptcies and the job losses, we were all feeling it at a personal level. After the wildly inflated prices paid for TV networks, newsrooms were now being emptied as the liquidators moved in. Frank Lowy would later admit that getting into television in the midst of the '80s boom had been a singular and spectacular error, but he certainly wasn't alone.

In an effort to control the boom that preceded the bust, interest rates had been driven up to 17 per cent. Business was paying 20 per cent. Paul Keating was dealing with the kind of blowout in the current account deficit and foreign borrowings that had caused him a few years earlier to speculate about banana republic status.

As journalist Paul Kelly reported in *The End of Certainty*, tensions within the government were starting to build—among senior ministers such as Trade Minister John Dawkins, Industry Minister John Button and Finance Minister Peter Walsh—over what they saw as difficult and unfinished business. The Accord with the trade unions had delivered wage restraint but the productive drivers of a high-growth economy—better work practices, a more highly skilled workforce and efficient infrastructure—all needed attention. Spending outpaced production, and inflation was running at over 7 per cent.

I had a taste of these tensions in an interview I taped with Button in the immediate aftermath of the 1990 election. Having won against the odds and with a looming recession, Button was cautioning against any false euphoria and told me the newly elected government could not afford a repeat of 'the missed opportunities' of the previous term.

After the interview went to air, Keating went berserk. He took Button's comments as a personal slight and called a press conference with the sole purpose of slapping down his colleague. It would take two leadership challenges but, as Prime Minister, Keating eventually incorporated in his One Nation program many of the productivity-enhancing measures advocated by Button and others.

What this public spat demonstrated was that alongside the egos and internecine rivalries there was nonetheless a genuine contest of ideas within the Labor government. And that spilled over into the parliamentary and public debate.

For all the incoming, the Hawke–Keating government was bloody good at defending itself against the Liberal opposition, whether it was led by Andrew Peacock, John Howard or John Hewson. And it wasn't just a show, a bit of debating legerdemain. The Labor crowd believed in what they were doing. Time and again, they were out there, telling the story of the great Australian change.

Keating's tutorials, whether delivered to John Laws on Sydney radio or to the public via Canberra-based journalists, were legendary—full of conviction and verve and the kind of imagery that stayed with you. He must have known that there were any number of Australians who would not have minded if he'd fallen down Mount Ainslie and never been found—certainly anyone who had lost a business and had to lay off workers—but Keating also knew that retreat from the whole vast project of the liberalising of the Australian economy was not an option. He would have killed his own credibility if he'd lost his nerve and buckled.

The major television interviews in the '90s, on programs such as *Lateline* and the commercial equivalents, reflected this contest of ideas. They were serious, well-researched efforts conducted by serious people. They were also feisty, irreverent and, at times, career-changing. The key political players certainly thought they would have insulted themselves and everyone else had they not properly prepared for a lengthy interview with O'Brien or Channel Nine's Laurie Oakes. Speechwriter Don Watson acknowleges this in his memoir, *Recollections of a Bleeding Heart*, and talks of the intense scrutiny that the PM's chief advisors expected and prepped their leader for in any 'mid-term examination' conducted by Kerry O'Brien, who by the early '90s was back at the ABC anchoring *Lateline.* By 1995 O'Brien had moved on to the prime-time ABC program, *7.30 Report.* I was chosen as his replacement to host *Lateline*, having rejoined the ABC after the commercial debacle at Ten.

It was a marvellous journalistic moment, with cheaper and more effective satellite transmission allowing hook-ups from all over the world but just ahead of the distorting high-octane madness of the 24/7 news explosion. It was a time when there was still … time. Time for research, for reflection and, importantly for a program such as *Lateline*, time to find the actual *decision maker* and not have to make do with the inexpert *expert*.

It was one of the most professionally satisfying periods of my career, one where I had the opportunity to interview leaders from everywhere and at all points on their personal trajectories. There were plenty of robust exchanges but my style was more inquisitive than interrogative. I hope I conveyed the impression that the guest was more important than me, and I like to think I gave interviewees the space to answer.

The Israeli Labor leader Shimon Peres sounded like a poet rather than a politician when I talked to him after his shattering loss to the conservative Likud Party in the elections of 1997. In the same year, New Labour leader Tony Blair was a man in a hurry just ahead of the tsunami-style win he scored against the Tories. And others—Madeleine Albright, Colin Powell, Fidel Ramos, Sir Julius Chan, Henry Kissinger, Chris Patten and Aung San Suu Kyi—all talked of the tensions in leading at a time of change.

The best of these interviews provided a point of illumination: they would produce a phrase or a pithy or passionate answer that seemed to get to the essence of motivation or action. Whether interviewing victor or vanquished, I was learning to recognise what I most admired in creative political leadership: the physical and intellectual effort, the call to service, and the wit to know when to junk conventional wisdom. Leaders, I discovered, do what they do because they can do no other. They feel the seduction of a great cause and the pull is irresistible.

Somewhere along the way, work and life had merged for me in a very agreeable way. I met my life partner Bob Hogg in the early 1990s. He says we danced around each other for ages but really the dye was cast that first freezing winter's night when we shared an indifferent Indian meal in a Deakin restaurant in Canberra. Bob was the National Secretary of the ALP, with a reputation as a successful and shrewd campaigner in successive state and federal elections. Labor had kept winning tight elections right through the 1980s and '90s—twenty-two campaigns over a ten-year period with Labor winning seventeen. Bob was a central player in forging the superior professionalism that kept wrong-footing the Liberals.

As I got to know him I could see the almost paradoxical mix of skills that he brought to the job and defined who he was. Bob was analytical but also instinctive. Never without hope but deeply pessimistic. Thoroughly immersed in the party's structures but somehow above them. Articulate but also capable of the kind of verbal longueurs that drive people nuts. Above all, he was a grown-up. He could look after himself and he wanted to look after me. I was hooked.

My friends always said I would never settle down with the local vet.

Chapter 3

DON'T THINK YOU CAN BEAT A PRIME MINISTER

THERE ARE TIMES when it's no bad thing to be under-estimated, as I'd discovered early on in my television career.

In February 2007, when I announced that I was seeking pre-selection to run as the ALP candidate in the seat of Bennelong against John Howard, it seemed to generate a collective intake of breath right round the country. Wayne Swan, set to become Treasurer after Kevin Rudd's 2007 election win, said it was a decision that gave heart to many in the Labor camp who saw John Howard as an almost unbeatable politician.

The conventional thinking, however, was that I could not win.

The Labor Party thought this, the fourth estate thought this, and even the bulk of my campaign team thought this.

It was never my thinking.

I didn't know I would win on 24 November 2007 in a seat that had only ever been held by the Liberal Party since its creation in 1949, but I knew I *could* win and that's what I set out to do. Every day throughout the long campaign of 2007 I went after votes, not as some kind of elaborate distraction to take Howard away from the national campaign, but in order to take the seat off him.

It was not a frolic or a quixotic tilt at the unachievable.

Howard took me seriously; he referred to me from the start as 'the Labor candidate'.[1] He wasn't taking any chances of further boosting my name recognition.

But for the most part, the Liberals mocked my pretensions. 'Madam Blow-In' was Tony Abbott's put-down—predictable enough from the Member for Warringah and then Health Minister.[2]

'It smacks … somewhat of a stunt … almost university politics.'[3] Thank you Andrew Robb, Howard's Minister for Vocational and Further Education.

South Australian Liberal MP Andrew Southcott said it was a case of 'Labor's hubris',[4] while one of his Queensland counterparts, David Jull, predicted that it was 'going to be interesting to watch' but the Prime Minister had 'been there for 30-odd years' and was 'one of the most immaculate campaigners in Australia'. For good measure, Jull added it wasn't a time for anyone to get their 'knickers in a knot'.[5] Quite.

From some of Howard's closest friends, there was a sniffy and seigneurial 'How could she?'

At one level all this was a hugely entertaining response from the party that supposedly lauds competition and a bit of risk-taking. At another, it reinforced, at precisely the wrong time of the political cycle, the sense of supreme propriety the Liberals have always felt they are entitled to exercise.

By 2007 the Liberal Party was complicit in so gaming the political system that any kind of leadership regeneration had been thwarted. Howard's desire for a seemingly limitless tenure in the top job was indulged by his party and aided by Treasurer Peter Costello's Hamlet-like prevarication about skewering his boss with a direct challenge.

There was a telling encounter early on in 2007 when my bloke Bob collided with Costello in the Qantas lounge at Canberra airport. 'Oh, look, it's the candidate's husband!' This mock greeting was accompanied by a burst of self-satisfied laughter and a sneer that Costello wore all the way to the gate. Bob enjoyed the moment in a different way: *Has the irony escaped you, Peter? It's Maxine who has the guts to take on Howard.*

I had no illusions about what I was up against. But there were some early signs that Howard had not only outstayed his welcome in the country's top job, but that voters in his own electorate were starting to think about regime change. Not long after I secured pre-selection, I was at the Rawson Street shops in Epping, a suburb in the north-west of the electorate where Bob and I were looking to buy a house. Without even basic campaign material at that stage, I was there, with only a few supporters, to introduce myself and chat to the locals. It was all pretty low-key. People were friendly but more interested in getting the Saturday shopping out of the way than in any long discourse on the state of the govern-ment. Plenty recognised me, which was a good start, but my radar went off when I spotted a formidable elderly woman heading towards me and making direct eye contact. She remained expres-sionless as she raised her walking cane off the ground, pointed in my direction and told me she had been voting Liberal for forty years. Think Lady Bracknell and you get the type. Every instinct was telling me that here was someone who would happily see Labor candidates fried in very hot oil.

She came closer, lowered the cane, and then made what amounted to a declaration, one that was audible to everyone pouring out of Coles. 'This time,' she said, 'I'll be voting for you.' I wasn't going to interrupt. 'Mr Howard has become a mean old man. Just like the one I have at home, only he is not running the country.' With that she was gone. I was so astonished I neglected to get her name.

In another chance meeting in a coffee shop in Eastwood, the geographic heart of Bennelong, I talked with a local Liberal Party grandee (they may have mocked me but they all wanted to meet me) and again I was startled to hear the kinds of resentments that were building against John Howard. 'Look, I have three sons, all in their twenties. They're beaut but they're boofheads. You know what I mean? Complete boofheads in the way only young blokes can be. And I would like to think that if one of my boofheaded sons got into trouble in a foreign country that my government would do everything to represent their interests and bring them home.'

This was another light-bulb moment. They're talking about David Hicks? In Eastwood?

It mattered little to this Liberal loyalist that Hicks had apparently allowed himself to be seduced by our enemies in Afghanistan. The point, according to my new friend (who bet so much on my winning in Bennelong that he was able to shout himself a new Lexus), was that Howard was breaching some basic conventions. The Prime Minister was being wilful in rejecting basic notions of justice and fair play and couldn't be bothered to get on the phone to his mate George Bush to get Hicks sent home.

There were multiple variations on this theme and it came down to one thing: at some deep level, Howard was provoking offence and discomfort on his own side. He was being cavalier with the system and playing the kind of crafty politics that was damaging to democracy.

The coffee shop chat was soon followed by a call from one of Sydney's super rich, a well-known eastern suburbs financier. I'd never met him but he came quickly to the point.

'You'll need money. I'll help you.'

'Well … thanks, but why?'

'I'm an old Ignatian. Howard has sold his soul.'

Now the state of grace of the PM wasn't on the playlist. Even allowing for Kevin Rudd's deep interest in all matters theological, Labor was not campaigning on the question of how long John Howard might have to spend in purgatory to atone for his sins. We were out there talking about the specifics—climate change, WorkChoices, an Education Revolution. They were all critical in the battle to take Bennelong. But these early conversations taught me the importance of the subterranean issues, the ones that lacked any definition and therefore attracted no debate. Politics is a visceral business and by 2007 the revelation for me was the extent to which a decent percentage of voters in Bennelong were starting to feel a deep sense of unease about Howard. They were concluding that their Prime Minister and local member had not only lost touch but was losing his moral compass.

When I look back on my door-knocking notes from 2007, there's a frequent entry. Constituents asked me point blank, 'Do you tell the truth?' It put me on notice that the 2007 campaign was going to be about more than who could offer the biggest bribes.

First and foremost, if I was to have any chance of changing a pattern of conservative voting in a seat where constituents had voted the same way in over twenty elections, I had to establish a good organisational base and to be very clear about why I was standing and what I had to offer.

At the centre of my campaign team was a group of individuals who became my indispensable 'brains trust'. They included senior NSW senator and former Keating government minister, John Faulkner; John Watkins, then the Deputy Premier in the NSW Iemma government and the local member for Ryde; Michael Butterworth, a member of Ryde Council and Labor staffer; and Jan Burnswoods, a Labor stalwart and former member of the NSW legislative council. In 1980 she very nearly took the seat of Lowe from one-time Prime Minister Sir William McMahon. She had every right to see me as a political parvenu, and for a while probably did, but she backed me to the hilt and brought a huge institutional memory and local knowledge to the campaign. Both Michael and Jan were critical in helping me to negotiate my way around what was completely new territory for me, the local ALP branches.

When we all got together for our first meeting in April 2007 we were also joined by Trish Drum. With a background as a lawyer and a journalist, Trish had contacted me when she heard I was running. 'Count me in,' she said. And we did. Throughout the campaign Trish's job was to make sure I didn't make mistakes or end up on the front page of the newspaper for the wrong reason. I didn't want to be Rudd's problem candidate.

We assigned roles, organised fundraising, worked out how to manage the flood of volunteers who were already lining up to work for me, prioritised local activities, rented office space and, above all, developed a strategy for running a high-visibility campaign that would be both effective and credible.

Getting national attention was not going to be a problem. Already Trish was inundated with calls for interviews, magazine profiles and speaking gigs. And every time Howard or Rudd came to Bennelong, the cameras were there and I made the national network news right along with them.

The suburban local press was another matter. When I took my first look at *The Northern District Times* and *The Weekly Times*, the latter run by the bowler-hatted and jocular John Booth, I assumed they were printed by the Liberal Party secretariat, given their enthusiastic and almost uncritical barracking for John Howard. Booth's editorial style in particular seemed to have been borrowed from North Korea, judging by the page after page of happy snaps of the PM being mobbed by joyous and grateful citizens of the realm.

I was getting my first lesson in the power of incumbency. If you've been the member for thirty-three years then you have instant entree to all the key local institutions—the RSLs and sports clubs, the press and the chambers of commerce. Over the years Howard had worked them assiduously and they backed him. As I told *Sydney Morning Herald* journalist Peter Hartcher, for his book *To the Bitter End*, local organisations 'felt proprietorial about Howard and he in turn felt he owned them'.

My candidacy landed like a bomb on these decades-long arrangements. I later learned of huge internal feuds on committees as officials debated whether or not to let *that woman* in the door. Time and again curiosity got the better of people. Once the wall was breached at one club or community group, then the invitations started rolling in.

I will always remember the gutsiness of Epping solicitor Robert Cameron and realtor Betty Ockerlander, who got in first and invited me to speak to the local Chamber of Commerce at the Epping Club. As luck would have it, I turned up the same week that Bob and I were settling on our new home in Angus Avenue, Epping, just up the road from the club.

She's really moving in. That got them talking. That and the fact that my new neighbours could see for themselves that I didn't have two heads, that I was not there to launch a personal jihad against Howard, and that my bid to represent them in the federal parliament was serious and considered.

I may not have won many votes that day but I was hugely encouraged by the fact that so many women turned up and that they were the ones who lingered after lunch and wanted to chat. About everything and nothing in particular. They were sizing me up, making intuitive judgments in the way that women do, but they were also signalling that no one should assume anything about their voting intention, certainly not on the basis of where they lived, how much they earned or how their husbands viewed the world.

Throughout 2007 I would attend hundreds of events like this: smallish gatherings where I had time to hang around and get a feel for people's concerns and they in turn could get a feel for me—what motivated me and what was important to me. It was actually the secret weapon of the campaign and hardly anyone noticed. Unlike Howard, I could turn up alone, and with the one precious resource that was denied to the PM … time.

I knew I was getting traction when I started to hear the feedback: 'She's worth listening to and she takes the time to listen to us.'

All of this might have been dismissed as an idle waltz up and down anecdote alley but for the fact that people could see that my campaign team was not just producing posters but delivering a community service. And we were doing it without indulging the hysterics and extremists who inevitably want to hang off high-profile events. Equally, we didn't stage-manage faux campaigns around the politics of protest.

By mid-year my campaign office in Eastwood was operating like a de facto electorate office. We were helping people with everything from housing and Centrelink payments to telco and disability services—the modern maze of inter-agency negotiations that is a nightmare for some people. Bennelong is in a part of Sydney where residents have higher than average incomes, so it can't be classified as a particularly needy area. Nonetheless it has its share of individuals with acute needs. My campaign office serviced those needs. We did this with competence and professionalism.

Lucienne Joy saw to this. A former journo, Lucienne was introduced via a mutual friend and we clicked straight away. She came on board early while she was waiting for the publication of her first novel. We had a pact. If it all went belly-up for me, I'd hit the road with her and flog her book. What a team we were! She organised the logistics for hundreds of campaign events. She'd send me off to retirement village morning teas armed with freshly baked cupcakes. Before I headed out the door to speak at yet another candidate forum, she'd remind me to B-R-E-A-T-H-E and to S-L-O-W D-O-W-N. She'd take a million calls a day, write almost as many letters and have a nervous collapse every morning when she saw the level of email traffic. She talked to me about life and love, the south of France, Roger Federer, the best spot for takeaway in Eastwood and why we were going to win. She laughed a lot. Behind the joie de vivre few saw the steel, but Lucienne's great gift was the way she artfully marshalled the efforts of the hundreds of people who wanted to be part of a campaign that was taking on Howard. She separated the professionals from the political tragics. Plenty wanted to sign up to do … nothing much at all really, except talk endlessly about *the last campaign*. They were politely redirected.

I can't say that my cramped little office in Eastwood ever hummed with complete efficiency but it was far from chaos central. We were running a professional, civil, positive campaign and we wanted foot soldiers who would sign on for this approach. And so they did. TAFE educators, landscape gardeners, nurses, teachers, public servants and lawyers. Some were ALP members; many were not. They were all there to get the job done and maybe, just maybe, to help make history.

We were buoyed by early positive polling, with Galaxy findings in May 2007 showing my candidacy had added eighteen points to Labor's 2004 vote and giving us a winning margin of 52–48 (remarkably close to the final result of 51.4–48.6). But there were also plenty of checks on any excessive optimism. Every day when we were out door-knocking we could see the mountain of Liberal-financed direct mail that oozed out of letterboxes and from under doormats. We couldn't begin to match this and we never did.

ABC viewership was high across many of the suburbs of Bennelong and that meant that a lot of people recognised me, but it was by no means universal. I knew I had my work cut out for me when I overheard a conversation between a couple of twenty-somethings who were working the checkout counter at my local Epping fruit shop, Martelli's.

There was the encouraging start: 'Isn't that Maxine McKew who came in a minute ago?'

Then the reply: 'Mmmm … you mean the one in *Home and Away*?'

Clearly there was work to do.

It was John Watkins, one of my key campaign generals, who played Mr Reality-Check: 'Don't get carried away. You'll be able to take a percentage point or two off John Howard but that's it. You won't win the first time.'

He wasn't being unkind or discouraging. He was simply stating the conventional wisdom: I might run Howard close locally, but in the event of a Rudd win nationally, Howard would quit Parliament and I would pick up the seat in a subsequent by-election. No one knew the area or constituents better than Watkins so it was a sobering political judgment.

It also fitted with the oft-reported view that my campaign was designed as an elaborate ruse to tie Howard down locally. A 'celebrity saboteur' was journalist Frank Devine's description.

Every time I heard this it irritated the hell out of me. *I'm fifty-three, I've sold my house in Mosman, I've bought and moved into Epping, and you still think this is a dress rehearsal?*

As the year went on, and the forums and crowds got bigger, I was emphatic that I was in it to win. The first time.

The one person who thought I could do it was Bob. Just as well because it was his idea in the first place.

*

There is nothing, and I mean absolutely nothing, orthodox about the way Bob thinks. He'd encouraged my nascent political ambitions right from the time the NSW Labor Party first started to make overtures about running me in a safe seat in western Sydney.

I'd given it serious consideration back in 2003 when the seats of Watson and Fowler were both mentioned as possibilities. The initial approach had come from Michael Easson, a one-time president of the Trades and Labor Council in NSW, whose wife Mary had served in the Keating government as the member for Lowe. I had a round of meetings with then Premier Bob Carr, who told me to 'go for it', and with the Sussex Street ALP chiefs Eric Roozendaal and Mark Arbib.

But why politics? Why cast off a successful career in journalism, where in spite of my relationship with a former ALP National Secretary I was respected as an authoritative non-partisan player?

Politics was central to my work and the way I lived my life. Interviewing the key figures on *Lateline* and for my column in *The Bulletin* took me to the inner boundaries and sometimes close to the centre of Australian public life. I liked being around politicians, finding out what motivated them and what they wanted to do with the power they had. If I had a defining touchstone in my approach to interviewing it was that I had a basic respect, rather than an instinctive cynicism, about the political process and about the players it attracts.

My starting point was that the modern Australian success story hadn't just happened. It had been argued and fought over and knocked into shape by a generation of political players. The best of them had the boldness and the energy to re-imagine the country through an altered policy mix that boosted our competitiveness without overt damage to the nation's social fabric. This had largely been a Labor effort. It didn't happen without pain. But it did happen, substantially without rancour and division, because at a critical point in time a group of senior journalists had the wit and the gravitas to analyse and explain the way Australia was changing. Paul Kelly, Max Walsh, Laurie Oakes, Kerry O'Brien and Michelle Grattan always kept the pressure on the political class, pinning them down on detail and exposing the inconsistencies, but at the heart of their work was an honesty about the need to promote a contestable but civil public discourse.

This was a big influence on me, and the headlines that a lot of my *Bulletin* stories generated or that my *Lateline* interviews provoked were the result not of 'gotcha' moments but of the time I took to encourage some genuine political candour.

Sounds arcane, doesn't it? Almost quaint. We now live with a media–politics dynamic that is almost completely conflict-driven and seems to chew up everything in its path. But at the time I was making my decision to switch from journalism to politics, there was still enough of a remnant of an understanding between the fourth estate and the political class that I didn't feel I was crossing over to the dark side.

Quite simply, I wanted to play a role in public life. I'd had thirty years of asking the questions. Now was the time to help formulate some answers. I had no personal animus towards John Howard, but certainly from the 2000s on I saw him as someone who was presiding over a lazy government that was wasting the once-in-a-generation prosperity coming from the mining boom. From 2002 the windfall from the generous prices the world was paying us for our minerals delivered an estimated $180 billion in revenue over and above the long-term GDP growth trend, and $75 billion of this exceptional bonus went straight out the door on handouts and tax cuts.[6] Where was the national re-investment in health, in research, in universities, schools and early learning, and in major infrastructure projects? Where was the co-ordinated planning across the states on everything from water management to developing an innovation economy? The questions were compelling but Howard and his team looked complacent. A spent force.

But at the same time that I was beginning to think about acting on my ambitions, and was being offered a way in, I knew that the federal Labor leadership team was a long way from being able to offer a winning alternative. I listened to John Faulkner, who warned of Labor's troika of problems: a crisis of leadership, organisation and belief. The revolving door of leaders—Beazley, Crean, Latham—seemed to point to a failure to resolve issues that went all the way back to the 1996 defeat. The party was locked inside its personal dramas at precisely the time when non-conservative voters were looking for a progressive, credible alternative.

Bob and I talked about all of this in the run-up to the 2004 election. There was the outstanding offer of a safe Labor seat, but while my heart was in it my head was telling me to back off. I just didn't believe that Labor was well placed to run a winning campaign against Howard. And if I don't believe it, you see it in my face and hear it in my voice. In my next life I'm coming back as Ms Inscrutable, but for now I'm stuck with being Ms What You See Is What You Get.

In the end the decision was made even easier by the sort of question that passes for normal in the Australian Labor Party. It was made absolutely clear to me that a safe seat could be secured but it was a highly conditional proposition. The then NSW ALP Secretary, Eric Roozendaal, wanted to be clear about the line of authority and asked me point blank: 'Who will own you? Us or your hubby?'

It was such a breathtakingly retro question in every conceivable way that by the time I got to the lift I'd decided to make a strategic retreat from all discussions. If the only path to Canberra was as someone's puppet, it wasn't for me.

Howard won the 2004 election, with an increased majority and control of both houses of Parliament. After the Latham experiment, the Labor Party returned to the safe hands of Beazley, but the problem of Labor's lack of appeal to a broadbased coalition of voters remained. Four Labor defeats in a row and there was still no hunger. No bottom-of-the-belly urgency to beat Howard.

*

There was nothing inevitable about Kevin Rudd's leadership. He had no factional base, he wasn't an institutional creature of the party, and he certainly didn't have the kind of natural blokey amiability that helps with the building of alliances.

But he impressed me from the get-go because he is a man of ideas, curious and intellectually restless. He is an internationalist with a view of the world and of Australia's role in it. He looks out, not in. And, like most Australians, he understands that the sun and the stars don't rotate around the Australian Labor Party.

I'd first noticed him in Washington in the late 1990s, when we were both participants at the annual gathering of the Australian American Leadership Dialogue, an event that brings together foreign policy experts and assorted others from the two continents. The quality of the discourse saves it from being a convention for well-qualified show-offs. What was obvious was that when Rudd spoke, he owned the room.

Rudd presented as smart, serious and hardworking. That's because he *is* all those things. But he is *not* a natural politician, not in the way that one thinks of Bob Hawke or Bill Clinton and the artless ease with which they both embraced power and drew people to them.

Rudd is his own creation. As a boy in the provincial backwater of Nambour in southern Queensland, he'd looked beyond his front fence and decided that he needed to know about China, and so he did. It was an ambition that took him to the ANU, not a natural choice for a Queensland teenager of the 1970s, and then to the foreign service.

His approach was always: *What's the goal and what's needed to realise the ambition?*

After the disappointment of his first failed tilt for the Brisbane seat of Griffith in 1996, he identified in a methodical way what he needed to do to win: apply his intellect to local policy solutions, marshall his energies to that end and win over the locals. Along the way he learned the same lesson that had sustained Howard through his long years in the wilderness. Politics, for the most part, is not a magical endeavour but is more about keeping on keeping on. Persistence, persistence, persistence. Rudd was good at this and after depressing election defeats—in 2001 and 2004—he would be out there on the Sunday morning after the poll explaining to whoever asked what the party had to do to win next time.

It was this kind of grit and doggedness that finally convinced the Labor caucus at the end of 2006, with a year to go before the next federal election, that if they really wanted to win, to finally put an end to the Howard era, then 'Kevin from Queensland' was their best bet.

I didn't hesitate when he rang in early 2007 and asked me to work for him. I'd already decided he had the clarity and discipline needed to run a winning campaign and that he was unlikely to be either intimidated or wrong-footed by Howard.

In September of the previous year, I'd decided that I was up for new challenges so I announced my retirement from journalism. I had absolutely nothing lined up and no expectations of other opportunities, political or otherwise. Some friends thought I was mad to give up high-profile work with no other prospects in sight, but my world had started to feel a bit like Groundhog Day and if I'd stayed that really would have driven me mad. I'm not much good at endless repeat acts.

The timing turned out to be serendipitous, but even as I signed off on what was my last *Lateline* in November 2006—with former Howard staffer Grahame Morris turning the tables and prodding me about what I was going to do next—Rudd was still weeks away from taking over the Labor leadership. At that point the Canberra press gallery wasn't even speculating about a likely change.

Someone else though was alert to the possibilities. In his memoir, *Lazarus Rising*, Howard records that when I announced on *Lateline* that I was leaving the ABC he told his wife Janette, 'She's going to run in Bennelong.'[7]

Howard and I crossed paths a few weeks later at the farewell dinner for ABC chairman Donald McDonald. I had been asked by McDonald to MC at what was a very elegant affair attended by the good, the great and the look-at-me's. There was a lot of affection in the room that night for McDonald, who'd been a more than able advocate for the national broadcaster. The McDonalds were close friends of the Howards so the PM was a natural choice as guest speaker. I delivered a lighthearted introduction, noting Howard's dawn-to-midnight interest in the ABC—'He starts the day with Fran Kelly and finishes with *Lateline*'—and we shook hands as I invited him up to the stage.

Every political pundit and member of the Sunday morning couch commentariat was there that night but if one of them had suggested that within a year I would replace John Howard as the Member for Bennelong then I would have said it was time for their bosses to reconsider their contracts.

Who could imagine such a thing? McKew running in Bennelong? Against *John Howard*?

Bob completely ruined my January 2007 summer holiday by musing aloud one Sunday morning. My bloke muses a lot. And it's amazing where his musing can take him. Or me as it turned out. On this occasion Bob was reading yet another story in the tabloids about Rudd's Herculean task in having to win more than sixteen seats for Labor to secure government. I was on my way out the door for a surf at Killcare beach when I heard: 'You could run in Bennelong. It's on 4 per cent and gettable.'

I can't remember what the waves were like that day, or the day after, or the day after that. I can remember from that point on I thought about nothing else.

Five words changed my life. *You could run in Bennelong.* Insane. An impossible ask. Vainglorious. History is against it. But this wild, dangerous, seductive idea wouldn't go away. It insinuated itself. Maybe. Democracy demands a contest. Australians love an underdog. What's Mark Arbib's phone number again?

Bob's reasoning owed everything to his background in Victoria where, as the state ALP Secretary responsible for John Cain's victory in 1982, he had pushed for regeneration and for fresh blood in contestable seats. Where others saw obstacles, he found new pathways. Where he came up against rigid doctrines and ossified structures, he made the case for modernising. He had enemies aplenty but over the years he had accrued a lot of respect for this approach.

His case for my running in Bennelong had a number of elements. First of all, we were in the neighbourhood. It was one seat across from where we lived on Sydney's North Shore and a move could easily be accommodated. Second, changed boundaries and a growing population of Chinese and Korean Australians meant that the seat could no longer be considered the conservative stronghold it was when John Howard first ran in 1974. By 2007 Bennelong was something of an aberration as the only non-Labor seat with such a high proportion of voters born in non–English speaking countries. Just over 40 per cent of Bennelong's residents speak a language other than English at home, twice the national average. But Bob could see something else that could not be gleaned from a strict reading of the census material. Suburbs in Bennelong were becoming attractive 'second home' options for young ambitious Sydney couples. Typically, once the first baby arrived those facing very high rents on the lower North Shore or the inner west would start to look at housing options in Denistone, Ryde or Epping. They were not traditional Labor voters and had higher incomes and mortgages than the national average. Critically, they paid attention to politics, not in an ideological way but issue by issue. Bob divined, quite correctly, that both Rudd and I had the backgrounds and profiles that would appeal to ambitious skilled and professional people who had an eye to the future and were wearying of Howard.

There was an important third factor that made Bennelong an attractive choice for me. In opting to run in a marginal seat, with no other competing senior member of the party or prominent trade unionist even remotely interested in seeking pre-selection, it was an open race with no debts or obligations. If I pulled it off, I wouldn't owe anybody or be owned by anyone. Not by a faction, a trade union or head office. That was important to me and a very different proposition from the 'safe seat deal' that was on offer in 2003.

By early February I'd stopped agonising and had locked myself in for the race of my life.

I took the idea to Rudd who wanted to announce it straight away. I slowed him down, attended to some important formalities (like taking out ALP membership), talked further with Arbib and Tim Gartrell, the party's National Secretary and Campaign Director, and finally issued a statement on the evening of Sunday, 25 February, about my intention to seek local pre-selection for the seat of Bennelong.

The news was everywhere on Monday morning, the start of another parliamentary sitting week and one that was going to cause even more dyspepsia for the government. Howard appeared on Channel Nine's *Today* show and promised 'to work even harder for the Australian people'.

Rudd said, 'I commend Ms McKew on her determination and courage to contest a seat held by the nation's most formidable politician. History is against us. Rarely has a political party ever won sixteen seats to claim government. It is almost an Everest-like challenge.'[8]

I had scripted what I considered to be some stirring prose to accompany my political debut, but as Rudd's advisor, Alister Jordan, correctly predicted, the major media focus would be on real estate. *Ms McKew is putting her Mosman home on the market and will move into the electorate …*

Sydney and property. A magic combination. Where you live is who you are.

Trish Drum was now joined to my hip and to my brain, prepping me on all our key messages on climate change, education, WorkChoices, etc. etc.

I had a daily prayer: *Don't let me be the one who stuffs up.*

The test came soon enough when the *Today* show thought it should even up its interview with the PM and invited me on to discuss the Bennelong campaign with Karl Stefanovic. All the prepping and the deep breathing and the slow delivery went out the window when Karl fired off a beauty from left field: 'Maxine, are you in love with Kevin?'

Thirty years of asking questions and somehow I missed that one.

The day was rounded off when I received a note on letterhead from Garfield Barwick Chambers. From the sanctum sanctorum of Sydney's legal elite came this message: *Even if you don't win it will be great politics and you will give the bastard an awful fright.*

What an exquisite reversal! Howard had been successfully frightening the bejesus out of Labor leaders for years, certainly since the brutal politics of the *Tampa* election of 2001. The brilliance of the 2007 campaign is that Rudd refused to play on Howard's preferred turf. He marked out his own ground and took his message about the future into every marginal seat across the country.

Above all Rudd got the *tone* right. When voters tuned into Rudd they heard and sensed someone who was reasonable, sensible and sincere—a safe, reassuring alternative to Howard, who by mid-year, along with the rest of his team, was sounding more and more desperate, even hysterical at times.

My local approach in Bennelong mirrored that of Rudd's at the national level. Howard's local constituents weren't angry with their representative of thirty years, but they were starting to think that their MP had outstayed his welcome. Throughout the long months of the 2007 campaign I kept wishing and saying, 'There is nothing mysterious about Bennelong.' It turned out to be right.

In the same way that there was national disenchantment with the style and policy neglect of Howard, I picked up the same sentiment as we door-knocked the suburbs of Gladesville, Eastwood, North Ryde, Epping and everywhere in between.

Door-knocking is a standard campaign tool. It costs nothing more than shoe leather, and serious candidates do it because it works. If a householder inches open the fly-wire door then you know you've got a chance to convince them of your bona fides.

I had a huge advantage as I took Labor's message door to door and street to street. My profile had been boosted enormously by the national press I was attracting. By July and August I was on the front cover or prominently featured in any number of magazines—*The Bulletin*, *The Australian Women's Weekly*, *The Monthly*, *Sunday Life*, *The Weekend Australian*—all of them positive pieces that lauded the plucky underdog.

Still I got the shock of my life when people would greet me before I even introduced myself. 'Oh, hi Maxine,' was pretty standard. Some invited me in for a cup of tea; others wanted me to linger to meet their young adult children who'd 'be back in a minute'. In Ermington one weekend, a young woman obviously in the middle of a family drama, yelled out, 'Mum, quick, get the camera for a photo with Maxine!'—and then proceeded to tell me that 'Dad has had a bit of a turn and we're taking him to the hospital, but look, great to see you ... '

In all these encounters, and at every other campaign event, I aimed to present a positive face and to never belittle my opponent.

But this was no ordinary contest. Many residents in Bennelong felt special because their local member ran the country. I had to convince people, some of whom had been voting for Howard for thirty years, that it was not an act of heresy to consider shifting their vote.

In the same way that upmarket retailer David Jones now *invites* customers to part with their dollars at the upcoming sale, I was asking people to *reconsider* their vote. All my instincts told me that a more muscular negative campaign based on a direct attack would not work.

Respect and courtesy. That's what I aimed for and I demanded the same from everyone who put on the purple—the *Strong Voice for Bennelong* T-shirts that were our recognised insignia.

Above all, and unlike many of the party faithful, I never took the attitude that people were somehow deranged because they had kept sending Howard back to Canberra election after election. I respected that choice, in part because I believed that ever since the defeat of 1996 Labor had failed to argue an effective case for change.

It's why I chose to have nothing to do with the leftover campaigners from the *Not Happy, John* crowd of 2004. It was a decision that annoyed the Liberal apostate John Valder, who thought I was pretty arrogant in rebuffing his offer of help. The 2004 effort was encouraging for the non-conservative parties, but the two-party preferred swing against the Liberals in the neighbouring seats of Bradfield and North Sydney was of a similar order to that in Bennelong: 2.7 per cent, 3.2 per cent and 3.4 per cent respectively.

That was the fright for the NSW Liberals.

Bugger that. I wanted to win. And that psychology drove everything. It was the critical ingredient in attracting campaign workers who were as serious as I was.

I built credibility, day by day, week by week, and after a while a lot of people started to think there was an alternative to the status quo. What I was doing was making it safe for people to switch their vote.

The remarkable thing is how flat-footed the local Liberals were. We all kept waiting for the Howard army to turn up in force. It never did. When Howard campaigned in the electorate he had more security personnel around him than supporters.

There was an early attempt to discredit my credentials via paid advertisements in the local press: *Representing your interests is not as easy as ABC.* This clunky effort rolled a couple of blocks down the main street and ended up stuck on a roundabout. It turned out to be so out of sync with public sentiment that it was quickly dropped and never resurfaced. Most constituents saw my background in journalism as a perfectly reasonable entry point for parliamentary representation.

There was something else in my favour: the fit seemed right. I liked Bennelong and Bennelong seemed to like me. I was on the same wavelength as the people I met, whether it was at the Coxs Road shops at North Ryde or any of Bennelong's other meeting points. Conversation was easy. I kept meeting people whose outlook wasn't that different from my own. People who were ambitious, optimistic, but had arrived at a point in their thinking about the nation where they were saying, 'We have to do better.'

The Liberals missed this. It was a subtle mood shift, a stirring of something in the soul. The social researcher Hugh MacKay had written at the start of 2007 that he detected 'a restlessness. A gnawing sense that we'd better take another look at the big picture'.[9]

Rudd was out there, day after day, urging, nudging, persuading Australians to take this step, and in the process, to engineer a major historic shift by putting an end to the Howard years. At the same time, I was asking Bennelong voters to play their part in this. There was a parallel logic to this co-ordinated effort.

It was also great national drama. There was a sense of moment about the race in Bennelong that had never existed before.

The Prime Minister, Mr Howard, is back in his electorate today to hold off the challenge from Maxine McKew …

I was forcing Howard to play serious defence in his own backyard for the first time. As he felt the pressure, the PM talked more and more about himself. About the decisions *his family* had made, not his party, and certainly not about decisions in the national interest. The more voters heard this, the more they said, 'It's not about you, it's about us.'

We didn't win over every house or every street, but there were days when the purple army would finish work, foot weary but euphoric, and come back to the campaign office full of stories of this person or that person who was definitely voting Labor for the first time. It felt as if someone had sprinkled fairy dust, such was the benign mood and sense of goodwill moving our way.

Of course, there were still enough true-blue conservatives who couldn't stand the sight or the sound of *that woman*. One kept calling Lucienne Joy and saying, 'She's had her fun, tell her to get back to Mosman.' One of the local Eastwood shopping centre proprietors wore his own T-shirt that read: *Walk away Maxine and keep walking.*

Best of all was the story that my Angus Avenue neighbours told. Apparently one elderly Howard supporter refused to believe that I'd moved into Epping and furtively parked her car in my street for days on end to track whether or not I really lived there. Who knows how many times she had to set an early alarm to spot my 6 a.m. exits as I headed off to do a meet and greet with morning rail commuters?

One section from Margot Saville's spirited account of the campaign, *The Battle for Bennelong*, summed up things nicely. Margot attended the final judging of the Miss Eastwood Granny Smith Festival Queen, the better to capture some local colour:

> Wine flowed freely and at 9 p.m. the door burst open and a very tall, fat man in a floor-length red gown entered the room.
> It was Ivan Petch, the Mayor of Ryde, in his mayoral robes,

which are trimmed with a kind of brown road-kill. Anthony Roberts, the Liberal state member for Lane Cove, immediately leapt to his feet, crying, 'Santa, Santa' and escorted Petch to his table, which included Greg Smith, the Liberal state member for Epping … the table made merry and when the MC mentioned other dignitaries, they all stood up and uttered long high-pitched ululations, like a private school war cry. Maxine sat on the other side of the room. A social anthropologist would be fascinated by this performance. It seemed to be sending her a message—this is our turf and you are not wanted.[10]

It was not hard to understand the fury of the local Liberals. The interloper was threatening the fixed cosy arrangements and lord-of-the-manor patronage system that had been in place for a long time. Again, it was all about *ownership*, and Bennelong was Liberal territory.

By mid-August Jennifer Sexton's *Bulletin* front-cover story was published, referring to me as 'The Smiling Assassin'. It was this kind of attention, a relentless media focus on the contestability of Bennelong, that was getting right up the noses of the local Liberal establishment. But when Howard supporters did start appearing on the streets towards the end of the campaign, they were snarly, loud and abusive. It didn't go over well in an area where people observe the courtesies.

I kept smiling but I didn't feel much like a killer. I just kept moving, from morning teas, to mums and bubs clubs, to forums, to schools and to shopping centres. Sustained by dim sum and banana smoothies, I dropped five kilos, and my moods were all over the place. I'd race from one event to the other, with the hits of Dusty Springfield played at high volume in the car: 'You don't have to say you love me, just be there to vote … '

Every day I'd wake up thinking that this would be the day that Howard would wheel out the heavy artillery—a crushing attack campaign, another divisive chapter in the culture wars or a seductive set of tax breaks.

It was all too late, of course. And voters knew it. They'd had enough of the Howard show of dog whistles and easy handouts and quick fixes. But still we weren't sure.

An interesting turning point was a Bennelong-specific program on SBS hosted by Jenny Brockie. We were contemporaries and had worked together on the early ABC *Nationwide* program but I expected no favours. Quite the contrary. Jenny's production team had invited an audience of Liberal, Labor and swinging voters and seated them in voting blocks in the studio. *The Australian*'s George Megalogenis was also there as a commentator, as was Howard biographer Peter van Onselen.

This was actually the first and only time throughout the entire campaign that I had a direct encounter with my opponent. But it was hardly an evenly matched event. The PM was interviewed at length by Brockie at the beginning of the show from Canberra, while the rest of us were in SBS's Artarmon studio in Sydney. I was seated, not upfront with the host, but in the audience with the Labor voters. But as things turned out, the staging and choreography of the show played to my advantage. I was sitting there *with the people*—I was one of the people, listening and talking—and for an hour on prime time the whole show reinforced the David versus Goliath nature of the Bennelong campaign. Goliath still had the power but I had the presence.

Megalogenis and Van Onselen wrapped up the show by reading from the conventional wisdom script: *She won't win but she'll pick up the seat in a subsequent by-election.*

The papers that picked the trend early were Sydney's *Daily Telegraph* and its weekend stablemate *The Sunday Telegraph*. Their published polling, from early in 2007, consistently pointed to the PM losing his seat for the same reason that Rudd looked set for a historic victory: Howard had stayed too long and was no longer in tune with the concerns of voters. Just after I secured local pre-selection in March 2007, I went and saw the editor, David Penberthy, to make sure he understood two things. First, that I would be running a serious, well-resourced campaign, not a celebrity circus. Second, that Bennelong was a winnable seat for Labor.

There was huge and understandable media interest in the Chinese and Korean communities and which way they would 'direct' their votes. It led to the incorrect and insulting view that there was somehow less heterogeneity among Chinese Australians or Korean Australians than among fifth-generation Anglo-Celtic voters, or anyone else for that matter. I came to the view that just about everything I heard about ethnic voting patterns in Bennelong was unreliable: respect for hierarchy and the allure of high office would ensure a continuing vote for John Howard; community leaders would deliver a 'block' vote, etc. etc.

A more accurate and complex read on the growing Asian community involved the origin and timing of the migratory journey. Whether Chinese, Indian, Korean or Sri Lankan, did they come from rural areas or were they urban professionals? Did they arrive twenty years ago or last year? Did they have recent memories of John Howard, the deliverer of prosperity, or more distant ones of John Howard the multicultural doubter? Beyond that, when it came to getting a fix on Bennelong's Asian voters I looked to the same kind of socio-economic analysis that political parties applied to all Australian voters: a consideration of income, age, gender, professional status and education level.

You only have to spend five minutes in Eastwood, the heart of Bennelong's Chinese and Korean communities, to realise that what unites families is the same set of interests and ambitions that drives migration to the area from other parts of Sydney: more affordable housing, easy access to the city and, above all, quality education.

I probably spent at least half of my campaigning time on the campus at Macquarie University, at the local TAFEs, or in Bennelong's schools, preschools and early learning centres. Labor's message about the need for an education revolution hit the spot with just about everyone, from Chinese seniors who were helping to finance their grandchildren's education to Denistone and Ryde families who wanted to keep sending their children to local highly competitive public schools and, not least, the principal and staff of Marsden High School in Ermington.

Marsden High is a school in the less affluent part of the electorate, located just off busy Victoria Road, that in the 1970s produced high-flyers like News Limited chief Kim Williams and RMIT Vice-Chancellor Margaret Gardner. Forty years later, when Kevin Rudd arrived at Marsden to promote his plan for investment in school-based trade centres, principal Greg Wann introduced him to a school community that represents fifty different language groups. There were polyglots aplenty—the Afghan teenager who spoke Urdu, Pashto and Dari; the Persian girl who was fluent in four languages and taking Extension English in her HSC. Wann didn't go out of his way to make a political point but he was moved that the leader of a political party and one who was bilingual himself had come to the school and talked firsthand with the students. In spite of repeat invitations to graduation nights and other special events, Wann said that Howard had never visited Marsden High School.

There may well have been a dozen good reasons for this, but it was seen locally, in a community that is still far from socially secure, as a slight, as insufficiently caring. And after eleven years as Prime Minister, in his own richly diverse electorate, Howard was no longer being given the benefit of the doubt on questions to do with race. There had been too much hesitancy, ambivalence. Too much carelessness.

They'd seen it with Howard's 1988 statement on Asian immigration. They'd seen it with his long indulgence of Pauline Hanson. And in 2007, right in the middle of the election, migrants saw it in the easy condemnation and casual dismissal of the rights of an Indian doctor, Mohamed Haneef. For long-term Asian migrants in particular it all added up to one thing: Howard's acute discomfort with *the other.*

By the time the formal campaign period began in October, many of the local Asian community leaders were openly endorsing my candidacy, among them Caroline Yi Xu, Justin Li, Wilson Fu, Hugh Lee and Jason Koh. They gave a variety of reasons. They could see the ALP was taking the seat seriously, they appreciated the time I had taken to meet with them and understand their concerns and, above all, they saw in Kevin Rudd a modern leader who moved with ease across cultures.

Rudd didn't have to stand and deliver speeches about tolerance and cultural diversity. It was there to see within his own family. One of the more arresting sights of the campaign was that of Rudd's daughter Jessica and her husband, Hong Kong Chinese Albert Tse, being gently teased by Bennelong Chinese residents about their status as newlyweds. As they moved about Eastwood they presented a near perfect snapshot of a changing Australia: a mixed-race, multilingual professional couple in their twenties with an eye on carving out a future for themselves in a region that would be defined very differently in the twenty-first century.

It was nothing you could capture in a campaign slogan and it was hard to pin down. It was what it was: a very powerful image.

What I came to appreciate was that for many Asian Australians the 2007 Bennelong campaign represented something of a liberation. Years of repressed hurt resurfaced and Howard suffered accordingly. No one ever said, 'It's payback time,' but one Chinese restaurateur did say to me, 'I've waited a long time for this.'

Howard had set the election date for 24 November and his hope must have been that the formal campaign of six weeks would make a difference and see a last-minute reversal of fortune. He certainly spent money with an eye to winning back crucial votes. A promised $2.4 million for a West Ryde Community Centre; $645,000 for the installation of security cameras in Ryde (an area with one of the lowest crime rates in Sydney); and a last-minute offer of $12 million for a recovery unit at the Royal Rehabilitation Centre at Putney. When asked by the hospital management to match this offer I refused, and told them the Labor Party wasn't in the business of making five-minutes-to-midnight decisions on hospital funding. Rudd was certainly promising a motza of electorate-specific spending up and down the east coast, across the country and in the regions, in order to secure the sixteen-plus seats needed for victory. But my one and only election commitment in Bennelong was the construction of a childcare centre in North Ryde to the value of $1.5 million.

None of this made a jot of difference.

Voters had shifted early. A *Sunday Telegraph* Galaxy poll published in the middle of August put the two-party preferred vote in Bennelong at 53–47 per cent in my favour. Journalist Glenn Milne reported that my primary vote, at 47 per cent, was coming from Liberal voters disaffected with the Prime Minister. It was also coming straight off the Greens vote, which was down dramatically from its 16 per cent high in 2004.

Three months later, in early November, Milne reported again 'that for the last six months the Prime Minister's political wheels have been spinning in his own backyard with Ms McKew poised for victory with 52 per cent of the two-party preferred vote compared to 48 per cent for Mr Howard.'[11]

On the question of the most influential issues, there was a distinction not recorded in other marginal electorates. Forty per cent of Bennelong voters rated management of the economy as their highest priority, and 30 per cent listed the honesty of the candidates as the next most important issue. Industrial relations came in third.

It explains why the final weeks and days of the campaign felt so quiet. Everyone had made up their minds. They'd been leafleted, door-knocked, stopped in the street, their fetes and festivals overtaken by a cavalcade of media, both domestic and international. They'd attended forums, drunk cups of tea, talked to endless pollsters and been in the spotlight for nine long months.

We all *felt* like winners and we could see the joylessness on the other side. But nerves were stretched thin in the final week as we sweated it out until polling day. My dominant emotion was of not wanting to let anyone down. Not to disappoint. What if I just missed?

I couldn't believe the spectacular generosity of the people who'd been working with me for months. Labor Party members like Rhonda and Giovanni Bicego and Iris and John Knight had campaigned for years in Bennelong in an effort to nudge the vote Labor's way. This time, with every cake that Rhonda made for campaign workers, and every poster that Giovanni and the Knights delivered to a suburban front yard, they dared to dream of a different result. There were many many other ALP branch members just like them.

There was the Young Labor crowd—Amy Smith, Tim Quadrio, Michael Richardson, Sally Sitou, Tim Cummings, Jerome Laxale—who never stopped. They were there at six in the morning at Epping station or at the Meadowbank ferry wharf; they could locate anything, fix anything, divert anything; and they seemed to be the carriers of the most amazing cross-electorate intelligence. Sometimes it was best not to ask.

There was John Range, or 'the Field Commander' as I came to call him. A local TAFE IT teacher, John was not a member of the ALP nor did he strike anyone as overtly political, but he'd come to the view that the country needed to change and he backed me to the hilt. We made use of his exceptional organisational skills and his easy manner with all-comers and he ran our astonishing door-knocking effort. Over thirty thousand households were connected through John's efforts and the wonderful team he pulled together. He drew up the rosters, drove the van, tried to maintain our secondhand office computers, and kept telling me I was going to win.

Then there were the office gals, or as Lucienne would say, *les femmes d'un certain age*. Many came from the inner west or the lower North Shore, they had a dollar or two, they'd loved and lost and tried again, and above all, they understood that life is not linear and fixed, but problematic. They used their heads but had never disconnected from their hearts, so that when they saw someone in need, their first instinct was to try to help.

Sitting at the top of all this was Michael Butterworth, my campaign director, who'd never felt relaxed and comfortable in Howard's Australia. This was his moment, to put an end to the supremacy and sense of entitlement of the Liberals who for years had felt they were the exclusive owners of the 58 square kilometres that made up Bennelong. Michael described our campaign to unseat Howard as *viral* and for nine months he nurtured the organisms that kept reproducing inside the host's cells. When the purple army and its legions all got too much for him, Lucienne would take him by the hand, tell him to breathe deeply and take him out for a toasted cheese and tomato sandwich.

It all added up to a liquorice allsorts of a coalition working on an unconventional campaign seeking a convention-breaking result.

Rudd had kept his promise to me and brought his national campaign into Bennelong again and again. Julia Gillard, Jenny Macklin, Penny Wong, Stephen Smith and other senior members of Labor's team had visited. Bob Hawke and Bob and Helena Carr were also extraordinarily generous and effective campaigners.

And then there was the supportive constituency that went way beyond the borders of Bennelong. It seemed half of Australia was rooting for me. They sent letters, cheques, handy tips, cartoons and poems.

The well-wishers even reached back across time with one email arriving, just ahead of polling day, from the great-grandson of Jack Holloway, the first Labor candidate to defeat a sitting Prime Minister. Eighty years before, at the beginning of the Depression, Holloway, determined to maintain workers' rights, had triumphed over Stanley Melbourne Bruce in the Victorian seat of Flinders.

Could history be about to repeat itself? Whether millionaire or pensioner, the support flowed in, and within the cramped and boisterous confines of our campaign office we received daily evidence from across the country that Australians had had enough of the Howard years. Not untypical was the $500 cheque I received from Margaret Johnstone, a Melbourne pensioner. The campaign donation was accompanied by the letter she sent to John Howard. It read:

> I refer to the attached letter regarding the recent Seniors' payment of $500. The pre-election timing of this 'bonus' troubles me. You urge us to trust you, Prime Minister, but trust is based on honesty. Where was honesty in children overboard, in weapons of mass destruction, in the AWB affair, in your core and non-core promises? Regrettably a pattern of deceit destroys trust.

Margaret then delivered the kicker.

> Coming as I do from a long line of thrifty, hardworking Scots I am determined to put your money to the best possible use. I have forwarded a cheque for $500 to Ms Maxine McKew for her campaign in the seat of Bennelong.

It was hardly a singular view. Quite the opposite.

And as if on cue, in the final days of the campaign the bad faith and trickery that had come to define the Howard years were amplified in a spectacular way in the Sydney seat of Lindsay with the Liberals distributing fake flyers claiming that the ALP was sympathetic to Islamic terrorists.

This time the scam was undone from inside with a Liberal whistleblower alerting the Labor camp. Is this the way it would end for a four-time election winner?

Come election day, I left home at about 7.30 a.m., ready to spend a long day at polling booths across the electorate and feeling confident about two things. First, that I'd run the campaign I'd wanted to run, with energy and verve, and that no one could be in any doubt that I was presenting myself as a serious alternative to the incumbent. And second, that the leader I'd signed up to work for eleven months earlier had done everything he said he'd do. The clarity and discipline of Kevin Rudd's campaign had held right throughout the year and he never blinked. Rudd would take us into the post-Howard years, regenerate the national spirit and give purpose to the prosperity.

John Howard voted in Ermington. Bob and I voted at Epping West Primary School, just across the road from Martelli's and five minutes from our home.

It rained on and off but our side didn't seem to notice. The day was boisterous, wild, argumentative, colourful, emotional and, ultimately, decisive.

It was followed by one of those nights of inextinguishable joy, where the purple army danced, hugged, jumped up and down, yelled, wept, hugged some more, and then for a few moments was silent as I finally made it through the crush and onto the stage at the North Ryde School of Arts Community Centre.

If ever there was a time when I needed to find the words to capture a unique moment, a moment that few had dared to believe possible, this was it. People would tell stories about this night. About where they were and what they felt and how it made them smile and laugh and dance with the sheer unexpected thrill of a win that would make the history books.

I was barely breathing, my mouth was dry, but somehow my emotions and brain managed to connect.

Through the crush of cameras, and with Bob, Mary, my sister Margo and her daughter Alex positioned up on stage with me, John Watkins handed me a microphone. I was live across the country:

> This has been an amazing night for Labor and, hopefully, a transforming night for the country. Bennelong is on a knife edge. But what you've all shown over the past months is that the contest matters. One thing is for certain. Bennelong will never be taken for granted again.

I stopped short of claiming victory, but whatever the final count I knew we'd won.

And it was a special kind of victory because our souls *had* stirred as we'd asked, 'What's the best we can be?' I'd been thinking for days about what I wanted to say. The campaign had changed me in a subtle but distinct way. It was because people had let me into their lives and told me things and on election night I wanted to talk about who and what we are—the extraordinary, amazing Australia.

> I spent thirty years interviewing Australians—admired and powerful Australians—but now I know I missed the best of them. To get to know them, you have to knock on front doors and talk to them in the street—and you find out so much more when you are not carrying a camera and a microphone.
>
> So I want this to be a victory for Sister Louise, now a resident at St Catherine's. She's ninety and blind but only last week she told me, 'Nobody is blind in heaven.'
>
> I want this to be a victory for Emily who is six years old and a student at Denistone Primary. She told her parents to vote for Kevin Rudd because he would be good for children. And you know, we need a great Prime Minister for children.
>
> And I want this to be a victory for Ali who's just completed his HSC exams—and Ali, maybe you're here tonight. Only a few years ago Ali was in a refugee camp in Pakistan waiting for passage out but he has now found a safe home, and a welcome here in Australia.

I knew we had generated huge expectations so I finished with the oft-quoted line from poet Robert Frost: *I have promises to keep and miles to go before I sleep.*

In the exhilarating days that followed, as we absorbed what we'd achieved—a 5.4 per cent national swing that would deliver an astonishing gain of twenty-four seats, and a 5.5 per cent swing to Labor in Bennelong, a seat we had never held—I received hundreds of letters and emails from Australians. The messages ranged from the ribald to the inspiring to the humbling.

From Sir Gerard Brennan, former Chief Justice of the High Court of Australia: 'You have vanquished a prime minister and have made a major contribution to the dawning of a new age—an age in which Australia may again become a free and confident nation, a nation in which fear and negativity have no place.'

From Gough Whitlam: 'Maxine the Magnificent—well done.'

From one of my Epping neighbours: 'Right from the start you talked about issues such as integrity and fairness and justice. You made us realise that idealism is not dead and that cynicism in the political process does not have to be the ultimate winner.'

And from an old journalistic pal: 'Maybe I've watched too many *West Wings* and read the Redfern speech too many times, but it feels like a long long time since someone in Australia has spoken like this. Good luck and I know you'll do the best to serve the community.'

And for sheer laugh-out-loud chutzpah, it was hard to beat the note and photograph sent by 'Sarah'. She and six of her female friends, all battle-hardened progressives and champions of multiple causes, had made a pact that if I beat John Howard, they would do the full monty and stand under the Sydney Harbour Bridge at Kirribilli.

Come the moment, they were on such a high that stripping off wasn't enough. A marking pen was produced and across twelve very respectable and very bare buttocks was written the farewell of the night: B-Y-E B-Y-E J-O-H-N-N-Y.

Rudd kept it clean and sent a text that read: 'You are a giant slayer.'

And one of Bob's old sparring partners from Victoria, former Senator Robert Ray, declared: 'The Labor Party will owe her for life.'

As for me, I'd finally worked out the answer to that question posed by Karl Stefanovic back in February in Channel Nine's Willoughby studios.

I *had* found a new love in 2007. Bennelong.

Chapter 4
GREAT EXPECTATIONS

I WENT FROM underdog to giant slayer in a night.

'Have you absorbed what you've pulled off?' News Limited journalist George Megalogenis asked me that question not long after the November win. We were at the Paperchain Bookstore in Canberra's Manuka. Megalogenis had asked me to launch the new edition of his book, *The Longest Decade*, and the event seemed to attract half of Canberra with people packed into every available space. There was an equal mix of excitement and curiosity about the new crowd in town, and about me as one of its newest recruits.

I knew what I'd done. I'd stood conventional wisdom on its head. It was all there in the figures, which in turn reflected the work we had put in at the local level, as well as the masterful campaign that Kevin Rudd had engineered at the national level. In forty-seven out of forty-eight booths across Bennelong, Labor had recorded solid swings that told a straightforward story: Bennelong, just like the rest of the country, was ready for change. Whether blue-collar or hi-tech workers, young families, female professionals, Asian immigrants or even diehard Liberals casting a once-only vote for Labor—they shifted allegiance in sufficient numbers to deliver an unambiguous result and a 16 per cent primary swing. After the distribution of preferences, Labor secured 51.4 per cent of the vote to the Liberals' 48.6 per cent. The only pundit who had made a correct early call, and predicted a Labor win in Bennelong right from the beginning, had been veteran election analyst Malcolm Mackerras.

The seat had been watched by the country with the kind of fascination and fixed attention normally reserved for a Melbourne Cup race. In turn, Bennelong seemed to revel in the spotlight and voters went into the polling booths showing little sentiment about expediting a prime minister's retirement.

With the exception of Western Australia, it was the scale and breadth of the national win that gave heart to Labor's true believers and astonished the party's hardheads.

Rudd, an outsider from Queensland, and leader of his party for less than a year, had proven to be an outstandingly effective campaigner. He had delivered seats not just in the predicted marginals but also in conservative regional and rural areas, in canefields and coalfields, in the inner metro areas and on the fringe of cities.

It was a historic win in every sense. Rudd had always talked of the need for 'an Everest-effort' and it wasn't hyperbole. In the two previous elections of 2001 and 2004, John Howard had increased the Coalition vote and in 2004 had even secured a Senate majority. Rudd began the task at the beginning of 2007 needing a 5 per cent swing, and after eleven months of relentless, focused campaigning, he over-delivered with a decisive swing of 5.4 per cent. It translated into a two-party preferred result of 52.7 per cent to the Coalition's 47.3 per cent. The swing to Labor in Rudd's home state of Queensland was 7.5 per cent, with the party securing an extra nine seats, which brought to fifteen the state's seat count in the House of Representatives.

Rudd became only the third Labor leader to win government from opposition in sixty years. The Labor historians would also note that the swing to Rudd was greater than that secured by Bob Hawke in 1983 and comparable in achievement to Gough Whitlam's 7.1 per cent swing in the 1969 election that almost delivered him victory.

There was a sweet symmetry in this because a good deal of Rudd's pitch for office reflected Whitlam's transformative social agenda—national investment in education, health, housing and urban development.

Whether it was Damian Hale in Solomon in the Northern Territory, or the Queensland candidates—Jon Sullivan in Longman, Jim Turnour in Leichhardt, Chris Trevor in Flynn; or the NSW newbies—myself in Bennelong, Mike Kelly in Eden-Monaro or Janelle Saffin in Page—we all knew that the primary reason we were set for new lives as federal Labor parliamentarians was because Rudd had been a champion game-changer.

It was Rudd who'd not only played with Howard's mind but who had reached out and connected with Australians of all types. And it was real. In between all the horseplay for the cameras and the exaggerated bonhomie that campaigns seem to require, amidst all this, voters could see that when Rudd talked about the uneven performance of our hospitals or the woeful state of public school buildings, he meant it. They trusted him when he said, 'I'm here to help.'

As the veteran Canberra writer Mungo MacCallum wrote in the 2009 *Quarterly Essay*, 'Australian Story, Kevin Rudd and the Lucky Country': '... for all his nerdiness and prolixity, there is something very Australian about him, and the voters recognise it. Rudd has given them back their Lucky Country—and this time not in a spirit of irony, but one of self-belief.'[1]

Importantly, Rudd had also given back to the Australian Labor Party a sense of belief in its own capacities, although his inclination was never to indulge this. On the night of the election he'd hosed down supporters by telling them they could have a strong cup of tea and an Iced VoVo on the way through but after that it was time to get down to work. Some found it hard to forgive him for being a killjoy.

Rudd knew from his time as a Queensland bureaucrat that the first few weeks of a new government are crucial; that the way the new regime uses power can set the tone and pace of what's to come. Labor was well prepared on this front, with John Faulkner, Penny Wong and Lindsay Tanner all having worked on detailed planning for the transition to government. There was to be no purge of senior public servants as there had been when John Howard came to office in 1996. There would be increased accountability, a detailed Ministerial Code of Conduct, a 30 per cent cut to ministerial staff, and a vetting of government advertising by the Auditor-General.

What I remember, above all, from this period is the sheer busy-ness and the sense of intensity about what we had taken on. The campaign had been full-on but we were now all on warp speed. Rudd called me just after eight on the Monday morning after the poll. We talked for about fifteen minutes. He was full of praise for the campaign I'd run and thanked me in particular for the way I'd handled myself on election night and subsequently. We then got down to the nitty gritty of the role I would play in the new government. We had no prior agreement. I had never said to him, 'If I beat Howard this is the reward I expect …' I had accepted at face value what Rudd had said, that he would choose on merit.

Then again, talking with a Prime Minister prior to the announcement of a new ministry is hardly like a normal job interview. And I was not without power in this negotiation. John Faulkner had already been on the phone, wanting me to con-sider a portfolio based around the promotion of our international development aid, an area set to be boosted. That was tempting, but my primary interest was in education. That was how Labor could make a difference for a new generation of young Australians. I put it to Rudd that I was keen to work on one of the key aspects of our education policy, the reform of early learning and preschool. Rudd himself had invested a lot in this and was a convert after reading Professor James Heckman's research about the economic and social benefits of investment in quality early learning. It was also a nice fit with Bennelong, with some of the best Australian research, teaching and practice underway at the North Ryde campus of Macquarie University.

I didn't push for a ministerial spot but I made it clear I wanted to be part of the executive and would serve as a parliamentary secretary. We left it at that. There were no further discussions and it wasn't until the following Thursday, 29 November, when the class of 2007 all assembled in Canberra for our first caucus meeting, that ministerial appointments were confirmed and announced.

Eighty-three Labor members of the House of Representatives along with twenty-eight senators (Labor's four newly elected senators were not sworn in until July 2008) walked into Parliament House that day. And whether rookies like me or long-termers who had served in government and then through the long years in opposition, we all sensed the possibilities, along with the sheer thrill of the privilege and opportunity to govern for all and do good things. We believed we would build the future, redefine the 'light on the hill' and put an end to the rancour and belligerence in our public life.

As Rudd walked into a cheering caucus room there may have been some who held back, but not many. Everyone who'd walked the streets and knocked on doors month after month knew the force of will it had taken to sustain a disciplined campaign. Applauding along with the rest, Greg Combet, newly elected as the member for the Hunter Valley–based seat of Charlton, lent over and said to me, 'Howard was bloody hard to beat.' You're telling *me*?

Beazley, Crean and Latham, their portraits on the wall of the caucus room, had all tried to get Howard's measure but had fallen short. Their unlikely successor was now being feted. Throughout the sustained applause, Rudd looked neither triumphalist nor burdened. I wondered if he'd even had time to pause, to be still for a moment and savour the win, to feel what it meant or could mean.

For now it was about *doing*. There had been a plan to win and now there was a plan for the first year in government. Hell, there was even a plan for the summer—and it didn't involve a long stretch at the beach or even a munch of an Iced VoVo.

Penny Wong was about to head off to Bali to join delegates at the United Nations Framework Convention on Climate Change. Ratifying the Kyoto Protocol was one of the first acts of the new government. Jenny Macklin was charged with the all-important consultations that would culminate in the historic Apology to Indigenous Australians that would mark the new Parliament, and Treasurer Wayne Swan would have to frame Labor's first Budget against the backdrop of hedge-fund collapses in the United States and an early warning from his US counterpart, Hank Paulson, that America was facing a meltdown in its housing market.

I fully expected that by day's end I would be working with Stephen Smith, who'd had carriage of education policy throughout 2007. I was in for a surprise and so was Smith. At the last minute Rudd offered Smith the Foreign Affairs portfolio and he accepted after a quick call to his partner Jane, to warn her of an even more intense travel schedule. Julia Gillard, as Deputy PM, would take on the super-portfolio of Education, Employment and Workplace Relations and Social Inclusion.

When I'd sat down with Rudd that morning, newly installed in the prime ministerial suite and seeing one member of his team after another in quick succession, he told me he was appointing me as a parliamentary secretary reporting to his office and with special responsibility for early childhood education and childcare. After repeated references to 'reporting as well to Julia', he sensed my confusion and finally said, 'Oh yes, Julia has education.'

So I was to have two bosses: the Prime Minister and his deputy. Life was going to be interesting.

Soon after, Gillard and I had an even quicker meeting. Every bit as methodical as Rudd, and as prodigious a worker, Gillard gave the impression of starting every day with absolute confidence about what she would achieve and a detailed plan for how she would do it. It was an approach that earned the respect of many senior public servants.

Given the big ambitions we'd promoted around what we dubbed 'the Education Revolution', I was keen to have a deep and meaningful discussion straight away about our policy approach and how we would engage with key stakeholders. But that was going to have to wait. There was only time for a functional chat about immediate tasks before she ended with a lighthearted crack about the fact that two childless women were now the policy guardians of Australia's children. Not something that had even crossed my mind, but perhaps Gillard was still thinking about Liberal Senator Bill Heffernan's tasteless remark about her being 'deliberately barren'.

When I got a chance I rang Bob with the news and told him the swearing-in was set for the following Monday. He seemed more preoccupied with dealing with the endless couriers dropping off flowers and baskets of fruit from well-wishers.

Back at Eastwood, Lucienne and others, in particular campaign worker Maree Faulkner, were trying to wind up the campaign activities, organise the physical move into the electorate office and deal with an avalanche of calls and emails with requests from all over Sydney, across the country and overseas. Everyone wanted to talk to the giant slayer.

Having pulled off what had seemed an impossible feat, the bar was being set even higher. The view was that I could now set my sights on a cure for cancer, a complete rout of the Taliban and reform of the Vatican. I'm not kidding. Numerous artists wanted to paint my portrait for the annual Archibald competition, international media outlets were still lining up for interviews, and there was even talk of a movie. There was a mountain of invitations to speak all over the country and constant urging to champion multiple different causes.

I made an early decision and stuck to it. Unless it was local or related to my portfolio work, then invitations, for the most part, were replied to in the negative. This caused a bit of grief because many people seemed to want me to be a national flag carrier for all sorts of things they felt were missing from our public life. I was, however, very conscious of having been irritatingly tagged 'the celebrity candidate' right throughout 2007, and I would have immediately morphed into the 'the celebrity MP' if I'd raced around the country making speeches and pronouncements on each and every favoured issue.

Winning Bennelong against the odds and being only the second person to beat a sitting Prime Minister was now a matter of Australian political history, but I wasn't going to spend any time boasting about it. Equally, I didn't want to feel burdened by it. I was determined to be what I'd said I would be: a strong voice for Bennelong and a local champion. Howard had been an attentive local member but not a particularly visible one, at least not in recent times. So for now, and certainly for the first year, the diary priorities would be Epping Boys High and not The Brisbane Institute, and talking to veterans at the North Ryde RSL and not students of political science at Monash University.

The odd thing was that while half the country seemed to be as high as a kite about what had happened in Bennelong, both sides still had scrutineers hard at work in neighbouring Chatswood, where the Australian Electoral Commission was supervising and checking each and every postal vote.

Howard had still not officially conceded, but I formally claimed victory a week after the election on Saturday, 1 December. I made a brief announcement outside Gladesville Public School before taking part in the annual Christmas parade. *The Weekly Times'* John Booth was there and he raised his bowler hat to me as he snapped away. In the end 'Boothy', as we all called him, had seen momentum moving my way and had predicted a win in a conversation with Margot Saville. This is how Saville remembered it in *The Battle for Bennelong*:

> I ask John who he thinks will win Bennelong. *The Times* has always been fanatically pro-Howard, but I want to know what JB thinks. He says he thinks Maxine will win because she has spent so much time and energy getting to know the voters—she has run an excellent campaign. I am gobsmacked … Howard really is in trouble.[2]

On the Monday morning after claiming victory, I was back in Canberra, this time with Bob, and we set off together to the Governor-General's residence at Yarralumla for the swearing-in of Kevin Rudd, as Australia's twenty-sixth Prime Minister, and his chosen ministerial team. In front of the Queen's representative, Sir Michael Jeffery, Rudd became only the second head of government to swear to serve 'the Commonwealth of Australia' and not the head of state.

There were forty-two of us in the capacious drawing room that day: twenty Cabinet ministers, a further ten in the outer ministry and twelve parliamentary secretaries. All selected by Rudd, not caucus, thus breaking with long-held ALP tradition. One-third of incoming ministers were appointed to portfolios that differed from the ones they'd held in opposition. There was talent aplenty and diversity as well, with a record seven women across both Cabinet and junior ministries. But only four members of Rudd's team had prior experience at the senior level of government: Bob Debus (former NSW Attorney-General), Simon Crean, Bob McMullan and John Faulkner. While inexplicable to me, McMullan's position as parliamentary secretary—instead of being in the ministry—suggested that factional backing still mattered. McMullan was non-aligned. That made two of us. Two out of forty-two. Three if you included Rudd.

We were seated in order of seniority so I was down the back with my new colleagues Mike Kelly, Greg Combet, Gary Gray, Bill Shorten and others. The senior ministers went first, with Rudd announcing their names. Each would recite the oath and then, seated in front of the Governor-General, sign the executive documents. It was a solid line-up: Nicola Roxon in Health, Lindsay Tanner in Finance, Penny Wong as Minister for Climate Change and, most encouraging of all, John Faulkner as Special Minister of State and Cabinet Secretary. It gave Faulkner, with his strong background and interest in administrative integrity, a wide brief to be the guardian who would keep the government on the straight and narrow. Rudd was to call him his 'wise owl'.

Soon enough it was my turn. I was wearing very high heels so I was conscious of not wanting to provide the 'falling into office' photograph by tripping up. But the trap for this young player was signing on the dotted line. The wrong one. 'That's where I sign,' I heard the GG say. *Good start, Max.* Down the back of the room where all the families were sitting, I could swear I heard a familiar sigh from Bob.

Minus this little snag (and the GG's aide-de-camp later graciously provided me with a fresh copy), it was a day I could never have imagined. After years of interviewing politicians, now I was one of them. From questioning to governing.

Right from the start I was intensely aware of the expectations we had aroused. During the campaign we had promised 'fresh thinking' and a different approach on a range of complex issues: Commonwealth–state relations, tackling climate change, reform of education and health. I knew from years of watching and commenting from the other side that delivery is rarely perfect, and that even with the best of reformist intentions, the gloss of any new enterprise soon wears thin. But as everyone enjoyed the moment of victory and swapped campaign war stories, and gathered on the front steps of Government House with the Governor-General for the official photograph, it was entirely possible to believe that we were set to create a better Australia.

Labor governments are elected to *do* things and we would be bold. The government was led by a man with a formidable intellect and an innate sense of decency. He had appointed a ministerial team of bright, energetic people. Collectively, we had a sense of mission and a plan for the future. If we kept our promises, got the implementation right, maintained our focus and communicated effectively, then there was every reason to believe we would all be making the return journey to Yarralumla for years to come.

Later that afternoon the entire ministerial team gathered in the Cabinet room. It was another first for all of us, with the exception of Crean, McMullan and Faulkner. As was the briefing from the outgoing (by choice) Secretary of the Department of Prime

Minister and Cabinet, Peter Shergold, on the transitional arrangements for the new government. Just about everybody was soon to find out that government is light years away from opposition and that there is no handbook.

I was too preoccupied with making mental lists to feel intimidated. There was much to do: detailed briefings from senior public servants, getting on top of all the literature and research on early learning and children's development, staff appointments, and preparation for a crowded parliamentary calendar. My approach to new challenges is always the same: head down, do the homework, and don't assume any question is too dumb to ask.

There was one piece of bad news that I was still absorbing. The leasing arrangements on Howard's old electorate office on Victoria Road in Gladesville were such that the bureaucrats in the Department of Finance insisted that I make it my base as well. I couldn't believe it. Positioned right on the edge of the electorate, the space that had served as Howard's electorate office was on the top floor of an uninviting coral-pink building and with the kind of security and unwelcoming reception area that was fine for a largely absent Prime Minister, but dead wrong for me. My preference was for a highly visible, shopfront-style office on a main street, accessible by bus and train, and geographically well positioned.

My multiple appeals failed. It was my first lesson in the limits of power. It would be two years before I was able to relocate to more suitable premises in Oxford Street, Epping.

It did, however, give Howard and myself a bit of a talking point in what was an understandably awkward exchange when we finally came face to face on Wednesday, 12 December, for what was the formal declaration of the poll results in front of Australian Electoral Commission officials in Chatswood.

It says much about Howard that he didn't absent himself from this, the final formal moment that marked the end of his parliamentary career and the defining period of his life's work.

My primary vote count was 39,408 to Howard's 39,551. With a strong flow of preferences, the final margin of victory was 2434 votes. As *The Sydney Morning Herald* said, 'closer to a boxful than a handful'.[3] It was a decisive win but I was on a thin margin—1.4 per cent—making Bennelong the eighth most marginal seat in the country.

You could run in Bennelong. Was it only ten months ago that Bob had said this?

A few feet from where I was sitting, with Howard beside me, the Bennelong returning officer, James Carroll, read out the results that made official my new status as the MP for Bennelong: 'Accordingly, under the provisions of Section 284 of the Commonwealth Electoral Act, I declare Maxine McKew duly elected as a member to serve in the House of Representatives in the Parliament of the Commonwealth of Australia, the division of Bennelong.'

Howard had dealt with more setbacks than most in political life but there can't have been too many occasions when he imagined an ending such as this. He got through it by observing the conventions. He made a gracious concession speech, talked briefly about the changed nature of the electorate and then wished me well.

I responded in kind, and thanked Howard for his long service to public life. In my first speech to Parliament I would also pay tribute to the former PM 'for being a great warrior for his beliefs'. And so he was.

As usual, the place was crawling with television cameras and photographers. Later I would regret that I hadn't noticed the bloke from *The Canberra Times* who was on the floor in front of me with a great view right up my skirt.

Howard and I shook hands and by way of small talk he asked about the move into the Gladesville office, and then remarked, 'It's not particularly well positioned.' If only those Finance officials could have heard this from the departing tenant!

The next day's headlines—'HOWARD OUT FOR THE FINAL COUNT'; 'HOWARD'S END'; 'HOWARD ERA ENDS'—were accompanied by a totemic photographic image that says much about the strength of our democracy. In a nondescript suburban hall, power had been peacefully transferred and the moment was recorded with the vanquished applauding the victor.

With *one* very important exception. In a tasteless editorial decision that would draw the ire of many a Canberran, *The Canberra Times* chose to use a low-angle shot that was dubbed my 'Sharon Stone' moment. There were limits to how visible I wanted to be as an MP! I had learned another lesson. Beware adventurous snappers positioned yogi-style on the floor and, just to be safe, put the short skirts in the back of the closet.

It was two weeks to Christmas after a year that had been non-stop. Getting involved in politics is like walking through a door to a completely new life. Your old ways, the habits and indulgences and friendships that have previously sustained you are still there, but you are constantly pulled in another direction.

I'd always thought of myself as an efficient manager of my own time. I'd worked to deadlines my whole life and juggled a range of professional and volunteer commitments. But day by day, as the diary crowded up, with each appointment tagged a 'must do', I was realising that the life of an MP is light years away from just about any other professional experience. I'd had thirty years in the communications business and understood the dynamics of public life. I was familiar with the way our national institutions worked and could call on an Australia-wide network of influence-makers. All this helped, and I didn't lack for confidence. But even in these early days of the new government I could see just how different my new life was going to be. On a daily basis I would juggle complexity, scrutiny, accountability and competing interests—and for the most part, I was on my own.

Rudd was already setting the cracking pace that would become the hallmark of the new government. Cabinet held its first meeting in Brisbane on 6 December and a Council of Australian Governments meeting, or COAG—Rudd's 'workhorse of the nation'—was set for 20 December.

I was doing the rounds of some of the exemplary early learning centres, including the gem in my own electorate, Mia-Mia at Macquarie University, and meeting with some of the key institutional and academic thinkers in the field. I had a terrific job, and an important one, and most of the stakeholders I met could see that I wanted to tackle the job with energy and creativity. The country's standout champions for improved children's services—Fiona Stanley, Frank Oberklaid and Collette Tayler—were all public enthusiasts for our reform agenda for early learning.

But the main focus was detailed briefings with the department—in this case, the Department of Education, Employment and Workplace Relations. Childcare, in line with our election commitment, had been incorporated into the Education portfolio as this reflected the higher standards and greater level of professionalism that we were intent on bringing to the sector.

Trish Drum was invaluable in this period. She was now commuting between her home in the Blue Mountains, the electorate and Canberra, getting together all the portfolio briefing papers and handling the liaison with the public service.

At the PM's request, all departments provided senior officers to assist new ministers for a period of twelve weeks until long-term staff arrangements were vetted and confirmed. Annette Laurie filled this role in my office. She arrived with a background in indigenous children's issues, a nothing-fazes-me attitude, and a very solid appreciation of streamlined process and procedure. Just what I needed. In the days following the swearing-in of the new government, she could see the way the world was crowding in and quietly said, 'Everyone wants to see you right away but with a few exceptions I'll hold them off until the new year.' Laurie was a treasure.

As was Vicki Rundle, the department's key specialist in early learning. Rundle and I would spend hours and hours together in the coming months as we worked through our election commitments, in particular how we defined and implemented the country's first set of national standards for the out-of-home care of young children. She had great presence and, with a broad smile that practically swallowed her face, could disarm the most inflexible of stakeholders.

Overwhelmingly these were blue-sky days. Summer days with Christmas ahead, and a vigorous new leader with a young family in The Lodge. Winners are grinners and our win nationally, along with mine in Bennelong, seemed to put a spring in the step of a lot of people, whether political agnostics or true believers.

Margot Saville, a lawyer and former ABC and *Sydney Morning Herald* journalist, had been signed on early by Melbourne University Publishing boss Louise Adler to write an account of a race that was always going to be in the spotlight, no matter the result. Saville shadowed both myself and Howard for six months and captured the weekly detail, the excitement, the frustration, the nuttiness and, in the end, the real contestability of a most unlikely political match-up. She wrote on the run, and within a fortnight of the election result, MUP was ready to launch *The Battle for Bennelong: The adventures of Maxine McKew, aged 50 something.*

It was heavily promoted in *The Sydney Morning Herald* with excerpts published in *The Good Weekend*: 'Read all about it—how she did it—the savvy campaign that toppled a PM.'

The launch was at Pitt Street's ArtHouse Hotel on 18 December. There was another that night, hosted by Banjo Books in Epping, one in Brisbane and another in Melbourne. It was standing room only at all of them. People lined up to buy multiple copies for Christmas stockings. They asked questions from the serious to the trivial but in all of them you could hear the hope and the not quite so audible plea: *Don't let us down.*

Howard's nemesis, Margaret Johnstone—the thrifty Scot who'd sent me her pension bonus payment—turned up at the Melbourne launch and took a triumphant bow. In Brisbane, Mary was there with all her mates. She'd loved the campaign and never seemed to doubt the end result. Mary had clearly had a bit of convenient amnesia about those indifferent school report cards, because she told journalists she was unsurprised by the result: 'She's always achieved what she set out to achieve.' For a generous rewriting of history, my sister and I thought this was hilarious.

And from a gentleman whose name I can't recall, but who told me he cast his first vote for Ben Chifley, came a story that was obviously going to be embroidered over the years until it was part of his regular bowls club repertoire. Disappointed by the over-promotion of a sixty-fifth birthday gift of sky-diving lessons, where he'd been told that sky-diving was 'better than sex', my newfound friend beamed at me as he told me that on the night of 24 November, when he realised that Howard was losing in Bennelong, he turned to his wife and declared, 'Now *that's* better than sex.'

Everyone who has read Saville's book has told me they love it. I still hear this years later. Except, of course, my mate John Faulkner. He is at his curmudgeonly worst as he dismisses a book that he says lacks any serious political analysis. I pat him on the head when I hear this and tell him he needs to get out more.

Of course I enjoyed the attention. Who wouldn't? I knew it would end soon enough and it did. But not before I spelt out my own expectations and hopes for the country.

In a long interview with *The Sydney Morning Herald*, I told writer Annabel Crabb:

> I think we're on the threshold of something fine in this country. Jenny Macklin this week has talked about the importance of saying sorry to the first Australians. And I know that the new Prime Minister Kevin Rudd, is very conscious that this be done in a very special way. It marks … a new generosity in the way we engage with the first Australians and I would like to think that Labor's win in Bennelong connects with that generous spirit in some way.[4]

Sentiments for a summer of trust. The first summer of the new Labor government.

Elaine and Brian, with baby Margo, Maxine in the foreground.

Grandparents Eileen and Joe Truda at the counter of their Scarborough store.

A bad hair day for Maxine, here with Margo in Brisbane, 1980.

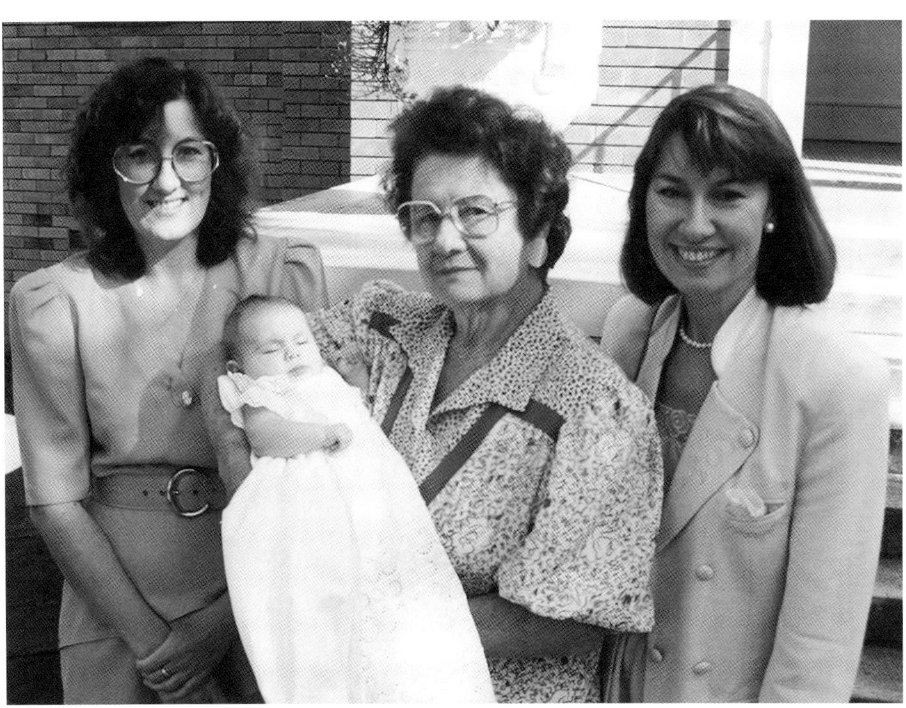

With Margo and stepmother Mary at the christening of Margo's baby daughter Alexandra.

In Washington DC as ABC TV correspondent, with John Hagan on camera, 1986.

In Rome for Channel 10, with Les Seymour on camera, 1989.

Taken for *Page One*,
Channel 10, 1990.

In Halong Bay, Vietnam, with partner Bob Hogg, 2004.

Farewelling the ABC, with Kerry O'Brien and Geraldine Doogue, 2006.

Countdown to election day, 2007.

Victory night, with Alexandra and Mary in the foreground, election day 2007.
© AAP Image/Tracey Neamy.

The poll is declared, with John Howard, December 2007.
© Fairfax Media/Brendan Esposito BBE.

Signing on, with Governor General Michael Jeffery and Kevin Rudd. Photography by AUSPIC.

Walk to the gallows, 24 June 2010. © AAP Image/Alan Porritt.

Electoral staff and Bennelong supporters, election night, 2010.

Election night, 2010.

Chapter 5

THE GRAND, THE BAD AND EVERYTHING IN BETWEEN

IT ALL STARTED so well.

13 February 2008 was one of those days—'a noble day', as it would be called—when it was possible to feel that history had turned a page.

The 361-word Apology to the Stolen Generations delivered by Prime Minister Rudd at the beginning of the forty-second Parliament took only a few minutes to read.

> We apologise for the laws and policies of successive Parliaments and governments that have inflicted profound grief, suffering and loss on these our fellow Australians. We apologise especially for the removal of Aboriginal and Torres Strait Islander children from their families, their communities and their country. For the pain, suffering and hurt of these Stolen Generations, their descendants and their families left behind, we say sorry. To the mothers and the fathers, the brothers and the sisters, for the breaking up of families and communities, we say sorry. And for the indignity and degradation thus inflicted on a proud people and a proud culture, we say sorry.

Australians are not always comfortable with big public declarations, with the defining moments that leaders try to grasp, but on this occasion, the country was more than ready. In classrooms and workplaces, in city malls with specially mounted outdoor screens, Australians stopped and listened and reflected. And as they did, they seemed to be at one with a Prime Minister displaying his humanity.

The Apology had been the subject of rancorous debate for over a decade, ever since Sir Ronald Wilson and Mick Dodson had concluded their 689-page *Bringing Them Home* report in 1997. Many of the cultural warriors of the right rejected outright the report's stark conclusion that the laws and practices that promoted the removal of Aboriginal children from their families 'were in breach of the international prohibition of genocide' and a 'gross violation of human rights'.[1]

John Howard never accepted this and, consistent with his position, was the only former prime minister not present in the federal parliament as Rudd, in the speech that followed the formal Apology, endorsed both the sentiment and detail of Wilson and Dodson's report.

I've heard Rudd deliver a lot of speeches and this was one of his best. As he spoke of removing 'a stain from the soul of Australia' there was absolute silence in Parliament.

The galleries were packed, as was the Great Hall and the public spaces outside. Inside, on the floor of the parliamentary chamber, members of the Stolen Generations sat alongside former Governor-General Sir William Deane and former Prime Ministers Malcolm Fraser, Gough Whitlam, Bob Hawke and Paul Keating. In 1995 it was Keating who'd got the ball rolling when he asked his Attorney-General, Michael Lavarch, to begin an inquiry that concluded a year after Labor lost government in 1996.[2]

It had taken a very long time to get to this point. And along the way there had been massive denial from the conservative side, and plenty of faux distinctions made between *symbolic* versus *practical* reconciliation. But there had also been the Sydney Bridge Walk in 2000 and huge gatherings across the country as a majority of Australians made the plea for a new spirit of generosity and partnership. Many of them had made the visit to Canberra that day. They wanted to be part of this moment.

As I would come to realise, when Parliament lifts its conventions and throws the doors open, it takes on a different aspect. It is more reflective of the richness of the nation and manages to convey meaning and relevance to a wider cross-section of Australians.

Ahead would be days of discord and nights of impenetrable boredom, and too soon, days *and* nights of career-destroying intrigue, but for now, at this moment, a majority of the nation could feel inspired through an act of genuine reconciliation with indigenous Australians.

It wasn't about guilt or about shame. It was about the record. Telling non-indigenous Australians the truth of what had happened to the nation's original inhabitants. Rudd captured this:

> There is something terribly primal about these first-hand accounts. The pain is searing, it screams from the pages—the hurt, the humiliation, the degradation and the sheer brutality of the act of physically separating a mother from her child is a deep assault on our senses and on our most elemental sense of humanity. These stories cry out to be heard, they cry out for an apology. Instead, from the nation's Parliament there has been a stony and stubborn and deafening silence for more than a decade … a view that instead we should look for any pretext to push this great wrong to one side. To leave it languishing with the historians, the academics and the cultural warriors as if the Stolen Generations are little more than an interesting sociological phenomenon. But the Stolen Generations are not intellectual curiosities, they are human beings, human beings who have been damaged deeply by the decisions of parliaments and governments.

There was sustained applause and tears shed both inside and out of the chamber as Rudd finished.

Father Frank Brennan, the Jesuit lawyer and indigenous rights advocate, watched a live streaming of the Apology from California and thought it 'Rudd's finest hour'. The next day he was delighted to see that the event made the front page of *The New York Times.* Brennan has since told me that what he recalls is the way the event captured 'solemnity, grief and even good humour', and how all that came together to mark 'a significant moment in the life of the nation'.

It was important, he said, that 'Rudd had sat down and heard the stories for himself, and that he and his wife, Thérèse Rein, had welcomed members of the Stolen Generations into Parliament, honouring them in the House of the people.'

There are many memories from that day, but I remember in particular catching Jenny Macklin's eye and mouthing, 'Well done.' As Rudd's Indigenous Affairs Minister, Macklin had spent weeks endlessly negotiating the detail of how this ceremony would be shaped and choreographed and she was entitled to feel a sense of triumph. But she would have anticipated it would not be long before we were being judged on how effectively we could work in partnership to deliver improvements in health, education, housing and employment—all areas where indigenous Australians experience huge deficits compared to the non-indigenous population.

Rudd would commit to reporting yearly to Parliament on what became known as Closing the Gap: the targets set for improvement in key areas such as indigenous life expectancy, mortality rates, and literacy and numeracy. This was accompanied by significant new investment across all policy areas with progress monitored by COAG.

But this was in the future. For many of us, particularly those of us experiencing parliamentary life for the first time, the high emotion and excitement of the Apology carried us through that first week and for quite a time after. Just as well, because we were discovering that no matter how tight the scheduling and how rigorous the time-keeping there simply weren't enough hours in the day for the meetings, events, briefings, media engagements, consultations and committees. And that was before you even thought about an occasional visit to the loo.

One day you're campaigning, the next you're governing. There is no training course and no one volunteers to guide you through the maze. You have to ask. Even then, they may not hear you as they race down the corridor to their next must-attend meeting.

Having spent the summer reading everything the senior public servants sent my way, I felt reasonably comfortable with the detail of the Early Childhood portfolio. The hard part was appreciating what my actual job was. The first reality check was finding out how few trained early childhood teachers were available. In the early months of 2008 I was so anxious about how the government would deliver on its commitment for universal access to preschool, particularly for children in remote Aboriginal communities, I felt I almost had to make a bolt to Fitzroy Crossing and teach the kiddies myself! That *wasn't* my job, but the sense of personal responsibility was enormous.

As was the sense of urgency about getting on with it.

We had an immensely ambitious agenda in early childhood, nowhere more so than in the area of indigenous education.

On a day when we had vowed to make a generational difference, Parliament House was full of people determined to see we got it right. After the formalities of the Apology, various leaders in their fields did the rounds of ministerial offices. Among the many who came through my door were Professor Fiona Stanley and Dr Chris Sarra.

I'd interviewed Professor Stanley years before for my column in *The Bulletin*, so I was familiar with the work she directed at the Telethon Institute for Child Health Research. While she could point to plenty of examples in her home state of Western Australia and elsewhere of innovation in social service delivery, her statistics, among the most reliable developmental data in the country, painted a dismal picture. On all the equity markers— health, literacy and social behaviour—our poorest children were going backwards, and this at a time of record economic prosperity. Her message was encapsulated in so many of our policies: early intervention is crucial. Get it right in the early years, for parents and infants, and we will start to shrink the equity gap.

Later in the day, indigenous educator Dr Sarra sat in my office and talked about his own mission: to reverse the low ambition that is the reality for so many indigenous children. Sarra had fought a lot of battles over the years, largely against a system that seemed to put a pre-ordained limit on children's learning potential. His fightback has been through the creation of the Stronger Smarter Institute at the Queensland University of Technology. The institute trains teachers to demand and expect the best from everyone, no matter their starting point. I've since met principals and teachers who've attended the leadership courses that the institute runs and they all talk about it as the most effective and career-changing professional development they've ever undertaken. And when it came to some of the more contentious parts of Julia Gillard's Education Revolution program, which would be rolled out later in the first term—issues such as national testing and the publication of results via NAPLAN—Sarra was a supporter. As he wryly admitted, 'I don't care about the argument that it's teaching to the test. In some of the schools I worry about, that would be a start.'

What I also remember from that day is how special Chris Sarra said he felt. It was as if his own country had validated him in a unique way and he had a refreshed sense of optimism about tackling some of the most persistent and complex of problems.

Bookending the day was Paul Keating. I didn't manage to catch up with Keating in person but I caught him later on the ABC saying it had been 'a day of open hearts' where the country had found its 'golden threads'.

That's how it was on one of the grandest of days in February 2008.

*

The popular conception of a federal MP's life is one of being driven around in white Commonwealth cars, using planes like other people use buses, taking advantage of overseas trips and constantly attending swank dinners.

There's truth in this, although in my case my diary managers were under strict instructions to keep the large formal dinners to an absolute minimum. No worthwhile activity or conversation ever happens at these look-at-me shows, and the after-dinner speaker, whether politician or business leader, can be relied upon to deliver a safe twenty-minute (if you're lucky) verbal bromide. I avoided them like the plague. Not a career-enhancing move I admit, but I didn't want Rudd's job.

But there's also plenty of real work. On any given day in my electorate office I might be required to be a social worker, psychologist, marriage counsellor, environmentalist, urban planner, immigration advisor or legal practitioner. It was all part of the fun of the job but you also quickly find out that a vast amount of your time can easily be consumed by people whose idea of the world is just a tad different from the way the rest of us operate.

A middle-aged man—I'll call him Christopher—turned up frequently at the Victoria Road Electorate Office. He saw it as his second home. As he said to me the first time he appeared, 'John Howard looked after me for thirty years. Now it's your turn.'

I was tempted to tell him that the Howard I knew had always encouraged self-reliance. But Christopher wasn't much of a listener. He just wanted a place to hang out and to tell his life story … over and over and over. When our patience started to wear thin, Christopher upped the ante and started threatening everyone in the office. Fortunately the Gladesville coppers were just down the road and came to our rescue.

Innovators that we were, we developed our own defence. Emergency Chocolate it was called and it was synonymous with those days when the combination of reason and wit just wasn't enough to get us through. Surplus supplies were everywhere and constantly being topped up. I reckon our EO was the sweetest office north of the Sydney Harbour Bridge.

I was at my happiest working locally. Unlike parliamentary sessions, you can develop your own rhythms, and it's up to you how entrepreneurial you want to be. Education was where I focused my efforts, and with forty-two schools, the Blaxland Road and Meadowbank TAFEs, as well as Macquarie University, preschools, specialist schools and language centres in my electorate, there was plenty of territory to cover. And local educators were hungry for information about our agenda.

Trish Hurley, a former teacher who had been one of my ferociously energetic campaigners throughout 2007, took on the role of co-ordinating visits, organising principal's forums and acting as the point person for the many aspects of the Education Revolution that we were rolling out: Trade Training Centres, the Secondary School Computer Fund, the National Curriculum and the new National Partnership Agreements with the states.

Above all, Trish organised *me*. With a folder full of detail she would bundle me out the door for an assembly at Epping Heights, then down to Epping Boys High for morning tea in the staffroom, then a catch-up with the preschoolers at St Dunstan's, ahead of one of dozens of meetings we would have with the staff at the Karonga Special School.

Karonga consumed a lot of our time and it was worth every minute. Principal Sue Dennett had been campaigning for years for additional funding to rebuild the appallingly named 'F' Block. It was a shocking eyesore and had been put up in a hurry in the 1960s with as much money as local parents could raise, then later transferred to the state education authorities. It was a disaster of a building and the whole place flooded every time there was a sprinkle of rain. And yet Karonga catered to the needs of some of the most developmentally challenged children in the state—children who would never move out of a wheelchair or utter a word or ever be able to toilet themselves. Every day teachers, aides and parents negotiated an unsafe workplace to help a group of young people with acute needs.

It was a dramatic example of the educational equity gap and one that for years no one in authority had taken much notice of. Building the Education Revolution (BER) money would help but would not be enough for the purpose-built facilities required.

Karonga reinforced my view of Bennelong: while it was not a particularly needy area, nonetheless there were individual pockets of great need. The school needed a champion, so the whole rebuilding project went to the top of my 'to do' list. It was one of the reasons I had got into politics: to fix things. It took two years of lobbying, but finally, NSW Education Minister Verity Firth, bless her, allocated a generous $3.5 million in the 2010 state Budget.

On the day the bulldozers knocked over 'F' Block Sue Dennett raised a glass.

Another great day. Perhaps one of the best.

*

What I liked about electoral work was getting the small things right. Fundamentally, people want the dignity of their lives recognised. Many are tired of being dismissed, of feeling lost in the system. They arrive, almost as a last port of call, at an electorate office, feeling that every other institution has spat them out. Often I would be meeting with constituents and Arthur Miller's hero in *Death of a Salesman*, Willy Loman, would come to mind: *Attention must be paid … a small man can be just as exhausted as a great man.*

I couldn't have achieved a thing for the Bennelong community without my magnificent chocoholics.

The best gift from John Watkins after the 2007 win was the wonderful Diana Waring. Having run Watkins' state electorate office of Ryde, Diana was the perfect person to help a neophyte like myself. She likes to remind me that when she took over the Bennelong office, it had six paper clips, three indigenous flags and no access codes for the printing machines. But nothing daunted Diana. She knew every inch of the electorate, was networked into every community group and seemed inexhaustible. It was never in her duty statement to spend Friday nights frying onions for our Saturday community barbecues but that's what she did. And much more.

Elizabeth Wulff was a serendipitous find. She arrived with a PhD in English literature, a head for public policy and the perfect temperament for the deep digging required to sort through a bureaucratic stuff-up. Constituents loved her. Many a Bennelong resident owes Elizabeth for the hours she would spend prodding a sometimes unhelpful or reluctant government agency, never giving up until she found a solution. When she cracked a big one, she would do a jig through the office! It was her persistence on behalf of the Australian Women's Land Army that secured appropriate national recognition in the federal parliament on the 70th anniversary (in 2012) of the formation of this magnificent corps of wartime workers.

Sue Pike, along with Lucienne Joy, completed the quintet that was our office for most of 2008. A lawyer and former teacher, Sue had done the hard yards during the campaign, so understood all the pressure points. She was a great organiser and prodigious researcher. There was always an absolute moral clarity with Sue, so any slippage in Canberra and she would give it to you with both barrels. And yes, she needed a chocolate top-up around four o'clock every afternoon as well!

The core of our purple army volunteers also continued to help out, and part-timers like the always cheerful Kaye Batten tackled the mountain of correspondence that was still coming in from all over the country.

It was a happy office because we all wanted the same thing: a return to generosity, tolerance and optimism. We'd had enough of the alternative. Throughout 2008 we were at one with much of the nation in anticipating something great; it was an Olympic-style spirit that would lift the nation. Rudd's huge and continuing personal popularity suggested that the rest of Australia was willing him to run a government that would reflect robust intellectual endeavour and convey confidence in our domestic and international discourse.

The early signs were promising.

Although it was easily mocked by some members of the fourth estate, Rudd's hosting of a 2020 Summit in Parliament House at the end of April that brought together a thousand thinkers and activists sent a strong message that we were serious about a contest of ideas. As Rudd said at the summit opening, 'Today we are throwing open the windows of our democracy to let a little bit of fresh air in.'

It was a rambunctious, occasionally chaotic weekend of discourse. At times, particularly in the governance session I co-chaired with News Limited's John Hartigan, it risked turning into the equivalent of the Christmas dinner where the post-prandial family arguments turn hostile. But in the end, whether banker or constitutional lawyer, teacher or retailer, all agreed that the old machinery was creaking. There was unanimity around the need to build a seamless national economy; to shape measured responses to the geopolitical transformation of the region as a result of the rise of China and India; to grasp the dynamic of climate change; to build strong healthy communities that left no one behind; and the need to tackle a big, long-delayed piece of national business: a vote to decide whether we should become a republic.

It was a national conversation.

I like to think that the Labor great we'd farewelled only the week before, John Button, would have enjoyed it. He would have lent the occasion his wit and wisdom before turning his charm on the most exotic-looking woman in the room. Button had been Industry Minister in the Hawke Cabinet and a true moderniser. He was a one-off, and combined an utterly engaging manner with political flair and rat cunning. But too soon, at seventy-five, he was gone. Dead from pancreatic cancer. On 16 April, in Melbourne's glorious St Michael's Uniting Church, Bob and I, along with many of the Labor family, honoured a man who, in the words of Les Murray, lived his life 'on a landscape as wide as all forgiveness'.

Button had called me after the win in Bennelong but we never had a chance to have a further talk about the political landscape we were traversing. I'm sure he would have told us to just get on with it. He hated political timidity.

My electorate was home to the Macquarie Park Technology Corridor, often dubbed Australia's Silicon Valley due to its emergence as a critical location in the north-west of Sydney for specialist companies in IT, medical research, communications and pharmaceuticals. And whether it was in conversation at the CSIRO, or at companies such as AstraZeneca, Medtronic or Cochlear, or over on the Macquarie University campus, at the almost-complete Australian School of Advanced Medicine, I heard much the same story. This clustered innovation group wanted to see Canberra provide a competitive research environment and more streamlined taxation, and support a tertiary education system that prized excellence and produced a pool of talented individuals.

Wayne Swan's May 2008 Budget represented the first downpayment for this sector, with investment in all areas of education and in particular the $11 billion Education Investment Fund for higher education capital expenditure. As a consequence, Macquarie University's successful drawdown of $56.6 million from this fund helped build the new Hearing Hub and turned the university into one of the busiest building sites on the North Shore.

But like everywhere else, the commercial heart of my electorate would soon be looking with alarm at a cascade of international banking and investment collapses in the Northern Hemisphere.

Swan had to frame his first Budget against a backdrop of falling global growth and dramatically altered forecasts being delivered by bodies such as the International Monetary Fund and the US Reserve Bank. The latter had already had to step in and save the Wall Street investment bank Bear Stearns when it suffered a run on its hedge funds.

In the book that recorded Australia's strategic avoidance of much of the crisis, *Shitstorm*, authors Lenore Taylor and David Uren recall Wayne Swan asking his hosts at the IMF and World

Bank meetings in Washington, at the beginning of 2008, if 'Bear Stearns is the end of it'. He was told it was only the beginning, and as he said to Taylor and Uren, 'That stuck in my mind.'[3]

In line with the government's rhetoric, Swan had been planning an inflation-fighting Budget, but as the news from overseas worsened, the options for harsh cuts in spending were wisely shelved. The Labor government delivered on its election promises—the tax cuts, the increase in the childcare and education rebates—and forecast a surplus that represented 1.5 per cent of GDP. Increased means-testing and taxes on alcohol and luxury vehicles were part of the package, but any further inflation-busting measures could have produced the adverse effect the government was trying to avoid.

So far so good. But while Australia was free of the subprime mortgage crisis that was causing pain and fury in the United States and elsewhere, there was just enough *corporate* subprime to worry a new government. Highly indebted operators like Allco, Opes Prime, Babcock & Brown and the childcare conglomerate ABC Learning all ran into significant financial difficulties as the lending merry-go-round came to an abrupt halt.

It was the last one that was of particular concern to me. With control of around one-fifth of the private childcare market, ABC's founder, Eddy Groves, managed to avoid mentioning why his company's share price was in free-fall on the day of my only meeting with him in the Deputy Prime Minister's office in February 2008. Groves' chutzpah was remarkable. With his house of cards about to collapse, he was still talking up expansion, telling us how he could run the government's retraining program for childcare workers *and* making the case for the soon-to-be-increased Child Care Rebate to be paid fortnightly direct to centres. It was a nice try, as it would have meant an injection of additional cash payments straight into ABC Learning at precisely the time when Groves was short of the readies. As it was, it was a classic case of public policy propping up a shaky commercial entity: an unchecked debt-laden conglomerate that had more to do with property deals than the economics of childcare and where the business model was under-written by hundreds of millions of dollars in subsidies from the Commonwealth.

I remember, in the early part of 2008, both Max Walsh and ASIC chief Tony d'Aloisio, in separate conversations, saying the same thing to me about Groves: 'You better have some good risk management in place.' What we had were a lot of departmental briefs. Dozens and dozens of them about the accreditation records and location of ABC Learning centres. There was also plenty of monitoring by the Department of Education, Employment and Workplace Relations (DEEWR) of the decline in Groves' share price, but red lights should have been flashing.

The jobs of sixteen thousand workers were at stake, not to mention the expectation that the childcare centres that parents relied on every day would remain operational. But remarkably there was no brief for the incoming government on a contingency plan in the event of a collapse of Groves' corporate empire. It was a rare miss by the department, but an important one.

I suggested to Gillard that we needed to pull together a group of individuals who, if needed, could deal with the financiers who had bankrolled Groves as well as expert personnel who were familiar with insolvency and corporation law. Gillard acted on this and as a result Michael Manthorpe was appointed to the task. Other public servants who had worked on the 2001 Ansett airline collapse were also recruited. Manthorpe was terrific to work with, always calm and methodical. He would later be awarded the Public Service Medal for successfully managing the transition of the failed ABC Learning to a newly created not-for-profit operation called GoodStart Early Learning.

But ahead of the appointment of administrators in November 2008, and after Groves and his wife Le Neve had sold part of their own shareholding to meet margin calls, the bloke who started out as a Brisbane milkman sprang another surprise. In June, Groves announced his centres would be increasing fees by an average of 11 per cent.

I had to hand it to him, the bloke had front. It was only a month after the Budget measure that was designed to make child-care more affordable by increasing the rebate for out-of-pocket expenses from 30 to 50 per cent, up to a ceiling of $7500. Yet here was Groves pushing in the opposite direction.

I was sent out to respond to the bad news on ABC Radio's *AM* program. I told reporter Alexandra Kirk that Groves owed parents an explanation.

> The fee increase by ABC Learning is disappointing. It's 11 per cent and that's nearly three times the inflation rate. I watched Mr Groves last night on *Lateline Business* and he had a lot to say about his debt levels, about his commercial empire, about his issues with the ACCC—so I'm assuming he will have just as much to say today to parents to justify this increase. Parents should be asking Mr Groves the question: what extra value will they be getting for the 11 per cent fee hike?

There was little we could do. We just had to cop it for the time being, knowing that the whole sorry saga was close to ending.

Gillard suggested that *working families* could rest easy. As she told *Lateline*'s Tony Jones, on 2 June 2008: 'We've indicated to child-care operators around the country that … the government will canvass all options at its disposal to deal with any unfair pricing practices that emerge.'

*

Working families. A useful campaign slogan but something we should never have carried into government. We bored the country witless with the repetition.

Either that or we offended people who felt they didn't fit this tight marketing definition—like my Karonga parents. Their work patterns were haphazard at best because their days and nights were consumed with the detail and drama of negotiating a half-way decent life for their disabled children. Were they *working families*? How about the self-funded retirees at the Ryde Eastwood Bowling Club whose volunteering was the glue that held so many community groups together? *Working families* didn't resonate with them either.

I certainly wasn't the only member of the Labor caucus to rebel against this kind of patronising and lazy language, but I was among the first to junk it. From correspondence, from newsletters and from interviews.

The backlash didn't take long. *She's not a team player.* No one says this directly to you, but the phrase is passed around and your staff are the first to feel they have been put in the icebox; or worse, to be loudly reprimanded, by the media 'minders' in the leaders' office, for breaches, minor or otherwise.

Some days I felt I was being treated like a wild horse that had to be broken in; on others, as the problem child who needed disciplining after class. One of Gillard's media acolytes testily told me to 'work on my exits'. Come again? Apparently, I was a bit tardy about making a quick getaway at the end of press conferences held on location—usually at a childcare centre or school—where you were required to break the land speed record and escape into an already accelerating Commonwealth car. God forbid that you might linger and try to explain a policy point or two to gathered journalists!

My staff were told on numerous occasions that 'the trouble with your boss is that she still thinks like a journalist'. Too right I did. I'd certainly changed professions but I hadn't left my analytical impulse at the ABC, so I always ran a critical eye over the daily missives that poured out of the PM's office. The ubiquitous 'talking points' represented the script that all MPs were supposed to memorise and reproduce. The plucky few who were called on to swell a scene or two in front of the cameras on each and every day of a parliamentary sitting week were required to (a) look straight ahead and speak with empathy to Labor's *working families* and (b) to pulverise the opposition for their shocking neglect and callous disregard for anyone but themselves.

It turns out I wasn't the only renegade team player who thought this was a moronic way for a government to communicate. As one of my colleagues, and someone who had been in politics for a very long time, said to me, 'When I turn on Sky TV and see a string of our backbenchers all saying the same fucking words that have been approved for that day, I just feel a kind of despair because you know no one knows what they're talking about. There is just no connection with the real world.'

As I came to realise, the world that seemed to count was the tight construct that existed in the minds of the government's media masters, a small group of people in the senior offices with more power than sense. In this particular universe, MPs, parliamentary secretaries and ministers, even though we had all taken an oath of office to serve the Commonwealth in good faith, were only deemed effective to the extent that we stayed in line and did what we were told. Those who demurred, particularly those new to Parliament, could find themselves at a distinct disadvantage. Or treated like an idiot.

It was a very odd way to work. Lower-level staff copped the brunt of it. Instead of collegial banter and a bit of negotiation around acceptable messaging, there was just control. And contempt for any kind of thinking that suggested that the electorate might be in a mood to hear their representatives sounding like an identifiable member of the species.

Were MPs intimidated by this approach? According to Arch Bevis, who'd held the Queensland metro seat of Brisbane since 1990, they were. He recalls a conversation he and others had on a particularly hot topic with the relevant minister. 'The minister made some effective points back to us and I remember asking him why he wasn't saying this publicly. The reply came back, "Oh the PMO [Prime Minister's office] doesn't want me to." To which the rest of us said, tell them to get lost, and if the PM doesn't like it, he has your phone number.'

As Bevis says, all too often it was a case of people who in any other environment acted like leaders but in government 'acted like lemmings'. As a result, we never developed an effective, let alone inspiring, language with which to govern.

It mattered less in the first year when we were riding high in the polls, but later, when we were grappling with massive complexities because of a vastly altered external environment, we handicapped ourselves by forcing everyone to behave—in the public sphere at least—like an operational robot.

Our Early Childhood policy was a case in point. When ABC Learning started reporting losses, it was obvious that the corporate fall-out would come to dominate headlines. Inevitably that would crowd out space for detail about the big agenda we were working on, the first national quality framework for the care and development of children. In the early part of 2008, there was a window of opportunity for the new government to explain the thinking behind our policy mix. There were plenty of new parents among members of the press gallery who were experiencing first-hand the mixed bag that was childcare. Why not talk to them? But time and again I was told by Gillard's office: 'That's not the story we want out there today.'

I complied with this until one day in early September 2008 when *The Sydney Morning Herald*'s Phillip Hudson made it across the parliamentary Maginot Line and sat down in my Canberra office for a chat about Bennelong. I can't imagine how it happened but I must have misplaced my set of approved 'talking points' for that day. Pretty soon I was telling Hudson about how Bennelong infants and preschoolers would benefit from what I was working on: a changed licensing arrangement whereby centres that looked after children would be required to lift their standards by hiring trained staff and improving care ratios. The existing high churn rate of staff pointed to a stressed sector with not enough professionals, yet it devoured billions every year in Commonwealth subsidies. To boost qualifications, we were waiving TAFE fees for diplomas and funding an extra fifteen hundred university places for early childhood teachers.

None of this was new and I had been talking about all of this in speech after speech since the beginning of the year. But it was below the radar until I made exactly the same points in a one-on-one interview. The fun and fireworks started when the story made the front page of *The Sydney Morning Herald* on 2 September. It was an accurate account of what I had said. While I was delighted that, finally, we were getting a story out about one of our big reform areas, I was about to find out that parliamentary secretaries are not supposed to occupy prime real estate in national newspapers.

In the PM's office, Lachlan Harris hit the phone around 6 a.m. and hammered his point: 'This is not what we wanted on the front page.' The PM's press secretary was not a happy boy. Not happy with me. His comment went to the heart of the way the government ran a 'command and control' system that assumed that a newsroom's editorial autonomy was a mere trifle and that ownership of the front page could and should be determined each and every day inside the PM's office.

It's one of the biggest distortions I've seen in my professional life. The political class, and it's true of all parties, invests a huge amount of energy in dictating the 'line' of the day. Far from being wedded to the idea of editorial freedom, politicians employ media minders to try to subvert this concept. It's a process that has been underway for a long time but the irony is that Rudd and Gillard have presided over a period when it has been done without any of the flair or finesse that might actually achieve the desired result.

Art conceals art. Communications strategies are vital for any kind of public enterprise, whether a corporation, a political party or a not-for-profit. But they should be servers, not drivers. Don't try telling this to the all-dominant media masters, however. They don't want to know and they are clueless about the way they are contributing to the dumbing-down of our democracy.

After the Hudson story, I was told to stick to regional radio. In the space of a year I went from having one of the highest profiles in the country to being one of the least visible members of the government.

When I surfaced for an appearance on the new ABC TV program *Q&A*, one of the first questions to me was via a video link: 'Hi, Tony, this is Chris from Perth. I've got a question for Maxine. Ever since the last general election she appears to have gone local. We don't see her much on TV, radio or in parliamentary debates. Is there a reason for this? What is she doing now?'[4]

The questioner was unwittingly highlighting the very conundrum that Lindsay Tanner has pointed to in his book *Sideshow*: it's not about what you do anymore, but about what you *look* like you're doing.

I tried to make light of it by telling the panel and the audience that I'd been let out of the dungeon for the night. It's certainly what it felt like, and the chains must have still been rattling because I didn't put in a particularly confident performance.

News Limited's Steve Lewis had a go at me as well and delivered a lovely anniversary present. In an article he penned for the *The Daily Telegraph* on 22 November, a year after my Bennelong win, his opening line ran: 'Perched in a fortress-like office three floors above bustling Victoria Road, Maxine McKew is running late and sounding defensive.'

What followed was a dog of a piece that suggested I was an invisible do-nothing MP. Lewis had been provided with a nine-page, single-spaced printout of my constituent-specific activities throughout 2008 but not a line of this was referenced. I realise now I was target practice, as Lewis, certainly from Labor's perspective, has proved to be a serial offender. Lewis was the journalistic conduit for the stories surrounding Treasury official Godwin Grech in 2009. That story blew up in his face. Learning nothing from that, in 2012, Lewis would be subpoenaed by the courts over his role in an even bigger story: the attempt to undermine the Speaker of the House, Peter Slipper.

In politics it's the negative stuff that hangs around and attaches itself like a barnacle to a ship's hull. We hate it. But overall I can't complain about the press I got. National writers—Lenore Taylor, Laura Tingle, Paul Toohey, Tom Dusevic, David Penberthy, Claire Harvey and Nick Bryant—all gave me a good run and represented my views in a dispassionate way. So too did the suburban papers in the Bennelong electorate. By 2008 they were covering all the local events I attended and without any of the narkiness and *who does she think she is?* tone that had accompanied the coverage of the 2007 election.

Truth to tell, I didn't want to have to worry about my profile. I certainly hadn't made the switch to politics to reproduce my previous life and be a constant presence on television. But there's no doubt that I disappointed people who seemed to want a whole lot more from the giant slayer. What should I have done? Given background briefings and traded information with preferred journalists in the press gallery? It's what a lot of my colleagues did, but it's not the way I wanted to work.

And the bottom line was this: while I had some very big ambitions for the government, I only had a modest set of ambitions for myself. I wanted to be a doer and to use every minute of what was a fantastic opportunity to work on the policies that would help shape the country.

So many of us felt this.

Bob Debus had been Attorney-General in the NSW Carr government, and then switched to the federal sphere in 2007 to give us a much-needed win in the Blue Mountains seat of Macquarie. With the fresh start promised by Rudd's leadership years, Debus told me earlier this year that he ran again because he wanted 'to change the political destiny of the country'. He told me he hated the way 'John Howard had deliberately busted the model of politics I believed in, by constantly undermining social justice and the rule of law'.

Rudd had appointed Debus as Minister for Home Affairs. With his long background in state politics, and blooded by the tough-as-nuts world of the NSW Parliament, Debus had seen it all. Of our early days in government he says that 'Rudd's intuition and impulses right across the policy spectrum were good. Really good. And we seemed to be moving credibly on the large policy initiatives that would permanently change the country.'

Debus also recalls that 'ministers hit their stride pretty quickly' and 2008 was the year that seemed to signal a decisive swing away from the Howard years. Nowhere more so than in the area of Commonwealth–state relations. A new Intergovernmental Agreement was aimed at boosting the effectiveness of government services, in areas such as education, training, healthcare and housing. There was a major rationalisation of the number of payments to the states, with ninety Specific Purpose Payments being replaced by six new National Partnership Agreements.

An area long neglected was that of housing, and it received a huge boost through these arrangements. Throughout the campaign, Rudd had talked about the national shame that was homelessness. As capital city real estate soared in price, those on low incomes or on the margins had a desperate time trying to locate affordable dwellings close to services. The fresh investment and different approaches rolled out by the new Housing Minister, Tanya Plibersek, hit at exactly the right time, when architects and social planners were rethinking design, location and financing. The $5.6 billion that was invested via the Social Housing Initiative helped to fund much-needed repairs and maintenance on eighty thousand existing dwellings, and saw over nineteen thousand new units constructed.

In many areas, including training, education and health, our first year in government laid the foundations for significant change and put some fairness back into the system. Rudd would be criticised for running too many inquiries, but how to argue with the appointment of Dr Christine Bennett and the creation of a National Health and Hospitals Reform Commission to consider the long-term health needs of the nation? Or Gillard's choice of Professor Denise Bradley to review our vast higher education sector? And the appointment of Professor Barry McGaw to chair the new National Curriculum Board, so that finally we could get some educational consistency around the country. They were all outstanding individuals, expert in their fields.

Rudd also backed Fortescue Metals chief Andrew Forrest and his private sector initiative, the Australian Employment Covenant, designed to source fifty thousand employment opportunities for indigenous Australians. This was in line with Rudd's oft-repeated line that 'Canberra doesn't have all the answers.'

We looked like a government that was open to the ideas of others, and to testing those ideas.

This was reinforced through regular Community Cabinet meetings that required the ministry, along with dozens of advisors and officials, to travel to different locations across the country. They were popular events, and in April 2010 one was held in Bennelong at Epping Boys High School. The hall was chock-a-block, and people were impressed that the government had come to them. They felt someone was listening.

And we were.

The problem was that we weren't listening or talking with each other.

Too little information was shared across the ministry, let alone within caucus, and the tight structures soon led to the emergence of the all-powerful Strategic Priorities and Budget Committee. The SPBC was dominated by the four key players at the apex of the government: Rudd, Gillard, Swan and Finance Minister Lindsay Tanner. It was proposed by the Secretary of the Department of Prime Minister and Cabinet, Terry Moran, and based on the Victorian system of Cabinet committees. The thinking was that the Cabinet structures of the past had lacked a strategic planning capability that was closely aligned with confidential Budget priorities. Relevant line ministers participated as required, decisions were taken then brought before the full Cabinet for endorsement.

There are rival views on this.

Griffith University's Professor Patrick Weller, whose life's work has been the study of the machinery of government and prime ministerial behaviour, both in Australia and in the United Kingdom, has told me that there is 'little that Rudd did that had not been done before'. He cites Malcolm Fraser, among others, as exercising command over his ministry, and elsewhere the tendency of prime ministers to wield power with and through a tight inner circle, or 'kitchen cabinet'. 'Many of the things that Rudd is accused of are standard practice among PMs,' says Weller.

Others see it differently. Craig Emerson served as Minister Assisting the Finance Minister on Deregulation in the first term. He was not in Cabinet but was junior to the Finance Minister Lindsay Tanner and says they developed a good working relationship. When it came to streamlining the many areas of regulatory inconsistency across the states that bedevilled business, Emerson says he also had strong personal support from Rudd and the economic advisors in the PM's office.

Emerson had studied economics at both the University of Sydney and at the ANU and completed a PhD under the supervision of Dr Ross Garnaut. Both worked for Prime Minister Bob Hawke in the 1980s, with Emerson having responsibility for trade and microeconomic reform. Transitioning to government at the end of 2007, with experience at the heart of a previous Labor administration, Emerson didn't fear argument: 'You need robust discussion in the Cabinet room. There should be a sense that disagreement is good because you are road-testing ideas. You need to do due diligence on a particular submission. That's what needs to happen because you are really dress-rehearsing the broader public and policy debate. It was common in the Hawke years for a Cabinet matter on one of the big issues to be carried over. As young staffers, when Bob would come back to the office, he'd say, "We need to do more work." So we would revisit the matter until everyone was satisfied. It was quite common. And the differing views of ministers were taken into account.'

That's the contest of ideas that Keating had talked to me about. And no one should fear it. The odd thing is that Rudd, in my experience, always had his ears wide open when it came to a good idea. One Cabinet minister I've spoken to says that he always found Rudd to be open and consultative, that he was a good chair of Cabinet, and didn't seek to dominate with his own views. But that minister also says, 'It's inarguable that the "gang of four" decided too much in advance'—and that meant that more broadbased discussion was limited. Rudd worried about leaks. Yet SPBC meetings were hardly intimate gatherings. Often they were crowded with officials.

So why was this tolerated? Having spent eleven long years in opposition, weren't ministers hungry for robust debate and the processes that would allow this to happen?

Apparently not.

A veteran politician like Bob Debus encountered too many people who were merely fixers and lacked a serious political compass. Having worked with both Neville Wran and Bob Carr, neither of them pussycats who could ever be accused of endlessly indulging subordinates, Debus says that they both headed governments 'where everyone started the day wanting to do things, to get things solved'.

Even in the first year of the government, Debus worried that 'there wasn't much collegiality. There weren't enough informal conversations where ministers swapped information. That shocked me.'

What Debus came to realise was that the class of 2007 had joined a caucus where members 'had been to hell and back over the previous ten years'. Even though Rudd gave the most senior appointments to those who had opposed his rise to the top, the resentments from the endless leadership wars of the post-1996 period were always close to the surface. It affected the way people behaved and whether or not they even spoke to each other.

It's an explanation but not an excuse. Surely, having won the glittering prize of government, the sheer scale of the win could have liberated people from the past and made way for a bit of mature internal debate? And when needed, the courage to speak truth to power.

Craig Emerson agrees this should have been the case: 'If you are a Cabinet minister and processes aren't working, you have a responsibility to speak up. I don't think you can sit back and allow that to happen. It's weak.'

Emerson was to find that even the relevant economic ministers did not meet on a regular basis, yet among them, they had brainpower and expertise to burn. 'I assumed for a long time that Cabinet ministers had their own interactions but they didn't.'

And from the perspective of someone who had seen plenty of *Sturm und Drang* throughout the Keating years, Arch Bevis says, 'Too many ministers were not prepared to exert their authority, either with their colleagues or with the Prime Minister.' As for fearing the wrath of the PM or a particularly unpleasant blast from one of his staffers, Bevis says, 'If someone wants to stand over you they only have as much power as you want to give them. My view is that too many people lacked guts when it mattered.'

Bevis also recalls earlier practices where legislation was discussed with relevant caucus committees *before* the bills went to Cabinet. He cites Keating government minister Laurie Brereton's 'quite radical IR changes around enterprise bargaining' being subjected to a lengthy caucus committee debate and change before they were signed off. 'That meant it gave the minister comfort in taking it to Cabinet.'

But after 2007, caucus committees were expected to rubberstamp ministerial determinations. Bevis recalls one minister who didn't even bother turning up for caucus presentations but sent her staffers instead: 'She wasn't Robinson Crusoe either, but after I did my block, things changed.'

It could have been different. On so many of the contentious policy areas rolled out in the first year—the education reforms, the creation of an entirely new industrial framework under Fair Work Australia, and the design of the carbon trading scheme—and the big ones ahead of us—the mining tax and the ongoing management of the vast stimulus package—all these issues cried out for substantial internal debate.

Consider the irony. As a government we were trumpeting a new respectful set of industrial laws for the rest of the country, rules that would re-weight relations between employer and employee within a collaborative framework, yet our own internal workplace culture was closed rather than creative. Some would say, and plenty did, *That's politics. Suck it up.* And then they blame Rudd. For everything.

But not Anthony Albanese who told me earlier this year: 'I didn't support Rudd initially. I backed Beazley. But from day one, Rudd included me as well as a host of others.'

Manager of Government Business in the House of Representatives (basically the chief enforcer, along with the Whips), as well as holding the Transport and Infrastructure portfolio, Albanese, or Albo as he's known, is an inner-western Sydney political warrior who is clear-eyed about his priorities. The job is to fight the Greens and to fight the Tories even harder.

Albo has always defended Rudd and says, 'If people had ideas, they were treated on their merits.' But he also says that 'Rudd's centralist instincts' needed to be checked and that 'the SPBC had too much power for too long. That could have been challenged and it should have been.'

These reservations and judgments would only come to the fore much later. During our first year in government we were focused on managing the fallout from the unfolding global financial crisis. On 15 September 2008, the fourth-largest investment bank in the United States, Lehman Brothers, declared bankruptcy with debts in excess of US$600 billion. The next day, former investment banker Malcolm Turnbull replaced Brendan Nelson as leader of the Coalition.

It was a move that that didn't make the slightest dent in Rudd's extraordinary hold on the Australian electorate.

Having made exactly the right call domestically with an immediate $10 billion stimulus package, designed to maintain growth through the early stages of what became known as the global financial crisis, or GFC, and then making the even bigger call at the UN General Assembly for the enlarged G20 economies to assert their authority, Rudd finished the year with an astonishing 66 per cent of Australians preferring him as Prime Minister.

Turnbull scored 19 per cent on the preferred PM rating, only three points ahead of the man he'd replaced.

The year 2009 would begin with the inauguration of the first African-American President in US history, Barack Obama. No new President had been dealt such a bad hand since Franklin Roosevelt claimed the White House in 1932. Ahead lay thousands of housing and factory foreclosures and an unemployment rate that would soar to 10 per cent.

But on this side of the pond, Rudd's triumph would be in keeping the nation working. Unemployment in Australia would peak at 5.8 per cent, way under the Treasury forecast of 8.25 per cent.

It was a singular achievement by a Labor Prime Minister who held his nerve.

*

We're all adaptive creatures but life as a new parliamentarian in Canberra's vast house on the hill required a particular kind of adjustment. I sometimes felt at the beginning of a new parliamentary week that I was boarding the Starship *Enterprise* for a voyage to a vastly different planetary configuration. And it wasn't always easy to sort out the Vulcans from the Andorians.

At the equivalent of orientation week, the induction for the class of 2007, any number of old hands tell you that your enemies don't necessarily sit on the opposite side of the chamber but are right beside you. Nobody laughs when this is pointed out. It doesn't even provoke a titter. And you find out why soon enough.

In a world with a unique set of rules, rituals and hierarchies, I was a bit of an odd creature. A relative latecomer to politics and with no allegiance to either trade union or faction, I wasn't *owned* as Eric Roozendaal had so artfully put it, and had said 'no' to the one and only invitation to join the NSW Right that had come after the win in Bennelong.

Most of my colleagues had been planning their political careers and staking out their territory for years. This requires a rare kind of single-minded devotion to the task of winning favour, doing deals, ignoring setbacks, surviving the treachery and identifying the main chance until, finally, the prize of a safe seat is secured. A lot of things get traded away in the process. And close encounters with the chief operatives who seek to manage and control this process can certainly take the edge off your idealism.

Lindsay Tanner has put it well in *Sideshow*:

> The democratic process is undermined by the dominance of cynical apparatchiks who are skilled at manipulating the levers of political power but believe in little other than their own career advancement ... it punishes idealists and activists, and elevates cynical machine-politics to paramount importance. It fosters politics without beliefs.[5]

On entering Parliament, a desperate race begins to secure a spot on the most prestigious committees, or better still in the ministry, forming alliances, getting noticed, trying to develop a signature point of difference, duchessing the media, and being constantly alert to the exquisite possibility of further advancement whenever someone ahead of you falters.

The most important thing to grasp is that it's a zero-sum game. Your promotion is someone else's failure. An arresting parliamentary performance by one individual usually represents a complete humiliation for someone else on the other side.

Everywhere you go, people are telling you what to do, where to sit, and when you have to be in the chamber; the order in which you speak, and for how long. And here's the thrilling bit: the nation's governing body doesn't believe in flexible working conditions. The hours when you are required to be in Parliament are long and fixed and you can't leave the building without *permission* from the Whip's office.

A lot of parliamentarians are entirely comfortable with these tight, institutionalised arrangements and are there for decades. But if you enjoy the civilising rhythms of a more normal life—breakfast with your family, mixing with work colleagues and friends, dropping by your local coffee shop, walking the dog, ending the day with your head in a good book—then the restrictions and demands of parliamentary life can come as a bit of a shock.

I remember early on, during a division (where the chamber literally 'divides' and votes on a bill), sitting next to Mark Dreyfus, the new member for the Victorian seat of Isaacs. As a former leading barrister, Dreyfus was learning to make his own adjustments. As we swapped war stories, he said the thing he missed most was the freedom to walk out of the building and go down the street for a coffee and a breather. I sympathised. As we chatted on during the interminable count, we were both so engrossed in our conversation that we walked out of the chamber in the middle of what was a series of divisions—easy to do if you are not paying attention. We weren't. But Roger Price, the government Whip, was. He came after both of us and gave us a good ticking off.

The Whip's office was like central station. The focus was a large bulletin board where parliamentarians listed their preference to speak on various bills. It was also the place that managed rosters for chamber duty and liaised with Anthony Albanese as House Manager of Government Business and with all the other relevant senior ministries. The office also kept track of everything from new births to important anniversaries. Presiding over all this was the Member for Chifley, Roger Price, who had been in Parliament since 1984. Roger ruled with an iron rod but had a very decent disposition. He was generous towards me and I only wish I'd sat down with him right at the beginning and said, *how do I get this right?*

Everyone else seemed to be able to juggle ten balls in the air at once, so what was my problem? It took a while for it to dawn on me that the constant running around by some colleagues, accompanied by multiple pronouncements on this, that and the other, added up to very little. But in a new environment it's easy to be spooked.

I had trouble coming to terms with the KPIs, but I would have sounded like a complete naysayer if I'd given voice to what I thought about the way Parliament measured success. For the most part I kept my counsel but it seemed peculiar that what was prized was volume. In every sense. Maximum number of speeches delivered in Parliament. Tick. The frequency with which you popped up on Sky News lambasting the opposition. Even bigger tick. The shrillness (or silliness) of responses in Question Time. Very big tick.

We had plenty of our own look-at-me offenders on our side, but for my money, the *Dancing with the Stars* winner is Barnaby Joyce, the National Party senator from Queensland. He has divined that what is truly important is the mangled *bon mot*—the nuttier and more inconsequential the better. He knows it will always get a run, and as a result his constituents receive a daily reassurance that he is on the job!

When it all gets too much, there's a wandering spiritual advisor available to all parliamentarians. Whenever I saw him, I thought of the poor put-upon Chaplain Tappman in Joseph Heller's novel *Catch-22*, who was always being wheeled out for a few snappy prayers before the wartime bombers took off. Given the speed with which leaders were being blasted out of their positions in Canberra, novenas were needed. Perhaps plenary indulgences.

When I wasn't required in the chamber for Question Time and other parliamentary and committee duties, I spent the great bulk of my time during sitting weeks doing what I loved: policy work. Most days it meant back-to-back meetings with a vast number of stakeholders and bureaucrats as we worked on the design of the new national standards and an Early Years Learning Framework.

Diane Callaghan managed my Canberra office and made sure meetings didn't run over time; and Kathleen Forrester, with a background in economics and time spent in consulting and at the Productivity Commission, was indispensable as my chief advisor and guide through the internecine rivalries of the various advocacy groups. The trickiest part of my role as parliamentary secretary was in negotiating the boundaries of the job. I was working to one of the most senior members of the government, Deputy Prime Minister Gillard, who was also served by other junior ministers and parliamentary secretaries, among them Kate Ellis, Mark Arbib (after he commenced his Senate term in July 2008), Ursula Stephens and eventually Jason Clare.

The arrangement works well when there are clear lines of responsibility, regular discussions with the minister, and generally an openness about the work at hand. When I switched portfolio areas in mid-2009, and worked to Infrastructure Minister Anthony Albanese, this was his approach.

Patrick Weller, in the book he co-authored with Anne Tiernan, *Learning to be a Minister: Heroic expectations, practical realities*, has recorded vastly different experiences of the relationship between senior ministers and their subordinates. In the Howard years, junior ministers complained of not receiving sufficient support from departmental secretaries, with all the attention focused on serving the portfolio minister. Where there are explicit duties that can be served by a single agency, junior ministers or parliamentary secretaries have a good deal of clarity about their jobs. Greg Combet, for instance, in his first job as a parliamentary secretary was responsible for the Defence Material Organisation. Similarly, Bob McMullan had oversight of Australian aid assistance.

Ultimately, it depends on the relationship you develop with a particular minister. As Weller says, his interviews with executive members of government revealed that 'some are cooperative, while others are toxic'.[6]

I had a workable relationship with Gillard, but it could have been a lot better. We never established a pattern of regular meetings, and not for want of trying on the part of my office. In the early days I put this down to the fact that she had an immense portfolio and was simply too busy.

It's a pity because, for the most part, I was one of her strongest supporters when it came to the big changes she was orchestrating in education. But she never included me in wider discussions or sought out my views on any of the substantive areas—curriculum reform, accountability, or tertiary education training. This last mentioned was critical to everything we wanted to achieve with infants and with school-aged children. It was certainly worth debating whether we set the bar too low when it came to entry-level scores for those wanting to undertake education degrees.

After allowing for genetic and parental factors, every report that's ever been commissioned cites teacher effectiveness as *the* key determinant of a child's academic success. Yet, unlike other high-achieving education systems, where the top 20 per cent of students are selected for intensive teacher training, Australia draws on a much wider pool. We don't do that in medicine, law or in communications. Given the scale of the equity problem we are dealing with—a two- to three-year learning gap between our brightest and most disadvantaged students—it's an area ripe for attention.

It was Brendan Nelson who drew attention to this. Nelson served as John Howard's Education Minister and had commissioned distinguished educational researcher Dr Ken Rowe to conduct an inquiry into the teaching of literacy. The report was released in 2005. But like so much else, the Coalition in government had preferred to wage an ideological battle with the Labor states, so little was achieved.

Nonetheless Nelson, in May 2008, in the only Budget in reply speech he would ever deliver as opposition leader, said this:

> The Coalition will require a number of conditions for the funding of Australian universities that train teachers. Entry scores to undertake teaching courses at university are embarrassingly low. The minimum university entrance score must be higher for entry to an education degree. Science, humanities and social science departments will be required to set and/or accredit relevant course content and assessment in education faculties.

Opposition leaders are accorded near equal status when it comes to a response to the Budget. All parliamentarians are in the chamber for the evening presentation, and the media pay increased attention. I thought Nelson had raised an important issue. It's debatable whether or not the Commonwealth should act on the supply side to influence entry-level standards, but at the time, I thought it was worth having the discussion. As we filed out through the big double doors at the back of the House of Representatives chamber I sought out Gillard and said as much: 'We should talk about that.'

There were plenty of other people vying for her attention so I didn't hang around. Maybe she hadn't heard. But late that night Gillard left two lengthy messages on my mobile detailing *her* approach to teaching accreditation. It involved the setting up of a new national body, the Australian Institute for Teaching and School Leadership, which would codify the professional standards that graduating and accomplished teachers would be required to meet, etc. etc. On and on it went, in a curt tone that suggested no further debate would be entered into. And it never was.

It was yet another sign that, as a government, we didn't care much about a genuine contest of ideas.

On the plus side, Gillard allowed me a degree of autonomy, especially when it came to the design of the new national standards for childcare operations and the formulation of the Early Years Learning Framework. Her own specialist advisors in Early Childhood were good to work with, although she had three different people in the role in the space of fifteen months.

In public, she was always careful to observe the protocols and when *The Sunday Age* did an end-of-year report card in November 2008 on the performance of some of the newbies, myself among them, Gillard was quoted as saying that I had 'done a lot of the heavy lifting involved in implementing the government's agenda and that it was inconceivable that we would be in the position we are without her work'.[7]

But behind the scenes, I never shook the feeling that Gillard saw me as an irritant.

Chapter 6

NOT JUST CHILD'S PLAY

THE CHILDCARE DEBATE in Australia over the last decade or more, certainly the public debate, has been around a predictable cluster of concerns: cost, service type, availability. Get these right, the argument goes, and more women will be able to remain in the workforce and thus help increase labour market participation.

This focus has driven a massive increase in subsidies paid to parents through the Child Care Benefit and the Child Care Rebate. The cost to the Commonwealth for 2011–12 is $4.1 billion.[1]

It didn't take long for me to realise that what this delivered was a very expensive babysitting service. And of variable quality.

I must have read a dozen or more reports when I started work in the portfolio, including the research of Deborah Brennan, Alison Elliott, Marilyn Fleer, Margaret Sims and others—all academics who had spent years researching both the practice and policy relating to the care of children. Not one of them was prepared to offer any kind of enthusiastic endorsement of the mix of services that was offered across the states and by both private and not-for-profit operators.

In a report for the Australian Council for Educational Research, Professor Alison Elliott from Charles Darwin University described 'a fragmented early childhood sector with a patchwork of services, little agreement on service types or functions, and a mishmash of funding and regulations'.[2]

When, at the beginning of 2008, I started visiting long day care centres—the service that had seen the biggest surge in demand—I could see the problem for myself: harried staff, stressed infants, and operators who complained about dealing with a mountain of regulation due to the overlap of state licensing and national accreditation. Most did the best they could, but demand was clearly driving a system more focused on efficiencies and profits than what was best for children.

In high-growth areas, it wasn't unusual for large centres to have to deal with dozens of babies and toddlers being dropped off, sometimes as early as 6.30 or 7 a.m., and still in their night nappies. Staff would be run off their feet trying to quickly change infants and get them ready for the day ahead. It was also not unusual to go into centres that were noisy chaotic places with too few staff able to provide much in the way of stimulatory care, or be available for the kind of responsive one-on-one interactions that very young children need.

Frankly, it was all pretty depressing. Then there were the departmental briefs pointing out how difficult it was to close shoddy operations, and how the national body in charge of standards, the National Childcare Accreditation Council (NCAC), struggled to enforce compliance. The NCAC was in charge of approving centres, but the ultimate sanction for consistent breaches, the withdrawal of the Child Care Benefit by the Commonwealth, had never been applied.

The really bad days threw up the horror stories, such as centres where supervision was so lax that children wandered off the premises. In one notorious case in western Sydney, a baby was completely forgotten and locked up in the centre when the owners finished for the night.

If all this was costing billions, where on earth was the money going?

Operators certainly weren't investing in their staff. Pay was low and training patchy. Thirty-nine per cent of staff had no childcare qualifications whatsoever. Fewer than 10 per cent had a bachelor degree in early childhood education. The wonder is that this was tolerated. But it was, and by just about everyone.

It's unthinkable in any other comparable sector. When a six-year-old child starts primary school, parents expect their child will join a class of a particular size and be taught by a university-trained teacher who is required to update her skills through ongoing professional development. Incredibly, when we came to office, no such expectations existed for the critical early years. Yet how well children perform in the first few years in school depends on the experiences and learning acquired from birth.

Time and again, primary school teachers, in schools across a range of social settings, tell you that they deal with children who suffer from language delay or who are trying to make the transition to school with exceptionally rudimentary language. Vocabulary use at age three is a predictive measure of language skills in later life, and if parents or professional caregivers have not provided a stress-free environment where very young children are exposed to rich language through repetition, rhyme and song, then children are behind the eight ball by the time they start school.[3] Some never catch up and as a result have a limited set of life choices.

None of this is a matter of subjective judgment. The research on infant brain development is in and it's persuasive.

Early in 2008, Melbourne-based pediatrician Frank Oberklaid, the founding director of the Centre for Community Child Health at the Royal Children's Hospital, sat me down for an arresting presentation on the plasticity of the infant brain. The most dramatic growth is in the early years. As a baby's neural pathways develop, the foundations for advancement in vision, speech and emotional control are set.

Elsewhere, the work of Dr Fraser Mustard, who'd advised both the Canadian government and the World Bank on the need for integrated early childhood programs, was starting to become more widely known. Mustard was invited to South Australia as Thinker in Residence in both 2006 and 2007 and had a major influence on that state's approach to early childhood.

Then there was the advocacy of Professor Ron Lally, one of the founders of Zero to Three in the United States, an organisation that translates the known research into a series of practical tools that can help caregivers.

As Lally says:

> The care of young children in groups is a profession. It includes both science and art. As a society, we need to make it possible for people to study the science and practice the art of caregiving. We need to release caregivers to provide the kinds of responsive care they know how to do or can be trained how to do, and to develop deep relationships with parents, children and other caregivers.[4]

At a conference on early education that I opened in Perth, Lally was the keynote speaker, and among the many graphs he showed, there was one that demonstrated with absolute clarity why Australia's expensive babysitting model had hit its use-by date. By the time an infant is nine months of age, Lally explained, the development of a baby's synapses means that they are at their peak when it comes to being receptive to language. That translates into what most parents do naturally: they talk to their babies. A mother changing a nappy is doing a lot more than dexterously wielding the wipes. She uses touch, sight, voice and laughter to convey comfort and a sense of belonging. Free of stress, the infant's tiny brain has room to absorb dozens of different messages that aid cognitive development. The experts call this 'joint attention sequencing'. It's subtle but important.

Think of your average childcare worker faced with a similar task. We'll call her Tanya and she works in Growthville in a centre that has been approved to care for up to ninety children. The centre is almost at capacity as new parents are signing up every week. Tanya didn't finish Year 12 but likes working with children and is thinking of undertaking a Certificate III training course in childcare. But she's already worried about whether she will last the distance. In line with the state ratios that the Growthville centre abides by, Tanya has to care for five babies. Often there is only time to soothe one crying infant before her attention is drawn to another. If that means limited interaction, then that's the reality. Five babies. No one has ever talked to Tanya about Ron Lally's 'science and art' of caregiving, but instinctively she knows she could be doing a whole lot better if the centre employed more staff. If Tanya gets frustrated and leaves, the infants she has cared for have to build trust all over again with someone else.

Ron Lally's research tells us that when a child loses a critical caregiver, he loses part of his sense of himself because he identifies with parents and other primary carers.

Halfway through 2008, the children's writer Mem Fox caused a storm when she was quoted as saying that putting six-week-old babies in childcare was the equivalent of 'child abuse'. Fox was misquoted—she said she was actually quoting a childcare worker—but the sentiment prevailed.[5] I didn't say so publicly, but I could see her point. Fox was giving voice to the voiceless, speaking up for babies, some of whom are in full-time care from the time they are twelve weeks of age. One million young children are in formal care for an average of twenty-three hours per week in fourteen thousand approved services.

When we came into government, we inherited this system.

Our challenge was how to design a system that trained young women like Tanya in both the science and art of caregiving, and provided an operational framework that was at least as professional and accountable as our school system.

I was hardly starting from scratch. An impressive amount of policy work had been undertaken by Jenny Macklin in opposition and, after Kevin Rudd became leader, by members of his staff, chief among them Michael Lye. A focus on Early Childhood was central to Rudd's conception of an Education Revolution.

He was familiar with all the research and encouraged Macklin to put together an ambitious set of proposals to reform the system.

The very first commitment—for universal access to fifteen hours of preschool for every Australian child for a minimum of forty weeks a year and delivered by a qualified teacher—was announced at the beginning of 2007 by Macklin and Rudd. That set the scene for multiple follow-ups, with Rudd a constant presence throughout the campaign in preschools and childcare centres doing high fives with the four-year-olds. It sent an important message: we were serious about a quality early childhood experience for children and there was a way to make it a whole lot better.

A week out from the election, Labor released its Plan for Early Childhood, a comprehensive suite of reforms. These included universal preschool for four-year-olds; the introduction of quality national standards for care services; a five star rating system; $73 million to boost the qualifications of the early childhood workforce; a national roll-out of the Australian Early Development Index (the AEDI is a set of tools that measures the development of children when they start school); an expansion of the Home Interaction Program in fifty disadvantaged communities to help parents prepare their children for school; and specialised services for children on the autism spectrum. There was also a commitment to improved services for young indigenous children to help close the gap.

The package addressed all the outstanding issues: the need to improve quality, to invest in training, and to provide transparency and more information for parents. Critically, it also recognised that a range of special needs had to be considered, along with a focus on children in disadvantaged communities.

The big hook was the promise to help pay the childcare bills. Labor's commitment was to boost the Child Care Rebate from 30 per cent to 50 per cent with payments made quarterly instead of yearly. Half of all out-of-pocket expenses—that is, the costs incurred above a family's entitlement to the primary Child Care Benefit (CCB)—would be paid, up to a ceiling of $7500.

Wayne Swan's first Budget in May 2008 delivered on this. From mid-2011, families have also had the option of having the rebate paid fortnightly. (The term 'rebate' is actually a misnomer as the payment doesn't come through the tax system.)

Many of the families that someone like Tanya sees at Growthville have a combined income of up to $115,000 a year and they have benefited the most from the changes in Swan's first Budget. In most cases, where the mother works part time, the proportion of disposable income being spent on childcare has fallen from 11.4 per cent in 2004 to 7.6 per cent in 2011.[6] Where there is a bias in the system, it is against the mother who chooses to work full time.

If by now you're thinking that we'd all be better off if this could be simplified, then you're dead right. Treasury Secretary Ken Henry, in his taxation review, has suggested that the CCB and the rebate be rolled into a single payment.

The 2008–09 Budget committed $2.7 billion to help with fee relief. In addition there was $126.6 million for workforce initiatives, and $533 million for universal access to preschool. This was further boosted at the end of 2008 with COAG endorsing the first National Partnership Agreement on Early Childhood Education with a provision for $970 million over five years. In turn, the states agreed to meet the requirement for full participation by Australian children in preschool by 2013. By any definition it was an impressive investment in the country's human capital.

With one exception. During the 2007 campaign, Macklin and Rudd had also promised to boost supply by funding the construction of an additional 260 long day care centres on either school, community, TAFE or university sites. Thirty-eight site-specific centres were promised during the campaign, to be built in identified 'hot spots' and conveniently co-located on school sites. It connected with an earlier Beazley idea 'to end the double drop-off'.[7]

The proposal had merit and was in line with what a lot of private schools were doing—offering parents a streamlined service from the early years right through to high school graduation.

But the earliest of briefings with DEEWR officials threw up the obvious questions. Who would build the new centres? Who would operate them? Where were the centres needed?

As I would discover, determining supply and demand in childcare is notoriously difficult. Parents in particular areas will complain loudly that they can't get young Alice into a centre without thinking seriously about having to resort to bribery and physical coercion. Yet, typically, when you take a closer look at these areas, you find that *particular* centres are in high demand and have long waiting lists, while only a few blocks away, other services complain about being unviable because they have dozens of places that they can't fill.

What this tells you is that parents are discerning when it comes to choosing a centre. Word goes out on the parental grapevine that it's worth holding out for Centre A because it has a good record at retaining caring staff, while Centre B down the road has a high staff churn rate. It all pointed to why we were determined to lift standards for all facilities, but in the meantime, how to meet the election commitment without further distorting the market?

This was never properly resolved and was allowed to drift. The thirty-eight centres announced during the campaign were given the go-ahead with $114.5 million being allocated in the 2008–09 Budget. Proposals for the other 222 centres were handled through an expression of interest (EOI) process run by DEEWR, with hundreds of schools and community groups identifying their interest in accessing funding to build a new early learning facility. But it turned out to be another case of dashed expectations.

As the EOI process was being worked through, the far bigger issue concerning supply was the unravelling of Eddy Groves' ABC Learning empire. Understandably both Swan and Gillard spent a good deal of time working out how much it was going to cost the government to keep the doors of ABC centres open after the group went into receivership in November 2008. Cleaning up after Groves—covering the operational and employee entitlements—ended up costing taxpayers a further $126 million.

From early 2009, an opportunity to meet our original election commitment was offered by way of the monster $16 billion stimulus to schools: the Building the Education Revolution (BER) program. Primary schools all over the country were about to be transformed, with up to $3 million available for either new halls or libraries. We already knew from the EOI process just how many primary schools were keen to add early learning centres to their sites. Why not marry the two and extend the guidelines of the BER funding to enable nominated schools to choose their preferred new facilities?

My office put this proposal to Gillard and her senior staffers and it was backed up by her own advisor in this area. But Gillard chose not to go with it.

Still, I had plenty to get on with. The first few months in the job crystallised my thinking. I needed to define what was meant by the 'high quality early childhood experience' that we'd promised. If we got that right, we'd be doing a hell of a lot to improve the working conditions of carers like Tanya.

The first important structural shift was the establishment of a separate Office of Early Childhood Education and Child Care (OECECC) within DEEWR. The senior officials I worked with, mainly Vicki Rundle and Trish Mercer, but a host of others as well, were highly professional, energetic and genuinely enthusiastic about our agenda. Rundle, in particular, was not only steeped in the literature of early childhood but also aware of all the structural faultlines in the sector and attuned to the points of resistance. She was never fazed. After yet another round of consultations, where inevitably she would encounter grumpiness from some of the sector's bottom-feeders, she would cheerily reassure me and say, 'We'll get there.'

The buzz of the job was in working through the complexity. How to get consistency in child–staff ratios across the country? How to encourage a large unskilled section of the workforce to take up training opportunities? And, hardest of all, how to get a very disparate sector—encompassing preschool, family day care, long day care, in-home care and out-of-school-hours care—all on board and supportive of better services for children?

For years, the smaller private providers as well as the not-for-profit centres had focused their rage on ABC Learning as it moved to dominate the childcare market. Understandable, but over time it had become an excuse to avoid addressing the flaws in the system. Less myopic were the peak bodies, and with one or two notable exceptions, most were pushing for change.

June McLoughlin was the chair of the industry's regulatory body, the National Childcare Accreditation Council, and I always appreciated her frankness. She described an organisation that was hitting the limits of its effectiveness. The NCAC had to monitor inconsistent regulations across eight jurisdictions. Where they encountered an egregious breach, they were powerless to act without the full co-operation of the state licensing authorities. So in discussions with June, I found she was more than open to the idea of significant regulatory change.

The revelation was Pam Cahir, a woman with a big, bubbly personality who had been battling for years for a higher quality of care. Pam headed Early Childhood Australia, the national body that served as an advocate in all matters relating to children. She told me stories that made my toes curl: childcare centres where children were kept for hours in restraints because of staff shortages; operators who cut corners and consistently got away with it. Her message was: improve the ratios, require the centres to hire more staff, insist on training, and bring it all together under a single national standard.

Cahir was also a key influence on the approach taken by the union that covered most childcare workers, the Liquor, Hospitality and Miscellaneous Workers Union. Under its national secretary, Louise Tarrant, the union (now known as United Voice) would run its own campaign for improved working conditions and backed the whole concept of our Quality Framework.

Complicating matters, however, was a bit of industrial demarcation and frankly old-fashioned snobbery. Preschool teachers were covered by the education unions and most taught children in small community settings over a restricted number of hours. Some of them turned their noses up at anyone who worked in a long day care centre, telling me, 'What we do is special.' I agreed with them. But I thought it was high time that their special offerings were also made available in a variety of settings and during hours that suited most working parents.

In some cases this was happening. Many long day care centres provided early learning programs, or claimed to do so. With no agreement on curricula, it was hard to determine the effectiveness or otherwise of what was available. And remarkably, New South Wales was the only state that required long day care centres with more than twenty-nine children to employ a trained early childhood teacher.

This then was the fragmented mishmash that Alison Elliott had described, and the reason that a country like Australia was consistently marked down in OECD reports on investment in early childhood.

To turn this around, I needed to see what a quality setting looked like. I needed champions. The best of the best.

The Lady Gowrie centres were an obvious place to start. They were founded by a woman born to privilege, the wife of a Governor-General, Zara Gowrie, who believed that 'children are our greatest hope'.[8] She opened centres at the outbreak of World War II to help the children of disadvantaged families—a radical idea for the time.

Gowrie has been a leading practitioner over the years precisely because it has never settled into any kind of fixed institutional rigidity. Places are highly sought after. When I visited their Brisbane operation in Spring Hill, Gowrie staff explained to me that they don't assume that every parent is available to pick up a preschooler at 2.30 in the afternoon on certain designated days. That's on offer, but so too is a wrap-around service, whereby parents who need longer hours of care can access exactly the same quality preschool program. In one room, four- and five-year-olds are picked up mid-afternoon; in another, right next door, children are cared for until 5 or 6 p.m. Throughout the day, and on slightly altered schedules, both groups experience play-based learning delivered by trained professionals. By providing both flexibility and integration, Gowrie has managed to eliminate the false distinction between care and education. Exactly what we wanted from all providers.

Equally, when it comes to the care of infants it's Gowrie New South Wales that meets world's best practice by insisting on a 1:3 staff-to-child ratio. I wanted to kiss them when they told me this. I never got over my discomfort at seeing very tiny babies in very large long day care centres. At Gowrie's Erskineville centre in Sydney, the babies' room is an intimate quiet space. The best I ever saw.

Then there was the serendipitous discovery, after becoming the member for Bennelong, that one of the standout centres in the entire country was located within the electorate on the Macquarie University site.

Mia-Mia is a place that everyone falls in love with, mainly because it doesn't *look* like a typical childcare centre. When director Wendy Shepherd greets you at the door, it's like being invited into a comfy cottage. Every detail, from the soft sofas to the fresh flowers on tiny wooden tables, is designed to eliminate any suggestion of institutional care. Outside, the garden is a green wonderland and a bit of a zoo. There's an abundance of birds as well as the resident chooks, Henny and Penny. They greet the toddlers every day. There is no fuss. And no one seems to run around wielding the Spray n' Wipe.

So what's going on here?

Shepherd and her outdoor teacher, Janet Robertson, follow an approach based on the Reggio Emilia philosophy that puts the natural development of children at the centre of everything. Teachers build lessons around the interests of the child. So from very early on, children are encouraged to be autonomous learners. This is now something that is incorporated into a lot of modern pedagogy, but it's based on tools that were actually developed in a small northern Italian town in the late 1940s as parents and teachers looked for ways to help children put the destructiveness of the war years behind them.

I was so impressed with Mia-Mia, as everyone is, that I would often talk about it in speeches I gave around the country. This is what I said about one of my visits:

> As Janet talked about her many visits to Reggio Emilia and as Wendy quoted Carla Rinaldi on the importance of listening, I realised after a while how quiet things were. In a centre full of children, everyone was fully engaged. There was no stress, certainly no sense of a busy over-scheduled institution. This is what I love about Mia-Mia and why it is a centre of excellence. Mia-Mia puts the rhythms of children and their need for calm, sustained engagement at the very heart of what they do. Mia-Mia strives every day for programs that reflect the patterns of children's thinking, not the preferences of adults. This takes great structure and planning, but none of that is apparent to the children.

Mia-Mia also provided better than mandated ratios, employed an early childhood teacher in every room, both for toddlers and preschoolers, and opened their doors at 7.30 in the morning. Their daily fees were comparable to every other service in northern Sydney, although, as a co-located facility at the university, some of their costs were lower.

The question was obvious. If lucky parents in this part of Sydney could access a premium service for their children, why not the rest of the country? The Mia-Mia formula was there for everyone to copy, if they cared to. It was grounded in a well-thought-out approach to early learning, and carried out by staff who knew what they were doing.

That same commitment to quality was apparent among some of the private providers.

Only a few kilometres away from Mia-Mia, in centres that she owns in Baulkham Hills and Top Ryde, Nesha O'Neil runs an operation that proves you can combine a great service for children and maintain a viable business. With bachelor and masters degrees in psychology and a diploma in children's services, O'Neil employs a number of trained teachers and encourages all her staff to upgrade their skills. In an overwhelmingly female-dominated sector, she also manages to attract suitably trained young men as carers. And they stay.

O'Neil is a dynamo and has an ambition that goes beyond her own business. She wants to see the sector shake off the resistance mentality. She runs a professional, quality operation, is open to all-comers, including children with special needs, and can't see why everyone else can't do the same.

So these were the good guys and I found them in all sorts of settings, in cities and in the regions and across the states. But there were also constant reminders that the status quo suited a lot of people. A reliable supply of ever-expanding subsidies from Canberra had bred complacency. Time and again the anti-change brigade would repeat its mantra: *a quality agenda is all very well but you can't impose it overnight.*

No, but it was high time to make a start.

With eight different systems across the country, any change would have to be worked through with the states and territories, and often across ministries. Childcare and preschool, in many cases, are split across community services and education portfolios. The care ratios for babies, group sizes for toddlers, and requirements for qualifications were different across the states, but the challenge was not so much in achieving a common standard, but a *higher* standard.

I met with all my state counterparts and everyone agreed it was time to do better. Most had done a lot of work in the area. Ministers and senior bureaucrats, including in many cases the all-important Treasury officials, had seen the Fraser Mustard and Ron Lally presentations for themselves. Tasmania and Queensland, in particular, were sufficiently concerned about academic under-achievement in their respective states that they were already rethinking approaches around early intervention. Queensland had the biggest job to do, and a long overdue one, in introducing a prep year so that all Queensland students had the benefit of thirteen years of schooling.

When I started out I was negotiating with wall-to-wall state Labor governments, and to a large extent with people I knew. In New South Wales, it was Kevin Greene and John Della Bosca. In Queensland, Lindy Nelson-Carr and Rod Welford. There was Katy Gallagher in the ACT. The Victorians had Maxine Morand in the portfolio. In South Australia, it was Jane Lomax-Smith. In Tasmania, it was David Bartlett.

The first Labor domino to fall was in Western Australia in September 2008 and while Colin Barnett's Liberal government would prove a far more ornery customer when it came to some aspects of the COAG agenda, his Education Minister, Dr Elizabeth Constable, was positive from the start. With a strong background in education, Constable didn't need to be jawboned by the Commonwealth about the importance of investing in the early years.

While we all maintained a dialogue at ministerial level, the officials across the states got to work in what became known as the Early Childhood Development Sub-Group, part of the Productivity Agenda Working Group of COAG. Do you want me to say that again? Slowly? COAG was becoming an overloaded beast of burden, but it was the only way to work through the fragmented world of early learning.

Within fifteen months, all the jurisdictions would sit down with the Commonwealth and agree on the uniform design elements that are now the legal requirement across the country. One national standard. One set of regulations for children in all out-of-home care settings. That was the original goal and, as of January 2012, it's the reality. They probably don't mention it during show and tell sessions, but Australia's youngest citizens and their educators are now operating in a seamless national economy.

The guiding document that helped bring the states on board is hardly a bestseller, but the report of the Expert Advisory Panel on Quality Early Childhood Education and Care (the EAP) represents a policy game-changer. It sets out the rationale for the major changes now underway in early childhood services across the country. Hardly anyone in the community knows about it, but analysts like Professor Deborah Brennan from the Social Policy Research Centre of the University of New South Wales have since acknowledged the worth of 'the arduous, unspectacular but crucial policy work done behind the scenes'.[9]

I had a free hand in determining the make-up of the EAP. I wanted a mix of thinkers and doers who were capable of designing a new structure that took account of the mixed market, but one that would also define the elements of a learning system that would give young people the best possible start in life. I was also clear about what I didn't want: a group who would waste time re-inventing the wheel or hit the phone in a panic and call in the consultants.

Alison Elliott, the head of the School of Education at Charles Darwin University, was an obvious choice to chair the body. Where others saw obstacles, Alison always seemed to be able to identify practical ways to nudge the system. She was doing this in the toughest place of all, the Northern Territory, where she was training up teachers, many of them indigenous women, and finding innovative ways to deliver preschool programs to remote communities. As busy as she was, she said 'yes' straight away. As did the other academic advisors—Collette Tayler from Melbourne University's Graduate School of Education, Karen Martin from Southern Cross University, and Monash University's Marilyn Fleer.

Sitting alongside the academics were the people who operated services. Their participation was critical, not just in constantly reminding everyone of the practical considerations, but as a demonstration of common cause across a very disparate sector. Some, like Barrie Elvish, the CEO of the C&K community-run centres in Queensland, had a well-developed bias against the privatisation of childcare, having watched in horror from his home state as Eddy Groves' empire spread. But he probably met his match in Helen

Keneally, who joined the EAP and represented a growing group of small private providers under the banner of Childcare Associations Australia. Helen had no truck with operators who cut corners and thought it was high time the entire sector lifted its game. The members she represented, like Nesha O'Neil and others, were already demonstrating that *private* could be synonymous with *quality.*

Two other practitioners were great assets: Joan Gilbert from South Australia, who catered for exceptionally disadvantaged families at CaFE Enfield Children's Centre in Adelaide; and Mia-Mia's Wendy Shepherd.

Rundle represented DEEWR as co-chair and kept her good humour throughout. The task was to define what a National Quality Framework would look like by considering three key aspects: an integrated system of licensing, regulation and accreditation; strong national quality standards; and a quality rating system.

In the meetings I had with the EAP I told them to think big. 'Don't second-guess and serve up what you think will be politically acceptable. Leave the politics to us and work on a framework for children that we can all be proud of.'

That's just what they did. And in record time. The EAP report was finished by August 2008 and accepted by COAG at the beginning of 2009.

In looking at all the international and local research, the EAP considered the drivers of quality, and the report quoted earlier work by Elliott:

> Evidence on the impact and effectiveness of early childhood education and care shows there is a compelling knowledge base which demonstrates that enriched learning environments are fostered by better qualified practitioners ... and that quality outcomes for children are most likely when competent qualified staff interact with small groups of children in enriched environments.[10]

Not surprisingly, the EAP report recommended improved staffing arrangements, with a 1:3 ratio for the under-twos, and significant changes to staff qualifications. Putting the emphasis where it properly belonged, on an understanding of children's development and education, the report called for the employment of at least one university-degree qualified teacher in every service as well as an upgrading of skills for other staff.

No one in the group was unaware of the challenge and the cost of increasing the supply of professionally trained personnel, but neither could they escape the evidence that children benefit from *the richness and appropriateness of staff interactions.*

Running in parallel with the EAP's work was the development of an Early Years Learning Framework. Called *Belonging, Being & Becoming*, it was the first document of its type to be made available nationally for use by the educators of young children. The EAP also recommended that services be rated against the application of the new curricula.

By mid-2009, with all the work in, relevant state ministers came together in Canberra for a meeting chaired by Gillard and myself to argue out the basis for the new standards. We didn't manage a 1:3 ratio for babies but reached agreement instead on 1:4, a big improvement on the 1:5 then applying in most states. Other ratios were altered for toddlers and preschoolers, and—the big change—higher qualifications at all levels got the nod.

A realistic timeline for implementation was set. All long day care and preschool services catering for twenty-five or more children would be required to employ a qualified early childhood teacher by 2014. In addition, at least 50 per cent of the staff in centres would need to have, or be working towards, a diploma in early childhood education and care, while the remainder would need to have, or be working towards, a Certificate III qualification.

An earlier date of January 2012 was set as the start date for a new streamlined regulatory system that would end the duplication of service checks.

There was the usual backing and filling throughout the day, part of the normal ballet of Commonwealth–state discourse, but as Vicki Rundle had always predicted, we got there. Gillard brought a calm rationality to proceedings, and with appeals at times to 'the collaborative spirit of COAG', she locked in a transformative agreement. Not a lowest common denominator agreement but one that raised the bar for everyone.

It reinforced for me an important lesson. Despite all the noisy static then dominating the public space, the bleating from the naysayers about prohibitive costs, etc., there was nonetheless a quiet integrity about the process as people just got on with it. The work—the detailed consultations and the back and forth across the states, along with the endless hours spent on new design principles—was handled, uncomplainingly, by conscientious officials and committed stakeholders, until finally the goal was in sight.

At the start of the 2012 academic year, I went back to the Graduate School of Education at Melbourne University and sat down for a chat with Collette Tayler. Her thinking had been critical to the work of the EAP.

Collette now conducts the E4Kids study funded through a $5 million research grant. The data she is collecting over a five-year period, through controlled programs involving 2600 children across the country, will inform future policy work and give us a clearer picture of the effectiveness of instructional tools for the very young. Collette is also helping to guide the work of the new national regulator, the Australian Children's Education and Care Quality Authority (ACECQA), as its deputy chair, and is providing the hands-on training for state-based regulators who will rate centres against the new standard. More than most she's aware of the pressure points but she says, 'I see this as a long process. The whole system has to gear up for a decade of professional development. But you know, if we hold our nerve, we are on track to do something remarkable.'

Chapter 7

PENNIES FROM KEVIN

T HE FIGURES WERE fantastic. Proof that the vast stimulus package was keeping the nation working. The July 2009 Labour Force figures showed that unemployment was at 5.8 per cent, when the Treasury forecast in that year's Budget had suggested it could hit 8.25 per cent.

While the news from the Northern Hemisphere was of bank collapses, factory closures and forced house sales, Australia, by contrast, was riding out the greatest economic convulsion to have hit global economies since the Great Depression of the 1930s.

You could feel the let's-pull-together mood and see the results in every community across the country.

In Bennelong, consumers went right out and spent their bonus cheques, so whether it was the large retailers at Macquarie Park or the Asian grocery markets of Eastwood or the speciality shops at Gladesville, businesses kept on trading. Six months after the cash splash of $21 billion that had been sent out to families and pensioners before Christmas 2008, and again in February 2009, two-thirds of it was spent.

'Pennies from Kevin' they called it as retail assistants rang up another sale.

From law firms to IT companies, medical service suppliers and construction companies, local employers told me that they were doing everything possible to hold onto staff. Hours were trimmed in some cases, but labour numbers held. Female workers actually increased their part-time hours to boost family income.

Australia's success in cushioning the fall-out from the GFC can be seen as an extraordinary collective effort. Most people could see that we were well served by the strength of our institutions, the banks and regulatory agencies, and in turn, that gave them the confidence to continue to spend. Business investment, which had been expected to fall, was maintained and mass lay-offs avoided.

And at the Ryde Business Forum, the main business lobby in Bennelong, or in conversations in shops or with service providers, I kept hearing: 'It's hard to get good staff so this time we'll do everything we can to hang onto them.' That sentiment played out right across the country, in towns and regions, and it meant that hundreds of thousands of Australians avoided the ignominy of a termination notice and the financial fragility that follows.

In early June 2009, the March Quarter National Accounts showed that the economy was still growing. It was a modest 0.4 per cent growth figure, but what would British Prime Minister Gordon Brown or President Barack Obama have given to have been able to deliver that kind of news?

On the key economic and political metric, that of unemployment, the differences were stark. Australia, the United Kingdom and the United States had entered the GFC with comparable levels of unemployment. Gordon Brown would lose an election to David Cameron in 2010 at a time when unemployment in the United Kingdom had moved to over 8 per cent. It would move higher still to 8.3 per cent, under the pressure of the Conservatives' austerity package. In the United States, President Obama, elected on a 'change you can believe in' platform at the end of 2008, had to deal with an unemployment level that soared to 10 per cent within a year of his election. Jobs have since been added to the US economy but unemployment is still over 8 per cent.

Rudd never stopped talking about jobs. Both at home and overseas.

Having argued strongly for an expanded representative global body of the G20 economies, when the relevant leaders met in London in April 2009, Rudd was a significant contributor. He pushed for enhanced regulatory mechanisms for financial institutions, for an expanded mandate for the World Bank and for a capital increase for the Asian Development Bank. He advocated support for emerging economies, an avoidance of beggar-thy-neighbour protectionist policies, and mechanisms to avoid currency and bond market volatility. But the point he stressed, over and over, was the need to save jobs. He told his G20 counterparts that a focus on employment growth would be a major test of the group's leadership. Rudd provided a paper to the 'G20 sherpas', as he called them, which outlined the Australian approach of short-term stimulus to maintain growth and employment, followed by longer-term strategies to lift global productivity growth.

Ken Henry, Treasury Secretary throughout the period of the GFC, has since acknowledged that it was Rudd who pushed the country's principal economic policy-making body to undertake the broadest possible scenario planning. As Henry told *7.30*'s Chris Uhlmann in May 2012:

> The intense interest that Prime Minister Rudd showed in the issues and the fact he got on to them early is a great credit to him actually … as early as 29 February 2008, which, is what, six to seven months before Lehman's collapsed—he asked me straight out on a VIP flight to Gladstone, 'What's the worst thing that could happen?' And my brain was not in that space about the possibility of a global financial crisis hitting Australia. So I think that's to his very great credit that he was so far ahead of where … we were in Treasury.[1]

For Rudd, at the midpoint of his prime ministership in June 2009, the national data vindicated the decisions he had put in place in the last quarter of 2008 and kept refining as the global situation deteriorated.

At his 3 June press conference, Rudd told journalists: 'Today, in the midst of the worst global economic recession in three quarters of a century, we have good news for the Australian economy, although we are not out of the woods yet.'

Both the Prime Minister and his Treasurer avoided any kind of triumphalism but, as Lenore Taylor and David Uren record in *Shitstorm*, Swan was conscious of the achievement: 'We were not hesitant. We were not meagre. We acted promptly, decisively and in a big enough way to make a difference. The lesson of history is that governments typically acted too timidly and too late in response to a downturn. We were determined not to repeat those mistakes.'[2]

It was Rudd, with the full support of Swan, Gillard and Tanner, who drove the scale and design of the government's response from October 2008 as the Australian share market was falling and local banks worried about access to finance. So often accused of researching the universe and delaying decisions, Rudd, in the space of a critical weekend, 11–12 October 2008, showed he had the ticker for a considered and rapid response. Rudd kept pushing Henry on the key questions. What are the lessons from previous recessions? What is it that will make the biggest difference? How do we protect the maximum number of jobs?

It was a long, exhausting process and bloody scary for a new government. It was Rudd's first significant test as Prime Minister and he didn't blink. He grasped the wider significance of what was taking place beyond Australia's borders. He took advice. He tested the arguments. He acted.

Given what was to come, a level of intra-party acrimony that has not been seen since the Labor split of the 1950s—with accusations against Rudd of dysfunctionality, of profanity and temper tantrums, even an absence of true Labor values—how curious it is that, at a time of maximum stress, no such claims have ever been made about the long days and longer nights of decision-making that saved the nation a mountain of misery.

In *Shitstorm*, this is how Ken Henry describes the back and forth of discussion, particularly the internal debate around the scale and breadth of the stimulus package:

> The discussion was a process of coming to a shared view of the seriousness of the situation. We were having our judgments tested as they should, by the politicians. We were testing their political judgments and all eventually came to a view that the costs of erring on the upside were much smaller than the risks on the downside—that we were confronting something that was quite extraordinary. What are the consequences if that assessment is right? What are the consequences if that assessment is wrong? … Everybody was aware that whatever the risks were, they were worth taking.[3]

The biggest risk, and still the most contested aspect of Australia's response to the GFC, was the size of the second stimulus package, where the overwhelming concern was to maintain growth and employment. Ultimately, for Rudd and Swan, it was a no-brainer. The credentials of a newly elected Labor government would have been shredded had it not done everything possible to save the jobs of Australians.

The International Monetary Fund was urging economies everywhere to boost government spending and suggested fiscal stimulus in the order of 2 per cent of GDP.

In February 2009, the government announced $42 billion in spending on projects that were 'shovel ready' and aimed at the broadest possible reach right across the country. The spending was consistent with Labor's nation-building ambitions and designed to give the maximum boost to the construction industry. With a huge backlog of work identified, $6.6 billion went into social and defence housing, and $3.8 billion was allocated to create the Energy Efficient Homes Package so that householders could install ceiling insulation. The biggest component, a budgeted $14 billion that would eventually lift to $16 billion, was for a school modernisation program that was known as Building the Education

Revolution, or BER. Again, state education departments had long lists of schools that needed new facilities or big licks of money spent on basic maintenance. It was the same with local government authorities, so $1 billion would be allocated to councils for small to medium scale local infrastructure projects—everything from libraries to sports facilities to bike paths. In addition there would be a further $22 billion spent on infrastructure for road, metropolitan public transport, hospital and broadband in the May 2009 Budget. Finance Minister Lindsay Tanner called it 'kitchen-sink-o-nomics', as the effect was the equivalent of throwing the kitchen sink at the economy.

For most of 2009 and into 2010, the standard kit for government MPs would be the hard hat and protective goggles as we hit the road, inspected building sites and repeated the mantra that we were *supporting jobs today by building the infrastructure we need for tomorrow.*

My own sod-turning skills were about to be tested, courtesy of a new job and a new boss.

On 6 June 2009, as we were absorbing the good news that the economy was responding positively to the twin stimulus packages, Rudd announced his first major ministerial reshuffle. Chris Bowen from New South Wales moved into Cabinet as Minister for Financial Services; Greg Combet went into the ministry to assist with Climate Change and Energy Efficiency; and John Faulkner took on Defence. Mark Arbib, having only begun his Senate term the previous July, became Employment Participation Minister with responsibilities to support the Prime Minister on Government Service Delivery. Rudd was giving his chief NSW numbers man overall supervision of the stimulus programs.

With the Early Childhood COAG agreement on track, I had already flagged my interest with Rudd's office about a move. From now on I would be working to Anthony Albanese as his parliamentary secretary with a mix of responsibilities across a combined super-portfolio of Infrastructure, Transport, Regional Development and Local Government.

Albanese had a long-held passion for building up the nation's infrastructure—particularly in the heavy transport areas of road, rail and ports—and with the nation-building component of the economic stimulus, he had the budget to act. Conscious that the business community had for years been calling for greater planning around nationally significant projects, he established Infrastructure Australia, a stand-alone body to advise on priorities and to develop protocols for the use of public–private partnerships. Albanese also set up the Major Cities Unit, which links national funding to agreed criteria around integrated urban planning.

Overseeing all this was Department Secretary Mike Mrdak, an exceptionally effective, quietly spoken public servant. He'd come to the job from the Department of the Prime Minister and Cabinet (PM&C), where he had responsibility for governance and Cabinet support. Mrdak never seemed rushed or chained to his BlackBerry, and as a result, he was more reflective than some others.

From the start, I appreciated the time Mrdak took to give me briefings right across the portfolio. Albanese encouraged this. There were also regular Monday morning meetings in the minister's office during parliamentary sitting weeks. They were all-in affairs, with senior staffers and officials sharing information, and all finished inside half an hour.

And my new boss? Albanese has a public persona as the macho boy from Marrickville. Cross him at your peril. I never had to test that, but I liked Albo. He encouraged collegiality in his office and had a generosity of spirit that was rare in Canberra.

In the weeks when the House wasn't sitting, I was on the road, visiting regional cities and smaller towns, launching stimulus projects, large and small, meeting with mayors and counsellors, and setting up the national network of fifty-five committees that became Regional Development Australia. This brought together local champions who worked in conjunction with councils and provided advice to Canberra on behalf of their communities. Everywhere I travelled, people confirmed the figures and told us the stimulus was working.

Locals were employed as councils were able to kick-start projects they'd had in the in-tray for years. Primary school communities were cock-a-hoop with the kind of money they'd rarely been able to extract from their state education departments. Regions that had put up with black spots or decaying rail crossings now had access to funds that would both improve safety and boost local efficiency.

But time and again in 2009, and more so as we headed into the darker political waters of 2010, I considered the paradox. Individual gratitude with a particular project didn't seem to translate into community satisfaction. In the early part of the crisis there had been the London Blitz mood of defying the global downturn, but just as it was starting to be obvious that we'd survived the worst, the public conversation became more brittle and suspicious.

The opportunity offered by the scale and breadth of the stimulus was unprecedented: to build a political coalition of support for a set of measures that saved the country from recession. This was entirely possible but we never managed it. We never owned the success and, as a result, never turned it into a big story about pride in Australian achievement. A story about looking after everyone.

Instead we harped on for too long about 'not being out of the woods' and, along the way, treated Australians as if they were a bunch of lost Hansels and Gretels. Our rhetoric was clunky where it needed a touch of the heroic.

No one wanted to be cocky but we should have been confident enough to turn a successfully managed crisis into the next chapter of the Labor story.

It's what Keating meant when he told me, 'We missed the opportunity to capitalise on the achievement by contextualising it.'

The government had a two-fold task: to save the economy from recession and to continue to implement all the pre-election commitments. Rudd had developed a narrative and any number of lengthy strategic documents to support the goal of growing the economy and 'building a stronger and fairer Australia'. But, friend and partisan that I am, even my eyes glaze over at the detail and dryness of it. I don't want rhetorical questions and dot points. I want a story, an emotionally alive story that grabs my head and my heart. Just like most people.

The ability to speak to people's concerns at an emotional level and then move on to make an effective policy point is something that Rudd understands. It was central to how he ran his campaign in 2007. It is the very opposite of dumbing-down. Get the master story right, and you have people on the edge of their seats and ready to absorb the arguments.

Above all, we needed to be effective, but instead we were overly prescriptive. Stimulus signs, whether on school sites or local council projects, had to be of a certain size and displayed prominently. Too often, we came across as know-it-alls and treated the states as subcontractors rather than as partners. When advice went to Gillard's office from the largest states of New South Wales and Victoria about the need for more flexibility around timelines for the delivery of BER money, it was rebuffed.

We failed to appreciate that when it comes to promotion, less is more. We carpet bombed people with information about the stimulus programs. It's there in the newsletters we sent out to constituents, with dozens of items detailing one spending initiative after another. Instead of a policy pitch, it's a shopping list—certainly not an argument about a changing world.

It was all too much. And yet not enough.

Perfectly capable of putting in a top performance and charming even the harshest of critics, Rudd went from one extreme to the other in attempting to explain the changes unleashed by the GFC. A long critique of neo-liberalism in *The Monthly* magazine at the beginning of 2009 was followed a few months later by exaggerated populism on Channel 7 with references to a likely 'political shitstorm' over the government's increased borrowings.

Rudd always put huge energy into these endeavours but he might have done better to channel the success of President Franklin Delano Roosevelt, who at the start of the Great Depression spoke to Americans in farm belts and factories and calmed their fears about his New Deal. As outlined in *The Political Brain*, FDR operated in the marketplace of ideas but had a powerful understanding of how to frame an argument that engaged his listeners. This is part of what FDR said in his second 'fireside' chat to the American nation in May 1933:

> Today we have reason to believe that things are a little better than they were two months ago. Industry has picked up, railroads are carrying more freight, farm prices are better, but I am not going to indulge in issuing proclamations of overenthusiastic assurance. I am going to be honest at all times with the people … I know that the people of this country will understand this and will also understand the spirit in which we are undertaking this policy. I do not deny that we may make mistakes of procedure as we carry out the policy. I have no expectation of making a hit every time I come to bat. What I seek is the highest possible batting average.[4]

We may make mistakes. If only we'd said something along the same lines.

Rudd was a puzzle. In private or in small gatherings he could be persuasive and sophisticated, but on other occasions, he seemed to struggle with deciding which Kevin the public should see. Large events convened by the Business Council of Australia and the like, where the Prime Minister was the guest speaker, turned into tutorials complete with slideshow presentations of complicated trend graphs. After knocking back a glass or three of shiraz, no one in the audience wanted to know. What was missed was the opportunity to enlist allies, to give everyone a pat on the back, and to speak to the unique elements that were delivering a much-envied Australian prosperity. Then, at other times, Rudd would get the tone just right and people would line up to shake his hand and to praise the government's efforts.

Rudd came to Bennelong in 2009 and addressed the Ryde Business Forum (without the slideshow) and was warmly received.

As were Lindsay Tanner and Craig Emerson when they talked to other local business groups.

Throughout the year, I spent a lot of time with the local chambers of commerce and with training providers, making sure they had the detail of what we were up to. Employment was always more buoyant in northern Sydney than elsewhere, and some newer businesses used the tougher times and the government's tax breaks to try different things.

Like culinary wunderkind Gena Karpf, who opened her patisserie, Sweetness, in March 2009 on Epping's Oxford Street. Within a year she had ten people working for her. Instead of trying to make everything, she specialised in a few stunning products. Her signature piece was her marshmallows—tiny pink and green cubes of pure sugary bliss, beautifully packaged in chic little handbags. Every weekend she took her trade to markets all over Sydney and via the cheapest method of all, word of mouth, Gena built up a distinctive business. She always said that having gulped hard and started Sweetness during a downturn, she could survive anything.

Gena and I ended up as neighbours on the Oxford Street shopping strip when we finally relocated our electorate office at the end of 2009. It was a move that turned my EO chocoholics into marshmalloholics! Waistlines were only kept in check by the weekend door-knocking we did throughout 2009.

The benefits of incumbency and a well-functioning office notwithstanding, I was very conscious of the fine margin I was on, so together with the core of the purple army volunteers, I was constantly trekking across the electorate and talking to people in their homes.

The mood was pretty good. In a conservative area, Malcolm Turnbull's leadership barely registered. The July Newspoll figures saw support for Turnbull collapse with only 16 per cent of voters prepared to register their preference for him as PM. Rudd, who would only serve for another eleven months as Prime Minister, was recorded as the preferred choice of 66 per cent of voters—an astonishing endorsement.

But the local scene was throwing up a more complicated picture. In the by-election that followed John Watkins' resignation the previous October, the state seat of Ryde returned the Liberal candidate Victor Dominello with a swing of 23 per cent.

Talk about volatility!

In the space of a year, the voters in this part of Sydney had turfed out a Liberal Prime Minister in a federal seat that had only ever returned a conservative, and then voted the other way and passed harsh judgment on the party of a well-regarded Labor Deputy State Premier.

And then Australia's oldest political party entered into one of the most destructive periods in NSW Labor politics.

Morris Iemma's victory at the state poll in 2007 counted for little when the party bosses, Mark Arbib and Karl Bitar, decided to move against him. Iemma lasted as Premier until September 2008. He was followed in the job by the very decent Nathan Rees, who in turn was replaced by Kristina Keneally in December 2009.

At precisely the time when constituents craved a bit of steadiness and reassurance, the political landscape was filling up with corpses. It tested the nerve of those left standing and probably fed a belief that bunkering down with a select few was safer than encouraging robust discussion across a wider group.

But fatally, Rudd bunkered down with the wrong people. In the tight decision-making quartet of the Special Priorities and Budget Committee, the dynamic that had worked well during the crisis period of late 2008 proved less effective in the implementation phase.

Tanner was an ally and a contributor, but Gillard and Swan would soon be causing problems for Rudd's leadership. Gillard did it by forcing Rudd's hand on the abandonment of the central election promise to enact an emissions trading scheme. Swan did it by proposing a mining tax he could never effectively explain.

On the most important issue for 2009, that of managing the flow of billions in investment dollars across housing, education and infrastructure to the states, the SPBC was found wanting. Where Rudd needed to hear from a range of voices, from those who might have cautioned about modes of delivery and the like, he instead relied far too much on Gillard and Swan. Both have their strengths, but once they have taken a position, neither is particularly interested in alternative views.

Rudd denied himself the one thing that might have made a difference: a robust contest of ideas across the ministry and across the caucus.

And consider the irony. Having boosted confidence, maintained growth and kept unemployment below 6 per cent—an achievement few other advanced economies could boast—the government would soon be defined not by its successes but by flaws in implementation.

It was one of the smaller stimulus programs, certainly in financial terms—the $3.8 billion home insulation scheme—that turned into a disaster. It was abandoned after dodgy operators scammed the system. Headlines about house fires and the tragic deaths of some young installers would give the Liberal opposition plenty to work with as they ramped up an attack against government waste.

The bad days for Labor hit soon enough when Tony Abbott replaced Malcolm Turnbull as Liberal leader in December 2009. With a curious amnesia about the profligacy and handout mentality of the latter Howard years, Abbott crafted a simplistic attack on the government over pink batts and school halls. With a clarity that was lacking on our own side, he turned an entirely appropriate public policy response into an exaggerated paranoia about deficits and debt.

Less partisan players and commentators see it differently.

In his book *The Australian Moment*, George Megalogenis is quite explicit, saying that the government's public spending on major construction projects 'sealed the Great Escape from the GFC'. But he also adds that:

… the short attention span of politics—and some frankly mischievous claims from the opposition and in the media that the stimulus was 'wasted'—is inclined to dismiss the government assistance as unnecessary. Nothing could be further from the truth, and the proof is in the response to Australian politicians and officials when they travel to economic and other forums overseas. The question everyone asks us is: 'How did you guys do it?'[5]

It was no mystery to Nobel laureate in economics Joseph Stiglitz, who has consistently praised Rudd 'for putting in place one of the best-designed Keynesian stimulus packages of any country in the world'.[6]

Stiglitz also attacks those who promote 'deficit fetishism' and says it makes no sense in a country such as Australia, where debt is low. Total net government debt in Australia is projected to be around 9 per cent compared with other developed countries that are looking at figures in excess of 80 per cent.

And in responding to a question about government waste in an interview with Kerry O'Brien on *7.30 Report*, in July 2010, Stiglitz said this:

> If you hadn't spent the money, there would have been waste. The waste would have been the fact that the economy would have been weak, there would have been a gap between what the economy could have produced and what it actually produced—that's waste. You would have had high unemployment, you would have had capital assets not fully utilised—that's waste … but what your government did was exactly right. So, Australia had the shortest and shallowest of the downturns of the advanced industrial countries.[7]

By the time Stiglitz delivered this verdict, Rudd was gone. Prime Minister for only two-and-a-half years, he was ambushed by his deputy and abandoned by a caucus too timid to back a leader who had saved the jobs of Australians in every electorate in the country.

Somewhat perversely, given News Limited's relentless attacks on the BER and other programs, *The Weekend Australian* recognised Rudd's contribution by awarding him their highest honour at the beginning of 2010, naming him as the newspaper's Australian of the Year.

Their citation reads:

> Far from being mugged by the global financial crisis, Mr Rudd rose to the occasion and displayed the leadership qualities that have defined Australians of the Year since the award was launched forty years ago. Combined with the underlying strength of the Australian economy and its banks, Mr Rudd's single-minded approach ensured that, unlike his contemporaries Barack Obama and Gordon Brown, his reputation has been enhanced rather than diminished by the GFC. The crisis served to define the government after a first year in power when it struggled to carve out a clear direction. Mr. Rudd was an economic neophyte, having never held such a portfolio in opposition. Yet his management of the crisis cemented Labor's economic credentials.[8]

In an accompanying story by Cameron Stewart and David Uren, there were references to the PM's 'epic gamble' and praise from Treasurer Wayne Swan, who described Rudd's activism as driven by his sense of Labor values. 'Working closely with Kevin over the past year,' he said, 'I've seen just how much the jobs and livelihoods of ordinary Australians have motivated him throughout the global recession.'[9]

But Swan would soon change his tune. Within five months he would have a new job himself, as Julia Gillard's deputy, having backed the move against Rudd.

Swan would go even further and rewrite history.

At the beginning of 2012, with the government grappling with the twin problems of minority status and collapsing support, and with Gillard prepared to test her leadership in a fresh ballot, Swan took the extraordinary step of condemning Rudd as 'somebody who does not hold any Labor values'.[10]

So much for the shared grand days.

For a lot of us it's hard to even summon up the memory.

Chapter 8

AMBUSH

Government MP: He treated some of the factional operatives like shit, which is to his eternal credit. He wasn't going to let them run his government and nor should he. He was contemptuous of them. They thought, we'll show you. And they did.

McKew: And that's the reason they moved against Rudd?

Government MP: I'm absolutely certain of it. For fuck's sake we had a four-point lead on Newspoll the week before he had his head chopped off. His personal ratings were down but he was coming off the highest levels ever seen in Australian political history. He would have comfortably won the election.

It's something to think about, isn't it? That a first-term Prime Minister was removed because he was insufficiently deferential to a small group of people who see themselves as the 'owners' of the Labor Party. Rudd refused to genuflect and kiss the ring. He was busy with other things.

On the evening of 23 June 2010, I was attending a dinner at the Korean Ambassador's residence in Canberra's Empire Circuit. In an elegant setting, a dozen or so of Canberra's diplomatic representatives gathered at the invitation of His Excellency

Dr Kim Woo-sang. With a significant Korean constituency in my electorate and with a bilateral free trade agreement in sight, it would normally have been an occasion for a free-flowing exchange of views and a *tour d'horizon* of regional economic and security issues. It was a pleasant way to spend a winter's evening in the national capital at the end of a parliamentary sitting period.

But this was a night like no other. From the time they gathered for pre-dinner drinks, the Ambassador's guests were absorbing the early evening news that Kevin Rudd, Prime Minister for two-and-a-half years, was now locked away with his deputy in his Parliament House office and living out his final hours in the nation's top job.

The national broadcaster broke the story. A tip-off to journalist Mark Simkin had led the 7 p.m. ABC news bulletin. Simkin spoke straight to camera saying: 'Federal government sources have told the ABC that MPs are being sounded out about a possible move against the Prime Minister. Ministers have been asked for their support and the push is apparently coming from Victoria.'

It was nothing less than a public declaration of war by the anti-Rudd forces.

There was the same disbelief at the embassy dinner as there was at Parliament House. I was completely distracted as courses were served and taken away, and as my dinner companions attempted to politely skirt the only topic of interest in Canberra that night. Then, finally, came a question from one of the diplomatic wives: 'Is Australia ready for a female Prime Minister?'

That stopped all the chatter in an instant and, as the only MP present, everyone looked at me. My response was short and prickly: 'We have a Prime Minister.'

It is fair to say I didn't do much to advance Australian–Korean relations that night. I made my excuses and left shortly after. By then it was close to 10.30 p.m. and I was in a filthy mood. It had not been an easy year for any of us but a power play by Gillard and the factional bosses at this stage of the electoral cycle seemed to me insane. For months Rudd had been focused on lengthy health negotiations and running a crowded agenda—but in the post-Budget period, his office had started to work through the complexity. Gillard's obligation, surely, was to help Rudd implement the big ambitions he'd set for the government's first term. Instead, she was getting ready to knife her leader. Only two years earlier Rudd had beaten Howard. How the hell would any of us explain it at the coming election?

All this had gone through my mind in the minutes after I heard the 7 p.m. news story. I phoned John Faulkner straight away. We shared the same view that a collective madness had taken hold. As Defence Minister, Faulkner had spent much of the day dealing with the tragedy of more Australian soldiers killed in Afghanistan, and then spent a long night locked up as the third participant in the marathon discussions that took place between Rudd and his heir presumptive, Julia Gillard.

Back at my flat in Griffith, I switched on *Lateline* and couldn't believe what I was seeing. Paul Howes, the National Secretary of the Australian Workers' Union and the latest look-at-me available anytime anywhere commentator, was telling the nation via Tony Jones that it was time to anoint Julia Gillard as Prime Minister. This set my blood pressure racing. *Who appointed this bloke as a member of caucus?* Howes told Tony Jones: 'This is a good government with a good record and we can't get our message out. We can't get that message out because there is a dark cloud over the Labor leadership and there has been for the last few weeks and months.'

An interesting choice of words by Howes: *A good government with a good record.* Exactly the same sentiments would be repeated by the new Prime Minister the next day. When had all this been worked out?

Then, for the benefit of *Lateline* viewers, Howes helpfully described how things work in the Australian Labor Party, in particular how the system of big union patronage was uniting to destroy the leadership of Kevin Rudd. Howes explained that he'd rung Gillard that evening to tell her the AWU's position, and added: 'It's not unlike the position of the Health Services Union. I've seen that Michael Williamson, who's also the National President of the Party, has also endorsed Julia Gillard's leadership.'

The HSU would soon be at the centre of a major national scandal surrounding its own leadership and alleged fraud, but right now, just like the AWU and others, it was busy telling Labor MPs in caucus—the ones they 'owned'—that it was time to back someone seen to be more sympathetic to their interests. That's how it works and Rudd never wanted anything to do with it. He'd tried to govern differently, without paying heed to the dominant factions and their union backers. He was never one of the 'tribe' and was now paying the price.

I knew instinctively that the events of the day wouldn't be going down well in Bennelong. A community that had made a significant shift in 2007 wasn't going to be impressed by an execution squad bringing down the leader of the party they'd voted for. They knew Rudd, but who were these other characters whose names were suddenly all over the airwaves as supporters of Gillard? Labor senators like Don Farrell and David Feeney barely registered with the average voter, yet here they were, seemingly at the centre of things. Farrell is from South Australia, where he is the flag carrier for the Shop, Distributive and Allied Employees Association. He's been in the Senate since mid-2008. Feeney, a right-wing powerbroker from Victoria with a background with the Transport Workers Union, took up his Senate seat at the same time. Karl Bitar, the transplanted NSW supremo and National Secretary of the party in 2010, was also part of the push against Rudd. And there were two others taking aim at the PM: Mark Arbib and Bill Shorten. Rudd had provided them with an elevator ride to the top, promoting both in record time. What explained their disloyalty?

I checked my phone. My support for Rudd was a given so I wasn't high on anyone's call list. But I put in calls to two people: Alister Jordan and Anthony Albanese. Both sounded despondent after a night of phoning on behalf of Rudd. From what they said, it seemed clear that the fix was in, that Rudd was the victim of an ambush that had been months in the planning. Earlier in the evening Albanese had met in Wayne Swan's office with the old Beazley loyalists, among them senior ministers Jenny Macklin, Stephen Smith and Stephen Conroy. All of them knew the price the party had paid in diminished authority for the leadership wars of the opposition years. Rudd had finally delivered them victory and their ministries, yet two-and-a-half years into government they were telling Albanese they were prepared to go along with the plotters for the sake of a 'clean break'. Fed up with them, Albanese told them they would wreck the Labor Party and left.

Albanese had also warned Rudd back in May, when the Budget was being presented, to watch his back. Albo's antennae had been twitching for months, ever since he'd watched Gillard's cross-border intervention in the NSW pre-selections the previous November. Altered boundaries had left Reid MP Laurie Ferguson without a seat, but as Gillard's chief standard bearer in New South Wales, the Deputy PM made it clear she wanted Ferguson 'looked after'. Gillard prevailed. Chris Hayes, who'd taken over from Mark Latham, was blasted out of Werriwa to accommodate Ferguson, but not before Albo told Gillard, 'Look, you're already seen as the heir apparent, you don't need your henchmen around here.'

By 11.30 p.m. the phones went quiet. For everyone. Rudd had called a late-night press conference to announce the convening of a special caucus meeting the following morning at 9 a.m.: 'It's far better for these things to be done quickly rather than being strung out over a period of time.' And he added that, if returned as leader, he would be sending a clear message to the right wing of the party, that 'we will not be lurching to the right on the issue of asylum seekers'.

I took one last call around midnight, from someone who worked in the hot-house of Parliament and was close to the action. He reminded me of Gillard's lack of generosity towards me; more than that, her pattern of condescension and the way her office had locked me out of some important policy development. Gillard may have had the words 'social inclusion' in her title but the concept never seemed to extend to me.

I didn't have to agonise. It wasn't about Gillard but about loyalty to a Prime Minister still serving his first term. Rudd had disappointed with his colossal misjudgment in April 2010 when he'd dropped plans for an emissions trading scheme. I'd told him so at the first opportunity and found his response unconvincing. But against that I saw a winning trifecta: a leader who had beaten Howard; who had taken us beyond the shame of our history and made a heartfelt apology to indigenous Australians; and who, in the face of a global financial crisis, had made the timely and bold calls that saved us from recession.

Next morning it was clear from all the media reporting that this was a minority view, and a small minority at that. In my notes from 24 June I wrote a curt couple of lines: *Class of 2007, where are you? Where is your memory?*

I had always felt like an outsider in Parliament House and on this morning never more so.

After a brief stop at my own office, I went straight to see Rudd ahead of the caucus showdown. It was just after 8 a.m. I didn't expect a crowd but nonetheless it was a shock to see how thin the numbers were as we gathered outside Rudd's suite. Damian Hale was there, pacing up and down; he'd won the Northern Territory seat of Solomon by a nose in the Kevin 07 campaign and brought his unique knockabout humour to Canberra. He was one of the few MPs who regularly faced the cameras each morning during parliamentary sittings and managed to sound authentic. He'd been rung by some of his colleagues that morning, urging him to keep his head down. It was a red rag to a bull to Hale, who went right out and backed his boss: 'I don't like people who tell me what to do.'

Some of the Queenslanders were there: Jon Sullivan, Chris Trevor and Claire Moore. The government whip Roger Price and ACT MP Annette Ellis arrived to provide moral support.

But there was only a handful of ministers—Martin Ferguson, John Faulkner, Anthony Albanese, Craig Emerson and Lindsay Tanner—who were openly backing Rudd.

The power had already vanished. When? Last night? Early this morning? Either way it had evaporated. The end was swift, brutal, almost silent. That was the shock of it.

I wanted a few minutes with Rudd, away from the others. Chief of Staff Alister Jordan opened the door to the PM's suite and there he was … no longer commanding and full of energy, but shattered and with a face as white as the wall. He was behind the desk writing some notes for the caucus meeting that was about to discard him. His wife, Thérèse, and children, Marcus, Jessica and Nicholas, were all in the room, every one of them red-eyed from crying. It felt like the loneliest place on the planet. Rudd stood up and came around from the desk and I put my arms around him. What do you say to a man who is about to lose the glittering prize of the prime ministership? I think the best I could manage by way of consolation was a banal, 'This shouldn't be happening.'

Only a few weeks earlier I'd been in this same room having a rare one-on-one over a cup of tea with Rudd. It was at the height of the torrid campaign by the mining companies opposed to the super-profits tax, and by then he was fighting on multiple fronts. At times, he looked friendless. I suggested he needed to reconnect with those things that had worked for him during the campaign in 2007: the focus, the discipline, the purpose. *Tell people what you've done. You didn't blink when the GFC hit. You honoured Labor's primary purpose and kept the nation working.* And, as tactfully as I could, I also told him to drop the extravagant rhetoric and speak plainly. No more 'revolutions' or 'greatest moral challenges'. Use verbs. Let them do the work.

Neither of us knew it, but it was too late. Too late for everything.

Albanese was watching the clock. It was close to 9 a.m., the time for the special caucus meeting that was about to anoint a disloyal deputy as Australia's next Prime Minister.

It's quite a trek from the ministerial suites, across King's Hall, and down the corridors to the caucus room. And every ghastly second of this gallows march was followed by television crews. We stiffened our backs and faked our smiles.

I was so angry I could have taken someone's head off. How had it come to this? Even allowing for the missed opportunity of a summer election and the wrong call on the ETS, I was walking beside a leader who'd had the ability to take on Howard and the wit and talent to beat him decisively. But on Thursday, 24 June 2010, Rudd was brought down by his own.

How many MPs in the caucus room that day weighed up the consequences? How many intuited that their parliamentary careers were on the line and that the government was headed for minority status after the election? How many realised that the electorate would apply a different logic and prove an unforgiving judge of these events?

I knew my fate was sealed. I operated on the principle that the whole idea of factional fealty was arcane and had rebuffed an early offer to join the NSW Right. It meant that I set myself apart from the Sussex Street machine, and that had been noted. Mark Arbib and Karl Bitar (dubbed 'KarlMarks' by some of the Rudd staffers) saw themselves as enforcers. When they kneecapped Rudd they expected caucus to comply, and most did. No one said anything about my non-compliance, but they watched and saw that I stood with Rudd—and that meant I was on my own. It had significant consequences when it came to the re-election campaign in Bennelong.

As caucus chair Daryl Melham went through the formalities, I looked around the room. Bob McMullan was seated not far from where I had perched next to John Faulkner. A former National Secretary, McMullan had witnessed the drama of Labor leadership battles many times before. He had been overlooked by Rudd for a ministerial position when we formed government in 2007 so there were no outstanding IOUs between the two. But he could sense disaster as he'd watched the progressive destabilisation of

Rudd and, earlier in the week, had pointed out the obvious to caucus nervous nellies: the latest Newspoll had the government on a winning lead of 52–48.

I looked at the faces of ministers; most were staring straight ahead. Penny Wong was crying. The key protagonists, Gillard and Rudd, were in the front row, a few seats apart and making eye contact with no one.

Rudd spoke first. In what was a remarkably dispassionate analysis, he acknowledged that many of the people in the room were fearful because of declining polls but made the point that this was after two years of spectacular ascendancy. Importantly, he placed on record the fact that Finance Minister Lindsay Tanner and Climate Change Minister Penny Wong had argued to retain the ETS, while the counter argument had been forcefully put by Gillard and Swan. But he then said, 'I made the call.' He talked of failures of implementation, in the school building and insulation programs. On the contentious mining tax, the issue that was causing maximum grief to the government, Rudd emphasised that this had been 'a collective decision'. He then went to the heart of the matter and talked of his deep concern that the federal parliamentary Labor Party was now being subject to the same kind of pressures and practices that prevailed in New South Wales: the routine and cavalier removal of leaders in an effort to shore up flagging support.

With a sense of where Gillard might be heading on border protection, Rudd pointedly said, 'There is no mileage in trying to out-right the right on asylum seekers.'

At one point Rudd's voice appeared to break. Sitting close to the podium that Rudd was gripping for support, Graham Perrett, one of the Queensland members who won the Brisbane seat of Moreton on the back of the Rudd surge in 2007, half stood and said, 'Are you right, mate?'

Poor Graham. Was he having second thoughts already?

Rudd finished by saying he would not contest the ballot 'because the interests of this party and this government must transcend the interests of any individual in it'.

And then it was over.

Julia Gillard's leadership was endorsed by caucus and, shortly after, she took the oath of office. The photos of the country's first female Prime Minister standing beside Governor-General Quentin Bryce on the steps of Government House suggested a new era of girl power and a fresh beginning. But it was a deceptive image. Those who'd orchestrated this moment never considered that there might be any kind of backlash against this lightning-fast grab for power. This sentiment was reflected in Barrie Cassidy's book, *The Party Thieves*, where one MP is quoted as saying, 'The night of the long knives would be forgotten. Julia will be PM and it will seem that it was always so. The dogs may bark but the caravan moves on.'[1]

A short time later Gillard faced her first Question Time and her tone marked the start of a new kind of politics. Her combative taunt to Tony Abbott—*Game on!*—thrilled her supporters, but it was a shallow quip, more suited to the soccer field than the parliamentary chamber, and did nothing to establish any kind of moral authority for the new Prime Minister. It was also a scene-setter for the crass 2010 election campaign, where the main players buried once and for all the idea of politics as a contest of ideas. It would be replaced by a contest of fears.

*

On 13 February 2012, along with three-quarters of a million other ABC viewers, I watched as Julia Gillard traded away a bit more of her credibility in an astonishing interview on *Four Corners*. No girlish giggles this night, only short sharp responses. Reporter Andrew Fowler had reviewed the events leading to Rudd's removal and was pressing the Prime Minister about two points: her knowledge, prior to June 2010, of private party polling that showed adverse results for Rudd, and of the pre-coup preparations being made by Gillard staffers for a victory speech.

This would not have been a revelation to insiders, but for most—that is, the politically alert who make up the ABC's demographic—the Prime Minister's evasions and legalistic answers emphasised, yet again, why Australians struggle to trust her.

Gillard told *Four Corners* that her staffers 'might have been casting in their mind where circumstances might get to'. She had 'no specific recall' of private polling and critically, she told Fowler, 'I made a decision to run for Prime Minister on the day I walked into Kevin Rudd's office and asked him for a ballot.'

Come again? Gillard exercises top-down control over her office. Her forensic attention to detail sets her apart and her careful planning of every career move is legendary. Politics is her life and she gives it everything she has.

I remembered some of my own experiences working to her office. A speech I'd prepared for a Sydney Institute presentation in early 2009 was vetted and parsed by three separate Gillard staffers before I was 'allowed' to deliver it. Nothing happened without Gillard's say-so. Her office was a machine, and an efficient one. It suited her perfectly and advanced her ambitions. Yet Gillard consistently represented herself as a last-minute conscript to the party leadership, as someone who was on the periphery of events right up until the final hours of the showdown against Rudd.

The voting public never bought this. The manner of Rudd's removal in June 2010 either bewilders or infuriates Australians. In turn, it has fed a sense of illegitimacy about Gillard's tenure and tainted much of what she has attempted since the election of 2010.

Gillard's backers, however, have been masterful in the way they have cemented a particular narrative about Rudd's deficiencies as a leader. For a long time the media reflected this with story after story denigrating Rudd as the worst kind of martinet, someone who had contempt for proper process, and a leader who ignored his ministers. But in the time since the June 2010 coup, a different and more complex story has emerged, one told by ministers and caucus members who feel they were manipulated into a rush of judgment against Rudd. They now see Rudd as the victim of an ambush carried out by a group of political mercenaries. The cost has been catastrophic. One young minister, now almost resigned to losing his seat, has said to me: 'I wasn't planning on finishing my political career just yet. But there's no doubt the events of June 2010 mean that the party is now on the edge of the cliff and that we are looking at a wipeout of a generation of Labor parliamentarians.'

Over the past year I have spent hours talking with former colleagues as they have reviewed in their own minds the events that have proved so devastating for the Labor government. My only criterion was to seek out individuals who are independent thinkers and who are confident enough about their own standing in the parliamentary pecking order to call it like it is. They are by no means myopic when it comes to Rudd. They accept that he can be a deeply polarising figure for many in the broader labour movement. But above all, they see plainly what the electorate sees: the diminished authority that is the direct consequence of a political organisation that casually discards its leaders. Their concerns are now focused on the survival of the government and the credibility of a 121-year-old party.

Given the way events continued to play out in 2012, with both the Gillard and Rudd forces locked in a *danse macabre*, interviewees, for the most part, spoke to me on the basis of anonymity. Others were prepared to be quoted.

I've asked them the questions that continue to puzzle me in the wake of Rudd's removal. Among them, at what point did the mutual seduction between Gillard and those opposed to Rudd begin? Why didn't a senior group of ministers intervene earlier and tackle Rudd about the way he ran the show? And why, in the end, was a majority of the caucus prepared to wave goodbye to a first-term Prime Minister and one of the Labor Party's most successful campaigners?

One Labor MP, in Parliament for more than twenty years, and someone who did not vote for Rudd in the 2006 leadership ballot, describes it this way:

> This was a very professional hit against Rudd. Don't let anyone tell you any different. This challenge was over before anyone had any time to think about it. It played itself out behind closed doors. Kevin was locked up for five hours. I've been through seven of these bloody things and we were all locked out. They herded everyone in a way that has come back to bite them, and the party. And there was absolutely no justification for it. We were not a bad government. The same people claiming we had lost our way were integral to the direction of the government. It should never have happened and the public have never been convinced.

Julia Gillard, in her first statement after taking over from Rudd, said that 'a good government had lost its way'. What did she mean?

It now appears that the first thing that was 'lost' was Gillard's faith in the government's ability to prosecute the case for an emissions trading scheme, or ETS. She wanted it junked and from the beginning of 2010 never let up in putting forward this point. Before parliament resumed for the year, Gillard was telling ministers, Kim Carr among them, that she thought the government should drop the whole idea of an ETS because it had become electoral poison. As Minister for Innovation, Industry, Science and Research, Carr did not agree, seeing it as a totemic issue for the government, and thought that the case should be argued out in a double-dissolution election. That had been an option for the government since the second rejection in the Senate, in early December 2009, of the legislation that would have enabled the establishment of the Carbon Pollution Reduction Scheme (CPRS). Others agreed with Carr, including John Faulkner, who for months had been pressing the case for an early election, and had been doing so long before the international climate change summit held in Copenhagen in late December 2009.

Rudd hesitated about the early double-dissolution trigger. He was still nursing his own disappointments in the wake of Copenhagen, where in spite of marathon efforts by himself and others, further progress at the international level had been blocked by China, India and Brazil. Member countries had agreed that deep cuts in global emissions were required to hold the increase in temperature to below 2 degrees Celsius, but there was no accord about a specific deadline.

Back home and looking forward to a brief summer break, Rudd found that his deputy was both scathing and cynical in the wake of the Copenhagen talks.

In early January, Gillard met with Rudd at Kirribilli House. They sat out on the verandah, with its glorious views of Sydney Harbour, and where the ambience can usually be relied on to promote easy talk and resolution. Not on this occasion. Gillard had a blunt message for her Prime Minister. She told Rudd that under no circumstances would she support the case for an election based on the need for action on climate change. She made reference to the potency of the bush campaign being run by Barnaby Joyce, the Queensland National MP. Joyce had been busy exploiting the altered climate change sentiment with exaggerated claims about the price increases that would flow from an ETS. Joyce had his followers, but was Gillard, the government's best performer in Parliament, really rattled by Joyce? Rudd argued his ground but found his deputy immovable, and from this point, the tone of the relationship between leader and deputy started to change. There would be a new formality. Rudd's chief advisor, Alister Jordan, who was in the habit of taking a regular Sunday night walk with Gillard during Canberra sitting weeks, noticed the shift as well.

Gillard never relented and throughout the early months of 2010 continued to pressure Rudd to abandon the ETS. She was backed by Treasurer Wayne Swan. Mark Arbib, annoyed at the missed opportunity of an early summer election and rapidly losing faith in Rudd's leadership, pushed for an amended ETS package with an altered timetable. With time running out ahead of the Budget, the joint advocacy of Deputy and Treasurer turned into a threat. According to one minister:

> In the end, Rudd did listen to Julia and Swannie and that proved fatal. However when your Deputy and Treasurer go so far as to say you won't have our support if you persist, to the point where the survival of Rudd's government depended on him dropping the ETS, it was pretty much Hobson's choice by then. But Rudd was weak. He should have told them to get stuffed.

This version of events conceives of Gillard not only as a prime architect of a decision that came close to wrecking the government's environmental credibility, but as a deputy who shirt-fronted her leader with an ultimatum. On one occasion, she sent a written message to Rudd that went to the absolutism of her position: she would have nothing to do with an election campaign that re-argued the case for an ETS.

Gillard could have handled things differently. Had she continued in a more traditional way as a supportive deputy, she could have helped the government negotiate its way through a complex policy. But instead, she decided to take on her Prime Minister on an issue that was central to his credibility, Rudd having dubbed climate change 'the great moral challenge of our generation'.

And where was Cabinet in all this? Notwithstanding the accumulating problems in selling the proposed CPRS, there were still plenty of ministers and others who were prepared to march up the hill, banners flying, to fight the good fight on an issue that had been central to the government's election in 2007. It had been a seminal point of distinction during the campaign—we were on the side of the angels in wanting to save the planet. We cared about the future, while Howard was stuck in the past.

What's astonishing is that Gillard, one of the government's better communicators at the time, and someone who took a lead role in the 2007 election campaign in lambasting the inaction of the Howard government on climate change, was not prepared to take on the rhetorical challenge in government. In the end she showed precious little conviction on the issue and instead took to heart the focus group anxieties being pedalled by the national secretariat.

The rest of us were desperate to get some easily digestable information out into our electorates. In Sydney particularly, with Tony Abbott's 'great big new tax' being taken up with ferocious enthusiasm by talk-show radio hosts, Labor MPs needed material to counter not just the sceptics but also those who simply wanted to get a handle on the practical implications of a cap and trade system. My electorate office handled an enormous amount of correspondence on this. I'd had both Penny Wong and Greg Combet as guest speakers at Bennelong forums in both 2008 and 2009. They were convincing advocates and got a good hearing from the locals. But the electoral mood on this issue had turned, and 2010 was a very different battleground.

It was obvious we needed a credible and commanding 'sell' but we never managed it. Local MPs who prepared their own explanatory materials for letterboxing and the like found they struggled to get timely authorisation. It's now clear why this never eventuated: it was sabotaged from the top. While the foot soldiers were still in the trenches, on the lookout for an opportunity to go over the top, some of the generals were getting ready to surrender.

In New South Wales, Labor supporters had seen it all before. The loss of nerve by the party's organisation when Premier Morris Iemma attempted to privatise the state's electricity assets had resulted in his ouster and replacement by Nathan Rees in September 2008. One NSW state MP describes this as the handiwork of 'the Sussex Street geniuses, Mark Arbib and Karl Bitar':

> Look, their most striking characteristic is their short-termism. You know, when in doubt, change the leader. They can always tell you what the mob is thinking. Bitar and Arbib see the

politics of climate change getting harder, so armed with focus group research saying people don't want to pay more for electricity, they team up with Julia and get Kevin to ditch the ETS. Then they see his numbers fall and knock him off. You know, these guys would have knocked Hawkie off in 1984 when he went into a funk over his daughter. Anna Bligh was spot on in calling this the NSW disease.

This same MP doesn't spare Rudd.

In the end he caved into them and that pissed off a lot of people. I still believe that if we had gone for a double dissolution, and I will believe this to my dying day, that we would have won the election. But we wimped it. Whatever views people had on climate change, they looked at us and said, 'You are not for real.' Remember, the framing of the 2007 campaign was about the past versus the future. And the big part of the pitch for a future with Labor was that we would deal with climate change. So in walking away from it, Rudd was repudiating a key part of his political persona.

It was worse than that. It made us all feel like political cowards. When Lenore Taylor broke the story in *The Sydney Morning Herald* on 27 April 2010 that the government was planning to shelve the ETS, we lost the moral and policy ascendancy over the conservatives. I felt it acutely in Bennelong as action on climate change had been central to my campaign pitch. Whether people were light green or dark, sceptics or believers, this decision marked the point where we lost our post-election cachet, where we looked and sounded like just another bunch of expedient politicians. In the weeks and months that followed, the attitude of constituents was: 'If you don't believe in this, what else don't you believe in?'

The leak to Taylor forced the issue. Rudd had let things drift. It had been raised in Cabinet earlier in the year and some ministers had pointedly asked Wong about speculation that the ETS would be scrapped ahead of the Budget. I understand Wong denied any such thing. Later, Gillard prepared a paper for the 'gang of four', the Strategic Priorities and Budget Committee, and this recommended that the government *not* advocate an ETS in the absence of bipartisan support. With Abbott leading the Coalition, having taken over from the pro-ETS Turnbull, that wasn't going to happen.

But the decision was still open. As one senior minister has said to me, 'We had not finally landed.' Another is convinced that, had the issue been argued out in full in Cabinet, 'there is no way Gillard would have won the argument'. The minister believes to this day that the leak to Lenore Taylor was designed to derail the Cabinet process and to destablilise Rudd. Further, that all the post-Copenhagen manoeuvring around climate change 'was designed to set up a potential challenge to Rudd'.

A full Cabinet discussion had been set to take place before the May Budget but, with the publication of the Taylor story, a panicked and unconvincing confirmation was eventually made by Wong. Rudd said publicly that 'it was a reasonable and responsible course of action' given the limited progress at the United Nations Copenhagen talks.

The first recorded Newspoll taken after the abandonment of the ETS showed a five-point turnaround in the government's fortunes. For the first time the Coalition was in front of the government with a two-party preferred vote of 51–49. The pragmatism of Gillard had won out but Rudd was paying the price.

If that wasn't bad enough, we were about to make things even harder for ourselves.

Of the 138 recommendations in Treasury Secretary Ken Henry's review of taxation, Swan had decided, in an election year, to act on Recommendation 45 and alter the charging arrangements for the country's non-renewable resource sector. Henry argued that the existing mix of Commonwealth taxation and state charges be replaced by a uniform resource rent tax, to be 'levied at a rate of 40 per cent, with that rate adjusted to offset any future change in the company income tax rate from 25 per cent, to achieve a combined statutory tax rate of 55 per cent'.[2]

Swan's announcement of this on 2 May, just a week ahead of the 2010 Budget, set the scene for an all-out campaign against the government by some of the biggest corporate players in the country, BHP Billiton, Xstrata and Rio Tinto, all of which felt blindsided by an uncompromising Treasurer. The resource companies had for some time conceded the case for a more streamlined approach and a higher level of taxation on the massive profits accruing to the industry. Resources and Energy Minister Martin Ferguson had forewarned the key players early in 2010 that a resource rent tax was in the offing, but kept telling them that they would be fully consulted on all the detail, and that revenue estimates from the new tax would not be in the May Budget. They were less than reassured and started to roll out a national advertising campaign against the government from 7 May.

Then with the release of the Budget on 10 May with forward revenue figures booked for what was called the RSPT—the Resource Super Profits Tax—and the revenue allocated to specific programs, the miners felt they'd been completely dudded. The acrimony unleashed by the miners' campaign, along with Abbott's opportunistic rejection of any proposal for increased taxation, was the dramatic backdrop to the events that led directly to Rudd's removal as Prime Minister. What the public saw was an embattled leader who seemed indifferent to the needs of the country's wealth creators.

None of us needed to see detailed polling to know that we were unsettling the electorate. Big time. I remember a community barbecue in Ermington that I organised for the weekend after the Budget. This is not a part of Sydney where people boast about the size of their share portfolios or worry about what they will say at the next BHP Billiton AGM, but I copped a caning from people who'd listened to radio shock-jock Ray Hadley that week about the government's assault on 'the wealth of the nation'. After an hour of this even the sausages and onions started to curl and look a bit grumpy. When we finished up that day I calculated that just about everyone in Ermington had received a bonus cheque from the government and had a job because of the massive stimulus applied at the height of the GFC. But like customers, voters are always right. Temporary gratitude had been quickly replaced by irritation over a lack of resolve on election promises or poorly explained new policies.

In the case of the mining tax, Rudd was more sinned against than sinner. He'd been explicit with his Treasurer back in November 2009 when he was first briefed about Henry's recommendation. Rudd, still juggling election options and with major outstanding policy work to be resolved around both the ETS and health reform, didn't want a contentious debate on yet another front. He laid down some key conditions for his Treasurer. Rudd told Swan that he needed to secure the support of at least one of the major industry players and that he needed to have the states on side. Neither would be easy. Long negotiations could be expected with the states, as they sought to protect their constitutional right to apply royalties.

Rudd trusted his Treasurer. But as West Australian Premier Colin Barnett has said, Rudd's 'jaw just about hit the table'[3] when Barnett told the PM at a COAG meeting in April 2010 that the tax was a dead duck. Western Australia would not compromise its powers over mining royalties. Rudd had assumed that the states, including Western Australia, were on board. Frustrated, Rudd called on the head of his department, Terry Moran, and asked him to fly to Perth to meet with Barnett and see if a compromise could be brokered. Moran met with Barnett and the head of WA's Department of the Premier and Cabinet, Peter Conran, on Wednesday, 28 April. That evening Moran dined with Conran but found that the West Australians were unwilling to give way for fear of disrupting the massive investment that was flowing to the state.

Come Budget week, it was clear there was tension between Rudd and his Treasurer. Swan had not delivered and Rudd had come to believe that he had been sold a pup. Rudd certainly had a right to expect that, when it came to changing the taxation arrangements of an industry that actually stirs more patriotism than resentment, his Treasurer was up to the job—that he would be across the complexity and take the time to build confidence in the sector around the government's objectives.

It should have been clear from the start to Swan and his advisors that the mining industry would arc up. The problem started with the title. A 'super profit', in economic theory, is one earned over and above the cost of capital, but the detail in Swan's Announcement Paper of 2 May was so imprecise that it gave rise to the concern that normal profits would be subject to excessive taxation. Chris Richardson from Access Economics pointed to the problem when he told a mining conference in June 2010 that the 'RSPT taxes effort and entrepreneurial expertise (at 40 per cent) as well as mineral resource rents'.[4] This seemed to be a distinction lost on Swan. Did he seriously want to inhibit risk-taking in Australia's boom sector? The miners argued that the reach of the tax was too wide, the scope for deductible expenditure was too narrow, and the uplift at the Commonwealth bond rate of nearly 6 per cent was too low. Some of the disquiet around these points might have been avoided if Swan had been offering the substantial trade-off proposed by Henry: a cut in the corporate tax rate to 25 cents. The big opportunity to improve the competitiveness of the company tax system was lost with Swan's modest offer of a 2-cent cut to 28 cents. This would be modified further to a 1-cent cut, before being dropped altogether in the 2012 Budget. And still unresolved to this day, under the reshaped MRRT (Minerals Resource Rent Tax), is the refundable credit for state royalties paid by companies. This has turned out to be an open invitation to the states to increase their royalty charges.

There was something else. As proposed by Henry, and promoted by Swan, the RSPT had some peculiar design features. I'm no resource tax expert but even I could spot them. In its original conception, Swan proposed that the Commonwealth should subsidise loss-making mining operations. Why? Still thinking like a journalist, I remember asking Swan about the rationale for this. Why put this burden on taxpayers? I was told to look for the explanation on the relevant website. Other ministers, far more knowledgable, already had their reservations. Craig Emerson, one of the most highly qualified economists in the federal parliament, wrote an entire doctoral thesis on the taxation of petroleum resources. He then had the chance to act on this and alongside his mentor, Professor Ross Garnaut, worked out the detail of what became the PRRT, the Petroleum Resource Rent Tax, which was introduced by the Hawke government in 1984.

Emerson constantly tried to buy into discussions but was blocked. The ANU-trained economist could see the problem. As he says, the RSPT 'is theoretically elegant but practically useless' because it ropes in the government as a co-owner and joint risk partner in the development of the country's minerals wealth. The industry didn't want a bar of this. Equally there was no shortage of external voices sounding warnings. Among them was Professor Sinclair Davidson, who put it plainly when he said, 'What will happen when taxpayers have to stump up millions of dollars to reimburse a company for a failed project?'[5]

Another view of Swan's original tax is that it's a design more suited to an undeveloped resource market in a country in Africa, but not for a mature resource economy such as Australia.

Throughout April, another key player, Resources Minister Martin Ferguson, kept operating on the basis that there would be a long period of consultation with the miners and a full Cabinet Expenditure Review Committee process but he was in for a shock. Three days before the 2 May announcement, Ferguson received his first full Treasury briefing, and for him, it raised more questions than answers. Ferguson pressed Treasury officials on the question of state royalties, but he was told that 'everything would be sorted out later'—and besides, the proposal was already with the printers.

Another colleague, West Australian MP Gary Gray, was also kept at arm's length. A former National Secretary of the party, Gray had tasted corporate life as an advisor to Woodside Petroleum and had helped the company rebuff a takeover bid by Shell. In government, Rudd gave Gray responsibility for Northern and Regional

Australia. Gray was familiar with all the key players, sensitive to the politics of the West, and had spoken in Parliament of the need for a rationalisation of the tax arrangements for resource development.

So a significant brains trust was available. The combined expertise of Gray, Ferguson and Emerson could have been harnessed earlier by Swan to work with industry, get the detail right and arrive at a sensible middle-ground position—one that industry could live with, and one that achieved the primary purpose of an appropriate return for the community from the right to mine the country's non-renewable resources. Again, a healthy contestability around some key concepts could have avoided much of the political pain visited on the government. The only other Minister who appears to have been included in the SPBC meetings that considered the RSPT is Chris Bowen, who was consulted over the superannuation changes that would be funded from the revenues from the mining tax.

The full force of the miners' campaign hit during Budget week. Full-page advertisements were taken out in the national dailies by the Minerals Council of Australia. Rudd knew he had a potential catastrophe on his hands and while he was saying publicly, 'All Australians deserve a fair share of our national wealth', he called in Ferguson and told him to sort things out with the miners. At this point, Rudd had stopped believing the reassurances he was getting from Swan.

Ferguson got to work. Meetings with key players such as BHP Billiton's managing director, Marius Kloppers, were conducted with Rudd and Ferguson. They worked through some of the more contentious points, the dimensions of the uplift for the tax, and how to assess the value of established investments. At the end of every meeting all the documentation went back to Treasury and to Swan's office. Swan was absent for some of the post-Budget period, attending G20-related meetings overseas.

On Rudd's instructions, Ferguson continued to work towards a settlement. Throughout this period, from late May to early June,

he kept getting a lot of calls. They came from Gillard supporters, ministers and MPs. *How close are you to a deal?* Ferguson was
picking up on the nervousness about the government, but he saw
no cause for panic. Still, the internal calls kept coming. Ferguson
remained confident throughout that a deal could be reached with
one or other of the major companies, or with second-tier players such as Fortescue's Andrew Forrest. A deal on coal seam gas
had already been secured and was ready for signature, and by
24 June negotiations were well advanced for agreements with
the North West Shelf Venture partners Woodside and Chevron.
A string of emails that have since been released under Freedom
of Information confirm this with reference to a 'changed tone' in
meetings with companies such as Xstrata and a willingness to 'do
a deal'.[6] A resolution was in sight.

But then Rudd took a call that changed the dynamics completely. Marius Kloppers phoned the Prime Minister to say all
bets were off. Kloppers explained that BHP Billiton's chairman,
Jac Nasser, wanted negotiations with the government to cease. No
explanation was offered, but it was the clearest possible signal to
Rudd that Australia's most prestigious company had its eyes fixed
firmly on the emerging leadership tensions. On 23 June, Swan,
having never offered any explanation for the flawed execution of
the RSPT, told Rudd that he was 'voting for change'. The next
day, 24 June, and within hours of Gillard taking over as Prime
Minister, BHP Billiton announced that it would immediately
suspend the company's anti-government advertising campaign and
begin 'to properly engage on all aspects of the tax'. It remains an
open question to this day how this 'truce' was brokered so quickly
and so decisively.

*

The parliamentary sitting weeks that preceded the June coup had
been joyless. Rudd acknowledged to his colleagues the multiple

problems for the government: border protection, the school building and insulation programs, the ETS and the mining tax. We were being defined by our opponents and it wasn't flattering. There was no shortage of frank discussion. Some of the contributions stressed the need for clarity, calm and consistency. Another minister wanted to see a less crowded agenda and said confidently, 'We have a decade of reform ahead of us.'

As a government we had efficiently run through shopping lists of achievements only to find, as one put it, 'that the buggers out there don't know it'. That was quite an admission given the oppressive and ridiculous control exercised by the communication teams in Rudd's office and elsewhere. All the attempts to corral the ministry into sticking to a cornball script whenever individuals appeared on Sky News, the ABC or anywhere else had led us up a garden path of diminishing returns. I didn't win any friends by frequently referring to the ubiquitous talking points as 'bilge'.

What we didn't know was that a handful of individuals were already involved in an elaborate shadow play. Rudd's personal popularity had taken a dive, with the early June 2010 Nielsen polling showing that the PM's approval rating had dropped to 41 per cent. That represented an eighteen-point movement in the space of two months. The two-party preferred result was even more alarming, coming in at 47–53 in the Coalition's favour. But Newspoll told a better story and suggested the worst was behind us. The poll recorded on the weekend of 18–20 June, only days before Rudd was replaced by Gillard, showed the government on a winning two-party preferred margin of 52–48, having moved ahead from the 50–50 two-party preferred result recorded immediately after the Budget. And considering all the negatives that Rudd was dealing with, he was still preferred as PM by 46 per cent of Australians, compared with 37 per cent who favoured Abbott. On another measure, that of net approval rating, while he was Prime Minister, Rudd averaged an incredible figure of plus 34.

But a very different picture was being selectively presented to ministers and caucus members. Internal party research purported to show the government's vote in free-fall, with a potential loss of up to thirty seats. Polling in government-held regional NSW marginal seats apparently showed a wipeout. There's one problem with this: it's impossible to reconcile with the published polling.

So what explains this disparity?

A favoured technique in New South Wales had been to treat qualitative polling as something more scientific. Instead of listening to the views of voters in order to glean the occasional insight that might inform the prosecution of a message, Bitar and Arbib were fans of an American approach that scored messages to a mathematical formula. Individuals in a focus group, for instance, would be asked to rate a particular statement from one to five. The exercise is repeated across different states and among different kinds of voters. The figures are added up and, hey presto, a collective judgment is delivered!

This leaves one MP deeply unimpressed:

> The people who engage in these techniques have no serious political compass, and certainly no sense of the history and culture of the party. They have an instrumental approach to the administration of the Labor Party that is almost entirely uninformed by principle. They actually think that when someone is doing poorly in a poll that that means they should not be leader. It does not occur to them that there are a lot of other things to think about when you make a judgment like this.

This is not an insignificant issue. In the time that has passed since Rudd's removal as leader, many caucus members have said they were conned. Manipulated. And a principal tool in the enterprise was research commissioned and owned by the Labor Party. As National Secretary at the time, Bitar has to take responsibility for this research that was used against the then Prime Minister. It draws a harsh judgment from many, but in particular from John Faulkner, who told me:

> For a party official to use party research to undermine a
> serving Labor Prime Minister—or any party leader for that
> matter—is quite improper and should never, never, be tolerated.
> Unfortunately, this is just what happened in 2010. I am aware
> of caucus colleagues who were shown or handed research.
> I consider this was just sheer bastardry.

This is a strong statement from Faulkner, who is a trusted figure within the party, and he maintains that trust because he is a man who keeps his counsel. He was a participant, not just a witness, in the long discussions between Rudd and Gillard that took place on the evening of 23 June, Rudd's last night as Prime Minister. Faulkner has never spoken about the details, and says he never will. But such is Faulkner's disgust and contempt for the way Rudd was undermined and the way that party research has been misused that, on this matter, he is prepared to speak on the record.

So what was this 'research' that was being handed around, and was it deliberately doctored to convey the impression that Rudd's position was terminal?

Rudd's Attorney-General Robert McClelland was shown research by Gillard supporter Brendan O'Connor. It was the week before the June 2010 coup. McClelland recalls:

> It was research that showed a perception word identification
> graph as to how Julia was seen by voters. The words were
> in capitals. She was seen in concepts such as as 'trustworthy'
> and 'visionary' but what I saw came without any statistics. By
> contrast Kevin was portrayed as 'not of the people'.

> McKew: And this made an impression on you?

> McClelland: It had some influence on me.

> McKew: But you thought Gillard would be a better Prime
> Minister?

> McClelland: Not necessarily. I thought she had a more per-
> sonable style. The fact is the numbers were rapidly flowing her
> way and I saw the result as inevitable. Indeed the rhetoric from

her key backers was that we needed to have an overwhelming vote endorsing her. I would also have to acknowledge the subconscious influence that tends to affect caucus members in those circumstances—it's easier to vote according to which way the wind is blowing. It is not a particularly honourable stance and I now regret not taking a stronger position—it wasn't a proud moment all round.

This is a very candid admission from McClelland. He is a man who is conscious of the deep Labor roots in his own family. His father, Douglas McClelland, served in the Senate from 1961 until 1987 and was a minister during the Whitlam government. McClelland's grandfather, Alf McClelland, served as a member of the NSW State Parliament in the Lang Labor government. By virtue of this long period of public service, McClelland grew up in an intensely political world and has met and mixed with every Labor leader going back to Arthur Calwell. His parents tell him that as a baby he was also shown off to an earlier leader, the legendary H.V. Evatt. Since 1996, McClelland has represented the southern Sydney seat of Barton, the same seat that Evatt won in 1940 and which catapulted him a year later into John Curtin's Cabinet as Attorney-General. It's a substantial heritage that covers the best part of a century of Labor history and activism. But for the past year, and certainly throughout 2012, McClelland has registered the deep resistance of Barton voters to Gillard's leadership. He now wishes that events had played out very differently in 2010.

If Kevin had been able to buy himself some time and two weeks earlier had said, 'Look, these self-serving bastards are moving against me and I need some decent people to sandbag around me'— I, along with others would have done it and I reckon the coup would not have happened. As it was, on the night, things moved so quickly.

McClelland also believes, as do others, that Gillard had planned all along to take over from Rudd in the second term, but with momentum moving away from the government, she decided it was time to hit the accelerator. The party research, which purported to show Gillard's superior leadership qualities, was central to her push for power.

I never saw it at the time, but I've since looked at this research closely. A good deal of it was commissioned by the Victorian branch of the party, billed to the national secretariat in Canberra and carried out by the ALP's preferred polling company, UMR. The fieldwork was carried out over five days from 4 June 2010. The parts that helped to persuade caucus waverers include the comments of 'soft voters' about Rudd's perceived deficits. *Rudd is not doing a good job. He lacks substance. He has no principles. His decisions are bad for the country.* Gillard, by contrast, was recorded as having an eight-point lead on a 'favourability' ranking against Rudd, but on the same measure Rudd was still well ahead of Abbott. The research also threw up positives for the government, with UMR concluding that, overall, the mood of the country was upbeat with 53 per cent of those polled saying the country was heading in the right direction. And on a critical measure—that of preferred Prime Minister—Rudd recorded a respectable lead over Abbott of 48–36. The two-party preferred figure was the alarming one, but it was based solely on the views of a thousand *soft* voters in half-a-dozen Victorian seats and came in at 48–52 in favour of the Coalition. The important distinction is that the equivalent two-party preferred figures in published Newspolls, for instance, are based on a representative sample across *all* voting groups.

In February 2012, Gillard said she had no 'specific recall' of having sighted the UMR figures or any other research, but one senior government MP has a very precise recollection. This individual was in the Deputy Prime Minister's office in the days prior to the coup. Gillard produced the UMR documents, by now two weeks old, and went through the detail and emphasised Rudd's deficits.

The MP now sees this as a 'conspiracy against Rudd'. He was aware that right-wing factional chiefs had been caucusing around the leadership. There had been meetings the week before the coup in the parliamentary offices of South Australian Senator Don Farrell. Separately, Arbib had decided that Rudd's position was terminal and that it would be impossible for him to win another election. According to some, Arbib was pushing for a quick strike, lest Rudd head off to Yarralumla and seek the Governor-General's imprimatur for an election.

At this point the MP, shown the research by Gillard, had a choice. He could have alerted Rudd. He chose not to and now regrets this. Like others, he feels he was manipulated by a group of individuals determined to see change at the top.

The anti-Rudd leaks had gone on for months: carefully placed stories about the PM's erratic behavior, his cussedness, profane language, lack of punctuality and log-jams in his office. There was truth in some of this but the context was never provided. Did any of it amount to a sacking offence? I was accustomed to taut tempers and egos from my days in television so it was water off a duck's back as far as I was concerned. As for the boys from Sussex Street and assorted union bosses coming over all faint and reaching for the smelling salts because Rudd's sense of *savoir faire* was not up to scratch, well, it does stretch credulity.

In actual fact, the charge sheet against Rudd was a convenient fig leaf. Closer to the mark is that Rudd started to tire of Arbib and Bitar's reductionist view of politics. As one NSW MP told me, it led to a shift in allegiance:

You have to understand that Mark, in particular, had appointed himself as Kevin's consigliere and these things, well, they become a devil's pact. Leaders strike a bargain with guys like Mark. You know, they say to themselves, I will call the shots in the government and you guys can get on with running Tammany Hall. It's a bargain. I will look the other way as you get on with the unsavory business of raising funds, getting the numbers at conference and all the rest. In turn the party in New South Wales has produced people who are very good at selling themselves to leaders as indispensable. But at some point Kevin stopped listening to them. And suddenly, they found in Julia someone who was full of admiration for their deep and compelling insights.

Rudd had appointed Arbib to work directly to Gillard as Minister for Employment Participation with special responsibility for Government Service Delivery. Arbib had oversight of the Office of the Commonwealth Coordinator-General located within the Prime Minister's department. That meant, as he told *Lateline*'s Tony Jones in June 2009, that 'most of my job is related to the stimulus package. That's the frontline of what the government is doing. My job has been to co-ordinate the construction, to work with the state governments, work with the local councils, work with the trade unions, work with the corporate sector, to get these projects out. I'm going to continue that work but now focusing on the jobs element as well.'

But the man on the 'frontline' had also managed to carve out a role for himself that went way beyond any prescribed duty statement. From his earlier position as NSW State Secretary, Arbib had backed Rudd in the 2006 move against Beazley, and in government expected that his counsel on policy and strategy would be taken seriously. For a while it was. But by 2010 Rudd had tired of what he saw as the haphazard and shallow advice he was getting on any number of issues—boat people, climate change and how to deal with the fall-out from faulty stimulus delivery. From Arbib's point of view, he was simply reprising the role he had played in New South Wales when Morris Iemma was Premier. One NSW MP says this amounted to 'bossing the Premier around with a string of constant phone calls saying you have to do this or that'. Rudd should have set out some very clear rules of engagement from the start and his failure to do so led to misunderstandings on both sides. Rudd eventually decided that most of what he was hearing from Arbib was classic NSW-style lunacy and cut him out. By June Rudd was not returning Arbib's calls.

Matters came to a head on Wednesday, 23 June, the day before Rudd was rolled, with a leaked story to *The Sydney Morning Herald* that was run by Phillip Coorey and Peter Hartcher. *The Herald* reported that Rudd's Chief of Staff, Alister Jordan, had been sounding out caucus MPs in an attempt to measure support for the PM.

'A classic stitch-up of Jordan' is how one player close to the action now describes this. The *Herald* story was used by the Gillard forces as the trigger for much that followed in the next twenty-four hours. It provided, I've been told, 'a primary point of indignation but it was totally manufactured'.

Gillard blamed the PM's office for the leak. Rudd's deputy was furious and chose to see the story as proof that Rudd did not believe her protestations of loyalty. That's what she told Rudd in a hastily called mid-morning meeting. Faulkner was party to the discussions; he was trusted as someone who would not breach confidentiality. A second meeting was scheduled for later in the day.

Was this a case of mock outrage by Gillard? It's obvious there was no mileage for Rudd in planting a story that revealed his insecurities and his questioning of his deputy's loyalty. None at all. But the anti-Rudd forces were in the ascendancy and, by day's end, it was their version of events that prevailed and not the rebuttal from the PM's office. To make any sense at all, the leak had to have come from Gillard supporters.

Jordan, as far as I could see, had been doing his job. Given the many fronts on which the government was fighting, instead of bunkering down, Rudd's office, by way of a range of activities orchestrated by Jordan, was more open than it had been in the past. There was a regular Sunday evening phone hook-up with all the parliamentary secretaries. I took part in these, as did others, and it was a way of getting direct feedback and exchanging ideas on how to get back on the offensive. Other Rudd staffers convened meetings in the PM's office on how to resurrect a credible emissions reduction plan around clean energy programs.

Numerous backbenchers from across the states and factions took part in these meetings. There was another group that met to discuss issues around population, immigration, and urban and regional development. I remember one such meeting where Rudd joined us for twenty minutes or so and did more listening than talking.

There is no doubt that people were worried about the coming election and there is nothing quite like the constant stomach-churning anxiety of a marginal seat member. In a short space of time we had traded away a commanding electoral position. In Bennelong, the local Liberals were targeting me over the perceived or real failings of the state government, and from the beginning of 2010 they rolled out their attack campaign on 'that woman'.

But every election is hard. And unique. Candidates need to get out there and argue their case. And hold their nerve.

Strangely, this was not the logic that prevailed. The negative stories, the forced policy reversal on the ETS, the adverse party research and now the framing of the Prime Minister's most important staffer all pointed to one thing. An early decision had been taken by a few aggrieved individuals more interested in their own ambition and power than in working to restore the credibility of the government. This is how one minister summed up what happened:

> The move against Kevin was well organised by a few and the rest were stampeded. The weakest, and most common response from caucus members was, 'Look, I don't want this to happen, but it is happening, so we need to go for Gillard because that is the way to end it'. That was the big pitch and most bought it.

With time to think about the extraordinary events of June 2010, one former colleague has told me:

> The decision to knock over Kevin took place in an intellectual and political vacuum. That the likes of Arbib and Shorten and Feeney did what they did raises questions about the way that a

new generation within the Labor Party has taken to behaving.
It's very different and I regard it as an unmitigated disaster.

The plotters would soon find out by way of the ballot box, and
the near-death experience of the government at the August 2010
election, that the brutish behaviour that now passes for normal
inside the corridors of Parliament House is seen in a very different
light by the electorate. Yet, remarkably, Mark Arbib still defends
his role in the events of June 2010. When he left the Senate, in
February 2012, he told *The Sunday Telegraph*'s Linda Silmalis that
'it was the right decision and I stand by it. I didn't make that decision on my own, but was one of the key people and I don't back
away from that—and the Caucus overwhelmingly supported it.'[7]

And Rudd? I think he is culpable as well. Where he needed
to charm, he scolded. Instead of cultivating loyalists among backbenchers, too often he ignored them. He is a leader who makes
few allowances for people who don't share his own obsessions or
can't work to his timetable. He had some exceptionally talented
and committed people in his office, but he also indulged too many
whose approach to politics was crude in the extreme and who did
nothing to enhance the gravitas of the Prime Minister's position.

For all that, an outstanding question for me has always been
why a group of senior ministers did not approach Rudd at some
point in 2010 and vent their concerns? They had all taken an
oath of office and had a responsibility to speak up. If there were
concerns about access, the direction of the government, process
and the like, why was this not confronted by a group of senior
Cabinet ministers? Furthermore, if Rudd had rebuffed sensible
proposals, it could have been made clear to him that there would
be consequences for his leadership. But no approach was ever
made. Was Rudd so intimidating that no one wanted to go near
him? In the view of one MP: 'Of course Kevin could be a shit. He
was never warm and leaders do need to give out a bit of love. But
I can't fault him on access. The fact is he had some weak ministers.
I never had any trouble seeing Kevin but I picked my time. Prime
Ministers are busy people.'

And one of Rudd's ministers is also dismissive of the argument that, as PM, Rudd locked himself away and was deaf to the views of others.

> There are opportunities all the time to talk to the PM, especially if you are a Cabinet minister. As far as I am concerned this whole argument about not having access to Kevin is a bit of an excuse by some who had nothing to say. It's true that Kevin threw Feeney and others out of his office and told them to get fucked when they were arguing to retain their old entitlements, but with Kevin, if you wanted to discuss ideas, they were treated on merit. But no one went to see him to say, 'Look, you are in strife here.' Not Gillard, not Swan. And think about it. Kevin had given Swan his head on the mining tax. He'd landed that tax and couldn't explain it.

Much the same sentiment comes from yet another minister:

> All this stuff about Kevin being a bastard and the government dysfunctional, all that was retro-fitted. It was all wheeled out later to justify positions. I sat in the Cabinet and not once did anyone raise the issue of dysfunction. Not once did anyone say, 'This is not working.' They say, 'Oh Kevin had the power to appoint ministers and no one wanted to offend him.' Well I'm sorry. My view is if you are a Cabinet minister you have to earn your keep. If you are scared about the PM it says more about you than it does about the PM. As for process, I always thought Rudd was a good chair of Cabinet. I found him open and consultative.

Robert McClelland puts a somewhat different view. He laments the lack of robust exchange across portfolios and among ministerial colleagues. Earlier this year he told me:

> There is fault on both sides. To be frank, Kevin was confident in his own abilities to the point where he did not delegate as much as he should have, either to his advisors or to his

ministers. Equally, he didn't invest enough time in relationships with some of the more knockabout people in the caucus.
But we were all weak. I think ministers on the whole were
pretty bloody weak and pretty bloody ordinary in terms of
being prepared to articulate policy ideas and to fight for them.
We should have been more forthright and direct.

Other ministers, though, point to a deeper problem with the
political culture of a parliamentary Labor Party that no longer
seems interested in cultivating and embracing a contest of ideas.
The disappointment for new MPs like myself and others from
the class of 2007 was that, having reclaimed the Treasury benches,
there was a hesitancy, an ambivalence about arguing out the big
issues. At times we seemed more interested in managing than governing. Too many ministers seemed technocratic in their approach
and failed to carry the electorate with the force of their arguments.

In fact, we attempted and achieved a huge amount.

As Prime Minister, Rudd would have inspired greater loyalty if
he'd put a bit more time into telling his caucus why it all mattered,
why we were there. The ALP has always been about a great cause,
and the reason the party has abiding affection for Whitlam, Hawke
and Keating is because they never flinched when it came to the
big call and deployed both intellect and personality in advocating
the reforms that shaped modern Australia.

Yet it is only Rudd who has the continued appeal and talent to
be able to knit together a representative majority, to argue Labor's
cause across classes and creeds. Rudd still starts work every day
believing that the right mix of conviction, impulse and intuition
across the policy spectrum can change lives for the better. But
since the leadership was taken from him, he has seen a succession
of poor judgments and opportunistic policy calls result in a record
collapse of the Labor vote. As for the hollow claims about 'tough-
ing it out', they don't wash with this MP:

> We have lost our people. It's our people who feel disillusioned.
> Remember, what Whitlam and Hawke and then Keating did

was successfully build a coalition around the Labor movement and the progressives out there. We've narrowed the base. We are now in a situation where a whole lot of policy is dictated by one seat in the south of Sydney, Lindsay. As a result we have pissed everyone else off. We haven't got policy based on principle or UN conventions or anything other than the lowest common denominator. You can't do that because it will always go lower.

This same MP despairs at where this approach has taken not just the ALP but politics in general. 'In the chamber it's like being back at university. I watch both Gillard and Abbott and it's like watching a couple of student politicians. They do nothing for me.'

And those who ambushed Rudd, the handful of individuals who believe they 'own' the party, did they ever for one moment consider that this might be the result? That their handiwork would diminish the ALP, erode the government's credibility, and boost Tony Abbott's fortunes.

I doubt it.

Equally I do not believe that Gillard can be seen as a passive player. She was impatient for the prime ministership and allowed others to create a sense of crisis around Rudd's leadership. She then cut down a Prime Minister in his first term and pretended it was in the national interest to do so. Since then, Gillard has been just as brutal in abandoning previous supporters, shifting Kim Carr out of Cabinet, as well as Robert McClelland, who was moved out of the Attorney-General's portfolio before being dropped from the ministry altogether when he switched his support back to Rudd in February 2012.

McClelland has watched support drain away from the ALP in his own electorate of Barton, even from people who have been rusted-on party supporters for generations:

I have never seen the Labor Party so on the nose with the electorate. The feeling is just incredibly intense. Voters were significantly inflamed by Julia Gillard's comment before the 2010 election that she then intended to present 'the real Julia' to the people of Australia. That was fateful. If people do not have confidence in the genuineness of the leader they will not listen to the message however it's presented. This is precisely the position the ALP finds itself in—people have literally stopped listening.

Gillard has been the architect of her own misfortunes. The struggles she has had since the disastrous election campaign of August 2010 to establish her own authentic brand of leadership can all be traced back to the early months of 2010. In forcing a policy backflip on a cause she herself advocated during the 2007 campaign, she has defined herself forever as just another political operator, and forfeited any claim to be seen as a leader of conviction. Her constant mantra of 'getting the job done' earns little credit. Even the effort, in many cases the hard-won, exhaustive, grinding effort that has produced legislative wins, is seen as tainted.

It's because there was never a plan for what to do next. Only a plan to knock off Rudd.

The voting public saw it for what it was: a brutal grab for power. And they've never forgotten it. One young minister who is now facing the premature end to his career says it's because Gillard's supporters ruptured the fine bonds of faith that support the relationship between the governed and those they elect as their representatives. 'There is something special about the prime ministership. As people see it, the choice was withdrawn from them. They may have turfed Kevin out, but they saw it as their right, and not something for caucus. So there has been a sense of illegitimacy about it that has never gone away.'

Only two-and-a-half years after the hard-won victory against Howard, Labor lost thirteen seats in the snap election of August 2010. Bennelong was one of them. I had an early sense of what was coming after hearing from one of my Angus Avenue neighbours, a young mother with children at an Eastwood Catholic school, how shocked she was by what she'd seen on television.

On the Friday after Rudd's ouster I had flown back from Canberra and spent part of the day in the Epping electorate office, supervising the shredding of all the brochures and posters that featured Rudd as leader and looking for replacement photographs. The king is dead, etc. It was a miserable business. After that I headed home, and as I parked in my driveway, I spotted Rebecca at her letterbox across the street and waved. She signalled back, walked over to the car and let me have it: 'I can't believe what Julia has done and I will never forgive her.'

Maybe she'd missed my solidarity walk with Rudd.

Rebecca had watched Rudd's tears at his farewell press conference the previous day and had seen especially the personal despair on the faces of his family. She had registered their pain and felt her own all over again. She told me: 'When Steve was retrenched late last year, we never saw it coming and I know what it did to us as a family. It's the same with Kevin and his family. How could Julia do it?'

Voters are always right.

Chapter 9

THE 'TRADITIONAL OWNERS' FIGHT BACK

THE RESULT DIDN'T take long. Bennelong was gone. Back to the Liberals as history repeated itself. Voters in the Victorian seat of Flinders were the first in Australian political history to turf out a sitting conservative Prime Minister in 1929, only to return Stanley Melbourne Bruce at the subsequent election in 1931. Seventy-nine years later, Bennelong did the same thing. Having swung against Prime Minister John Howard in 2007, three years later voters reverted and once again voted conservative. On this occasion they chose a different John. Former Davis Cup tennis champion John Alexander reclaimed the seat for the Liberal Party. The two-party preferred vote came in at 53.12 per cent to 46.88 per cent.

The local paper, *The Northern District Times*, enjoyed pointing out that the result meant that 'John's the name'—with Bennelong having been represented first by Sir John Cramer then by John Howard and, after a three year interval, by John Alexander. The 'traditional owners', as the local Liberals kept calling themselves (with little sense of the insult it could cause) were back.

As for the *giant slayer* of 2007, I was now a political footnote.

Gillard's rush to the polls for an election on 21 August 2010 had been a disaster. Within two months of the destructive despatch of Rudd, voters in Bennelong and across the country had the rare thrill of witnessing a campaign where neither Gillard nor Abbott managed a positive or inspiring word between them.

No wonder the mood at the booths on election day was lethal. My own wasn't much better. I felt like a fake every time I opened my mouth. Everyone knew I'd backed Rudd and, whenever asked, I continued to make supportive statements about his leadership. At the same time, I had been out at railway stations in the mornings, and in shopping centres and elsewhere during the long days of campaigning, urging a vote for Gillard and handing out literature that proclaimed the banal campaign message of *moving forward*.

In the working-class suburb of Ermington, voters were so taken with this idea that they moved their support across to the right, and as a result we sustained some of our biggest swings in the booths that serviced the western edge of Bennelong. The Labor base was the first to go. In one of the largest booths at Eastwood, the same Chinese voters who had backed us enthusiastically in 2007 now spurned us. Most were horrified at the way Rudd had been brought down and were quite open about it. They told us, 'We left countries where this sort of thing happens in the middle of the night.' When it happened in Australia most people thought there was something crook about it. They still do.

On election night, I didn't string it out. The ABC's Antony Green called one Labor loss after another. First, the inner-city seats of Melbourne and Brisbane. In Tasmania, Denison was gone. In Western Australia, Hasluck. Solomon in the Northern Territory. Then a swag of seats in Queensland—Bonner, Flynn, Longman, Dawson, Forde and Leichhardt. In New South Wales, the losses were in Macquarie and Bennelong, but right across Sydney— in some of our safest seats—margins were slashed. There were significant regional disparities, with an improvement in the vote in Victoria and South Australia, but with an overall result that reduced Labor's eighty-three seats to seventy-two. Tony Abbott very nearly managed to make Labor a one-term government.

There was no more faking with this kind of a wipeout. Our election night get-together for supporters was at the West Epping Bowling Club, just five minutes from our home in Angus Avenue. I'd told my advisor Erin Dale earlier in the evening that if the ABC election-night anchor Kerry O'Brien wanted to interview me, then she should say 'yes'.

When Bob and I arrived at the club at about 9 p.m. the worst thing was looking at the shattered faces of my supporters. The incredible people who'd stuck with me: John and Donna Range, Andrew and Gai Bristow, Peter Egan, John Fowler, Giovanni and Rhonda Bicego, and so many others. They'd taken abuse all day on the booths but held their ground against a relentlessly negative campaign from the other side. I felt I'd let them all down. Worse … something inside me felt broken. What had it all been for? My staff were in tears. They'd worked so hard in responding to each and every constituent concern and they'd done it with grace and energy and good humour. Tomorrow they would be clearing out their desks and reworking their CVs.

I made a concession speech and thanked my supporters. As soon as I finished, the ABC technicians fitted me with an earpiece and I was live across the country:

O'Brien: What do you have to say about the nature of the national campaign, the quality of the national campaign and how it has affected you?

McKew: Kerry, there are some very big questions for the Labor Party tonight given what has happened. We shouldn't be on a knife-edge tonight and we shouldn't be losing colleagues all over the country. I couldn't help but think today, as I was out on booths, booths that I was on in 2007, the difference between the hope and the joy and the great expectations that we generated three years ago and the sullenness among many voters. I think we have been a good government but clearly not good enough. Now your question was about the national campaign. I would argue that I'd still be the member for Bennelong tonight if we had run the same kind of professional, targeted, clear, disciplined campaign that we ran in 2007. Clearly this national campaign has left a lot to be desired.

That was 'burning the bridges' comment number one. Another was coming up. And the minute I said it I felt liberated.

O'Brien: You were one of the few who stayed with Kevin Rudd at the end of his prime ministership. Do you think that there would have been a different outcome if Kevin Rudd had remained Prime Minister?

McKew: I don't know Kerry, but clearly you cannot have the removal of a Labor leader and a Prime Minister and then two months later have an election and not have that play into the outcome. But could I just give you an idea of what I think happened nationally … I think our problems actually go back to last year when we never quite claimed victory over the global financial crisis. I think the singular achievement of the government has been the fact that we have a national unemployment rate of 5.3 per cent. Everyone I know has got a job. Everyone in the suburbs around here is working. We kept the nation working. That's an extraordinary achievement. But that was not the central message of our campaign.

I still stand by every word of this. I was labelled a 'sore loser' by some of the headline writers the next day, but I wasn't so much sore as sorry. Deeply, deeply sorry and miserably sad about the squandered opportunity. Had I really said at the end of 2007 'that we were on the cusp of something fine in this country'? It now sounded ridiculously idealistic. We had been so careless. We had broken something precious: the faith that people had put in us. The power-hungry smart alecs who had moved against Rudd assumed that the electorate would just 'cop it sweet' and attach little significance to deposing a first-term Prime Minister. The pre-campaign attitude had been that 'the coup' would be seen as just another bit of personnel restructuring and oh, by the way, we'll throw in some counselling if you need it. It was a massive miscalculation and was followed up with a low-rent, timid, inglorious campaign that shamed us all. Bennelong saw the betrayal and the subsequent defeatism for what it was and voted accordingly.

The next day colleagues rang. *Sorry to lose you. Don't take it personally. You were on a thin margin. Nothing you could have done would have delivered a different outcome. Stay in touch.*

Then there are the friends who have never called. People we've known for twenty years. Haven't heard a thing. They must have lost our phone number.

Gillard did call. And it was Bob who picked up the phone. Bob hates to see Labor lose, but he hates cowardice and incompetence more, and for weeks he'd been raging about 'the fuckwits running the national campaign'. Fortunately, he managed to engage the brain-to-mouth filter on this occasion and spared the PM a full-on lecture. She had enough problems, clinging to the wreckage of a vanishing majority, and about to face the long negotiations that would be needed to form minority government.

Before he handed the phone to me, Bob was emphatic about one point. He told Gillard that it was the late announcement of the $2.6 billion Epping to Parramatta rail link that had ensured Bennelong was delivered back to the Liberals. Votes shifted as soon as the announcement had been made made. As did the bets. Sportingbet Australia detailed the way the odds on a Labor victory in Bennelong turned around dramatically in the last week of the campaign: I'd been backed at $1.60 with Alexander on $2.60, but by election day this had reversed, with $1.40 for Alexander. I'd drifted to $2.80. One of our mates, a seriously dedicated punter, sent an email when he saw how the betting was going: *Bob's not laying off is he?* He wasn't, but by this stage, things were so grim that even the ever-loyal Louis, the family dog, had started giving me disappointed looks.

I can only claim to have been wise *after* the announcement. The rail link was an important extension of the Chatswood to

Epping line in a busy Sydney growth corridor and had been on the drawing board of the NSW Labor government for a decade. That was the problem. It was on. It was off. But when we revived the commitment, just ten days out from the election, and even with strong backing from the Ryde Business Forum and the Epping Chamber of Commerce, voters saw it as a bribe. They thought it was too much money, promised too late and by a party that had a very mixed record on transport infrastructure delivery.

There was also the appalling imagery. Gillard made the announcement not in Bennelong but in Parramatta, with a giggling Kristina Keneally in tow. Keneally was seven months away from leading NSW Labor to its worst ever defeat. Instead of maintaining our distance from the NSW government, our triumph, during a tight national campaign, was to get into bed and be seen to be snuggling up close to this shambolic outfit.

I didn't say any of this to Gillard. We exchanged best wishes and I like to think we both meant it. In spite of everything, I wanted her to be Prime Minister, not Tony Abbott. She sounded unbelievably tired. Her voice, always flat, seemed to have nothing left in it. I told her I was grateful she had come into the electorate the day before the election and opened the new multi-million-dollar shopping complex at Top Ryde. We'd only just managed to pull this off as a celebratory community event. But the viciousness still cut through with some full-throated protesters yelling out, 'Gillard, you backstabber!'

At the electorate office, on the Monday following the election, we started to rip apart everything we had taken three years to put together. The office would soon have a new tenant. Most files were shredded, but we packed up treasured photos and memorabilia from constituents. The task was joyless, but there was plenty of black humour. Some of the EO staff had seen it coming. Diana, Sue and Lucienne could smell defeat. But Trish, Elizabeth and Kaye believed right up to the end that we'd be OK. Cynthia Moncrieff, who had joined our team the year before, was as exhausted and crushed as everyone else. Campaigns wring every last ounce of energy out of you. And when it ends in defeat, your feet feel like they are cased in cement and your brain is mush. As we filled the packing boxes and took the calls that kept coming in, a curious thing happened. The office started to fill up with flowers and fruit baskets. It was a bit like being present at your own funeral, where suddenly people want to sanctify what you've done. There were lots of thank you notes: *You did a great job*, etc. Some came from the other side: *Thank you for what you did for our school. Of course we vote Liberal.* Another lesson. Gratitude, even affection, doesn't necessarily translate into votes. News Limited journalist Paul Toohey had got it right in a profile he did during the campaign: 'Bennelong,' he said, 'doesn't feel like a Labor seat.'[1]

But outside the cocoon of the fast-disappearing electorate office, it started to feel very different. In the days and weeks after the election, it was as if someone had put a knife through me. And it was still being twisted. I'd walk into the supermarket or across the rail bridge to Oxford Street and people who passed me avoided eye contact. They seemed embarrassed to have me around. *It's not personal.* That's what your political mates keep telling you. But it feels intensely personal. I tried to reason it out. *Nobody has shot me. No one in my immediate family has a terminal illness. Bob still loves me. I'm resilient. Louis has lost the hangdog look and appears back on form. He's moved on. What's wrong with you, Max?*

In his book *Lazarus Rising*, John Howard devoted a couple of lines to his 2007 defeat in Bennelong: 'The swing against me in Bennelong was the average pro-Labor swing in NSW … I lost a marginal seat.'[2]

I wish I could be that economical. The most accurate one-line explanation of why I ended up as a parliamentary oncer is that I was done in by the two Rs: Rudd and rail. In the end just about everyone in Bennelong was cynical about whether or not the Epping to Parramatta line would ever be built, but they weren't cynical about Rudd. They felt they'd been disenfranchised. One of my constituents, Rod Miller, wrote to me in early September 2010 and seemed to express what many were feeling:

Voters believed in 2007 they they had elected Kevin Rudd as PM, and that, for better or worse, he should be allowed to serve his full first term. They felt betrayed and incensed when that choice was taken away from them by a few smart operators, who decided what was best for themselves. A small unrepresentative group of powerbrokers set themselves up as kingmakers (or queenmakers) and it was to hell with the people and the country.

Members of the Bennelong Chinese community reacted in exactly the same way. Justin Li, a young Hong Kong–born Chinese lawyer, who sits on Ryde Council as the only Asian-born representative, told *The Northern District Times* that he was 'shocked at how abruptly it all ended for Kevin Rudd'. He went on to say:

> Despite some recent mistakes, I know he was still popular among the Asian community here. For one thing, Rudd's mastery of the Asian language and culture made our community more proud of its heritage. He was focused on the economy and on education—these are bread and butter issues for the Asian community.[3]

The big swings against us were in Queensland, Western Australia and in metro Sydney. It's only when you analyse what happened to Labor's vote in Australia's biggest city that you can begin to understand Tony Abbott's continued rage and fury about the legitimacy of the government. Had Abbott been better served by his NSW Liberal campaign team he would be Prime Minister today. As it was, the Liberals applied the blitzkrieg approach in Bennelong, where the two-party preferred swing away from Labor was 4.52 per cent. Daryl Melham just held on in Banks in Sydney's south-west but saw his vote shift by 8.92 per cent. David Bradbury in Lindsay, based around Penrith on the far western rim of the city, is now on the finest of margins, having lost 5.16 per cent of his vote at the 2010 poll. The most dramatic swing, 13.81 per cent, was recorded in Fowler, one of Labor's safest seats. And in an arc across western and southern Sydney it was a similar story. In Chifley, a 7.34 per cent swing. In Kingsford Smith, 8.1 per cent. McMahon, 5.96 per cent. Parramatta, next door to Bennelong, was down 5.49 per cent. Reid, 8.16 per cent. Watson, 9.06 per cent. And Werriwa, 8.32 per cent.

All up, it put the average Sydney swing at just under 7 per cent, a sobering result for a city where one in three residents is foreign born, and where there is a historical pattern of migrant loyalty to the ALP. It was small comfort at the time, but when I look at these figures, I find it all the more remarkable that we held as much as we did, and that our loss of votes in Bennelong was less than elsewhere.

The recriminations didn't take long. Former NSW Labor Premier Morris Iemma said it was 'the most inept campaign in living memory' and called for the sacking of the National Campaign Director and ALP Secretary, Karl Bitar. Iemma, along with many others, was appalled by what had been a values-free campaign with a slavish adherence to focus group research. We had confusing messages on climate change and asylum seekers, and one top-of-the-head suggestion after another. A citizen's assembly. A new detention centre in East Timor. A never-explained concept of a 'sustainable Australia' hammered by Gillard. Someone had sent her out to say that we couldn't just 'hurtle down the path to a big Australia'. What did this mean? Were we going to wind back immigration numbers or not? We didn't say. I think Iemma is right when he says that the subliminal message we managed to send to Sydney's immigrants throughout the 2010 campaign was: *We don't want you.*

The campaign smarties, of course, were trying to appease voters in monocultural Lindsay but, with a 5 per cent drop in David Bradbury's vote, that idea needs to be rethought. Ever since Liberal Jackie Kelly took the seat off Labor's Ross Free in 1996, Lindsay has developed an absurdly mythic status in New South Wales as *the* seat that has to be appeased and won by the party that seeks to govern. The Liberals saw it as the natural home of John Howard's *aspirationals*, and a part of Sydney that is only interested in two things: low interest rates and strong borders. Labor campaigners in New South Wales have co-opted this view to the point where too many issues are viewed, almost exclusively, through the prism of the so-called 'typical Lindsay voter'. A Charter of Human Rights? Don't think so. It won't play well in Lindsay. Recognition of same-sex marriage? Nup. It won't play in Lindsay. One of my Sydney Labor friends describes the 2010 campaign as 'a five-week national by-election for Lindsay'. He has a point. For soul-crushing bathos, it was hard to beat Gillard posing as Coast Guard Commander-in-Chief on a patrol boat off Darwin at the start of the campaign in early July. Who was right behind her? The Member for Lindsay, David Bradbury. Both seemed to be scouting for stray boats lest one slip through our impressive naval blockade and make it up the Nepean River to Penrith. God forbid!

The folly of this was captured in *The Sydney Morning Herald*, after the election debacle, with one 'disillusioned Labor politician' quoted as saying: 'The rednecks voted against us because you can't out-redneck the Libs but we had a collapse of traditional migrants who we brought here who thought we were no longer sticking up for them…. We walked away from them so they walked away from us.'[4]

We also broke the oldest and most important campaign rule. We never gave people a reason to vote *for* us.

In my campaign notes from early August I observed: 'This election is about legitimising the coup against Rudd. JG is only talking about herself. She says, "I am in the fight of my life." It's not about you, Julia. Campaign is completely dopey. Why aren't we talking about jobs?'

The campaign should have been crafted around *economic salvation*. But, of course, that would have meant acknowledging Rudd's central role in managing the GFC and saving Australian jobs. That became the great unmentionable of the campaign. And while we nibbled at this issue, with candidates talking about the maintenance of local employment, the fact is the mood had soured by 2010. That in part was due to the poor defence we mounted as Abbott went for the jugular on waste and mismanaged stimulus spending.

Locally, the confident outward-looking Bennelong of 2007, the community that had voted for change and fresh investment in the nation, was, three years later, wanting to bunker down. Retirees had seen their superannuation balances go south. Families were still working, but their spending patterns were changing. Thrift was the new god and debt was something to be avoided. As asinine as it sounded, Abbott's message of *Stop the waste and pay back the debt* hit the right psychological mark. His campaign pitch was a clean steal from US Republicans, who have developed a near monopoly on the marketplace of emotions.

This was evident at a pre-election candidates forum in Bennelong. It was sponsored by Everald Compton, who had spent thirty-five years as Chairman of National Seniors Australia. Compton was certainly no Labor ally, and on our side it was felt that he had never given the government much, if any, credit for the significant pension increase that had been delivered in the 2009 Budget—it amounted to a $32 a week increase for single pension-ers and $10 a week more for couples. It was a smallish gathering, certainly compared with the huge numbers who turned up to our forums in 2007, but it felt like half the local Liberal Party had piled into the function room under the library in North Epping. It was a very strange evening. I pointed out that the Liberals would be making things harder for business, with a rise in the corporate tax rate to fund their exceptionally generous Paid Parental Leave scheme. John Alexander said it wasn't a *tax*. It was a *levy*. Nobody in the room mocked this hair-splitting except for myself and the very decent Lindsay Peters, the Greens' candidate. At this point, two of my staffers, Sue and Elizabeth, who were parked up the back of the hall, started exchanging sardonic texts: *Time to beam us up Scotty. No friendly life here!*

But it got worse as I hit my rhetorical stride on employment.

> The nation is working. When the GFC hit, we didn't blink. We stood by the banks, put cash in people's pockets, and kept the construction industry buoyant. You can see it everywhere you look in the suburbs around here. As a result unemployment has been held to 5 per cent. That's an extraordinary achievement, not a happy accident. It's because we acted quickly. Compare that with the United States where unemployment is 10 per cent—

Before I could get the next line out, there was a sharp interjection from an unhappy constituent in the front row: 'Who cares about the US?'

I remember how the insularity of that comment shocked me at the time, but it shouldn't have. The fault was mine. The zeitgeist had changed by 2010 and I needed to connect with people's concerns about their own finances and speak to a shared sense of fate and purpose, not lecture them about comparative economies. As American psychologist and neuroscientist Drew Westen points out in *The Political Brain*, 'People vote for the candidate who elicits the right feelings, not the candidate who presents the best arguments.'[5] Outstanding leaders manage both. Among contemporary politicians, former US President Bill Clinton is a master at appealing to the heart *and* engaging the head. And in the 2007 campaign, it was Kevin from Queensland who managed this fine art as well.

So when I look back on the 2010 local campaign, I know I made mistakes. And yet … how did it happen? How the hell did it happen? That's the three o'clock in the morning question. How did I manage to beat a Prime Minister, only to be beaten three years later by a tennis player?

I can blame the incompetent national campaign, Rudd's poleaxing and the incoherent messaging, but there is no escaping the fact that I made some very big calls in 2010 that had a direct bearing on how the local campaign played out in Bennelong.

In the end we are our choices. I stand by the ones I made and I live with the consequences.

Choice number one was defying the party bosses and refusing to run a negative personal campaign against John Alexander. Before I even met with them, Sussex Street was well down the path in planning a Bennelong campaign that would target the business background of my Liberal opponent. The raw material for this was hardly something that had to be pulled out of the bottom of a filing cabinet. There had been no end of press commentary about Alexander's court battles over a development at White City in Sydney's prestigious eastern suburbs. The 1400 members of one of the city's oldest tennis clubs had been sufficiently enraged by Alexander's takeover tactics that they sued in the NSW Supreme Court. Alexander won that case but the decision was reversed when the NSW Court of Appeal determined that Alexander's companies were guilty of a breach of fiduciary duty and of 'unconscionable conduct'.[6]

The whole saga was very Sydney: a mega-million-dollar property redevelopment of an iconic sporting venue where one-time tennis greats like Lew Hoad, Rod Laver and Margaret Court had played, and with some of the biggest names in Sydney business circles, at one time or another, wanting to get their hands on it.

By January 2010, just over a month after Alexander had secured pre-selection as the Liberal Bennelong candidate, the ALP Sussex Street bosses, Matt Thistlethwaite and Sam Dastyari, wanted to involve themselves in the White City drama as well. And me.

Having been asked to come in for a 'tactics' meeting, when we all sat down together in the ALP headquarters' board room, I realised this was a first. Head office had pretty much left us alone in 2007. They'd certainly backed us, with generous resourcing and with personnel, but Bennelong had always been regarded as the icing on the cake: great if we could pull it off but never at any stage was it top of the 'must win' marginal seat list in New South Wales. In 2007 Bennelong had trophy value, not strategic value. But three years later, in a tight national race, Bennelong had their attention. And so Sussex Street wanted a big say in how to run the show.

The first item for discussion was the research. I am always sceptical about the material shown to candidates. No one wants to talk up your prospects lest you get too confident and slack off. But assuming what I was shown was legitimate, things in Bennelong were finely balanced. I was ahead, but not by much. The seat was contestable and the Liberals were getting ready to throw everything at it. They had picked their candidate early, they were better organised than they had been in 2007 and they had a powerful motive: I had humiliated them in their own backyard and they wanted revenge. Alexander was already out and about talking of winning back 'this sacred ground for our Liberal Party'.[7]

The Sussex Street game plan, as outlined by Dastyari, was to discredit Alexander from the get-go, to get in early with what is known in the trade as a *shit sheet* (and we wonder why voters are cynical about politics); this would aggressively go after Alexander and define him as a 'dodgy developer'.

As this was being explained, one of the office acolytes appeared and helpfully distributed a flyer that had already been printed up. Copies were handed around the table. Some creative genius had been hard at work.

On an A4 sheet, printed in menacing red and black, a set of *facts* was set out in bold type. It was based on some slender truths but with some significant inaccuracies. The central charge was that Alexander was a highly questionable character and the text suggested that no sensible person should even consider voting for him. The pièce de résistance was the artwork, which included some grainy black-and-white mug shots of the former tennis player that made him look as if he was headed for a police line-up.

I didn't know whether to weep or laugh. I started by pointing to the obvious. That it was a crude piece of propaganda that could soon be negated by a High Court judgment. Alexander was anything but a shy litigant and was seeking to have the NSW Court of Appeal judgment reversed by the country's highest judicial body. But Sussex Street had already anticipated this and their answer was a beauty: *Don't worry. All you have to do is to create a bit of doubt.*

I tried again. It would blow up in our faces. Just like the fake Islamic flyer handed out by the Liberals in the seat of Lindsay at the tail end of the 2007 election. But Sussex Street had thought about this as well: *Your name won't be on it.*

My, my, they'd thought of everything. Sure enough, when I looked again at what was in front of me, there, in tiny print at the bottom, was the authorisation: *M. Thistlethwaite 377 Sussex St Sydney.*

What was being suggested was from the dark arts box of tricks but it was standard operating procedure. Define your opponent before he defines you. There was nothing illegal or even particularly irregular about what head office wanted me to do. But as far as I'm concerned, this sort of 'campaigning' is corrupting. Candidates in tight races are told to get out there, go hard, go negative. It nearly always rebounds and the people who prosecute these kinds of attacks invariably end up with their own reputations in shreds.

With that sense of cold clarity that descends when you are presented with something that is completely at odds with everything you believe, I left Sussex Street that day thinking a couple of things. The party in New South Wales was led by people who had no qualms about running an accusatory personal campaign ahead of a High Court judgment where there was a more than equal chance of Alexander's contractual arrangements being vindicated. If the situation were to be reversed, would I want anyone doing that to me? Hardly. *Standard operational procedure* for me was the very opposite of what I was being asked to do. At all times during the 2007 campaign, when I had been up against one of the most successful Australian politicians, I'd insisted on running a civil, positive campaign based on the issues. Anyone who had wanted to get their rocks off by yelling insults at Howard had never made it onto our list of volunteers.

It's not that I thought that 2010 would be an easy re-run of 2007. Far from it. Retaining Bennelong was always going to require a different set of strategies. But I wasn't about to let anyone change *me*. There is really only one way to operate in politics. You have to be clear about who you are and what you believe in. There are plenty of necessary compromises, but you have to be rock solid about the things you *won't* bend on. And the bottom line for me, after the Dastyari–Thistlethwaite pitch, was a revulsion against being turned into an attack dog with a tawdry charge sheet on an opponent. *This* was the best that the brains trust of the NSW ALP could come up with? And it would be orchestrated by a couple of jokers half my age with a glib answer for everything and a political horizon that didn't extend beyond the walls of their own offices? Not for this girl. There would be no more meetings on this or any other topic with Sussex Street. I was signalling yet again that I didn't want to be *owned* or directed by the faction bosses.

In May 2010, John Alexander won his case when the High Court determined that there had been 'no breach of fiduciary duty' in relation to the commercial arrangements over White City. Had I done the bidding of Sussex Street three months earlier and created 'just a bit of doubt', I lay London to a brick that Dastyari and Thistlethwaite would have been nowhere in sight when Channel 7's cameras turned up seeking an explanation for the political slander I'd launched against my opponent.

So what about my opponent? Having first tried for pre-selection in 2009 in neighbouring Bradfield and missed out, John Alexander was clearly keen on political participation. But he was hardly a natural. Journalist Nick Bryant noticed this in a profile he wrote for *The Monthly* and published in July 2010, just ahead of the election. Watching the pair of us at a fund-raising morning tea at Holy Cross College in Ryde, Bryant wrote: 'Whereas McKew works the room with Clinton-like gusto, Alexander seems unacquainted with the requirements of retail politics. He stays in a self-delineated comfort zone close to the entrance. Perhaps he is just naturally shy …'[8]

He may not have known how to comfortably press the flesh, but Alexander turned out to be anything but shy when it came to targeting Howard's giant slayer. There was never a direct hit, but for six months he rode piggyback on a very nasty Liberal-directed protest against the provision of much-needed federally funded public housing. Within weeks of Alexander successfully securing pre-selection in Bennelong in December 2009, posters appeared overnight on telegraph poles in parts of West Ryde, Epping and Eastwood: 'STOP MAXINE'S GHETTO STIMULUS'.

It was hardly elegant signage: black bold print on a yuk-green background. And there were plenty of them. Someone had been busy. It took our supporters a day or so to tear them all down. There was nothing to connect the posters to Alexander, but a website address was listed: www.raid.org.au. The website no longer exists, so if you google it you won't find it. But if you keep digging and look carefully, you'll see a link from 2010 to the website of Victor Dominello, the NSW Liberal Member for Ryde. RAID stood for Residents Against Inappropriate Development. It seemed to me it was a Liberal front, a faux protest group designed to have a shelf life for as long as it would take to get rid of *that woman*. It should have been called RLAM—Resident Liberals Against Maxine—because that's what it was.

Alexander had been clear about his strategy from the start and told reporters, including Nick Bryant, that he wanted to harness the backlash against the state Labor government. As he said, 'There's a very, very strong feeling that the state government has really been pathetic.'[9]

He had a point. But the irony was that the $49 million in federal stimulus funds directed to the refurbishment of existing public housing stock, as well as the construction of new dwellings in suburbs like Ryde and elsewhere, was as good an example as you could find of Canberra working with the NSW government to address the chronic undersupply of decent affordable accommodation for low-income people. It was a policy that had *Labor values* written all over it. Certainly, in Bennelong, it worked a treat with well-designed landscaped villa complexes completed in record time. It has meant that pensioners and single parents with limited choices have a decent roof over their heads. At the Bennelong Community Cabinet meeting in April 2010, Housing Minister Tanya Plibersek dealt with the one complaint about costs by pointing out that the average cost of construction for a dwelling unit had been $270,000.

But that didn't cut it with the local Liberals. It wasn't about the facts. The whole noisy business was designed as a distraction, a convenient way to channel local frustrations. It was about getting under my skin. The Liberal ratbaggery went on for months, with Sunday street corner meetings and banners that proclaimed: 'HOMES NOT GHETTOS'. When interviewed, Liberal protesters trotted out the approved script: *We're not opposed to public housing but … etc. etc.* A newly arrived alien would have been forgiven for thinking they had landed in Rio or Sao Paulo and were witness to an attempt to redesign the crowded *favelas*!

Colin Kerr, the editor of the local *Northern District Times*, noted the nature of Alexander's campaigning, saying:

> For a politician hoping to be Bennelong's member in Canberra, to be talking about these issues seems to be what I would call hyper-local … he's brought it down to a very local level, joining protests on phone towers and housing. These are state issues, not federal issues … but he's probably counting on the very bad smell from the NSW government leading in to this federal election.[10]

He was, and Alexander would ride the anti-state-Labor sentiment all the way to the 21 August poll.

Of course, where I was concerned, the Liberals tried to have it both ways. The busy ghetto-builder Maxine was also Invisible Maxine. One of Victor Dominello's staff members, Caroline Beinke, gave this idea an interesting nudge during the July–August 2010 campaign, when she posed as 'an ordinary voter' in Eastwood. With a sad look down the lens of a Channel Nine camera, Ms Beinke, a former Liberal candidate who had run against Peter Garrett in the seat of Kingsford Smith, talked of how 'utterly disappointed she was with how Maxine McKew has or has not represented the people of Bennelong'. At the time I was about fifty metres away from her, further up the Eastwood Mall, and being interviewed by a rival network about how I was 'representing the people of Bennelong'.

But journalists who took the time to seek out genuine representative community leaders came up with different responses. Paul Toohey, writing before the formal start of the campaign in an article for *The Daily Telegraph* published on 26 June, quoted Brad Chan, the president of the Australian Asian Association of Bennelong: 'Alexander,' he said, 'is just not as visible. He's still finding his feet. I'm not sure if he's approached our member groups but I don't hear about him.' By contrast, Toohey noted that: 'Everyone calls McKew by her first name. People feel they know her.'

In a *Sun-Herald* article the previous November, journalist Stephanie Peatling came to much the same conclusion and sought comment from the local business community about the extent of my local activism. Andrew Bland, the president of the Ryde Business Forum, described me as a 'vigorous local member' and went on to tell Peatling that I had impressed the local business leaders by my willingness to come to events and to understand the community. Bland also offered this observation: 'She hasn't just come from the party machine. There was a large contingent of people who would have voted for John Howard. Without naming names, I can see where she has won people over.'[11]

There was more of the same in a full-page profile in *The Weekend Financial Review*. On this occasion it was Tom Dusevic who had a good look at what I was up to in August 2009. Dusevic knew Bennelong well, having covered the 2007 campaign, and after taking local soundings he commented: '… those groups with which she has built the strongest relationships—Asian migrants, seniors, health workers, local clubs and teachers—confirm she is present and approachable.'[12]

Closer to the 2010 election, Claire Harvey wrote a 'Sunday Agenda' piece for *The Sunday Telegraph*'s 4 July edition and remarked on my 'three years as a passionate advocate for needy local schools and for nationwide education reform'.[13] A few weeks later *The Daily Telegraph*'s David Penberthy hit the local shopping centres and it was a similar story. Penberthy quoted a young mum, Leanna Ralla, who said, 'Maxine has done a good job on education. Our daughter has got her photo with her in the pamphlets they've been sending out.'[14]

I've quoted the above because it puts paid to the nonsense pedalled by a few that I sat on my hands for three years and morphed into Maxine McWho. The truth is that for a lot of people in Bennelong I was just plain Maxine, and that's how I liked it. I was ambitious but not overly so. I wanted to take a bit of time to find my way. That's what I'd done as a journalist and my success had been gradual, not instant. But there is no time for that kind of incremental approach in today's world, and certainly not in politics. It's all about instant judgments and demonising the other side. Then it's about securing the *next* promotion as fast as you can. There are no points for quiet achievement and the winners in this game have an almost narcissistic attachment to self-promotion. The barely disguised bragging is everywhere—on a politician's web page, in press releases and in newsletters. Topping it all off is the ultimate personal PR tool of social media, where at any time or anywhere a political player can draw attention to her/his unique and indispensable contribution.

Here's the funny thing. Having spent thirty years working in communications, I find all this pretty grotesque. As a rough rule of thumb the biggest political show-offs have the least to offer. But I do appreciate the irony. There is no doubt that the spectacular national press I received as a result of my decision to take on Howard was a big factor in my success in the 2007 campaign. But that kind of attention turned out to be a very mixed blessing in terms of how my performance was perceived. 'Maxine gets down to work' was never going to be a sexy headline for anyone. But to this day I mark myself down for not being able to find a way to meet, at least in part, the very considerable expectations that people had for the giant slayer.

What I can point to is what I delivered for Bennelong. Eighty-eight million dollars went into refurbishing local schools through the Building the Education Revolution program, and whether it was the almost complete rebuilding of St Charles' Primary School on Victoria Road or the six new classrooms of Eastwood Public or a small school such as Epping Public on Norfolk Road being able to construct its first-ever assembly hall, it was transforming. We micro-managed the details from our electorate office and Trish Hurley had BER state co-ordinator Angus Dawson's number on speed dial. Dawson was incredibly responsive to local needs, so with constant intervention and a bit of lateral thinking, the Bennelong schools, by and large, got what they wanted. If the project engineers wanted to knock down everyone's favourite tree, we saved it and negotiated an alternative site. You get the picture. We were all over it. It's been a once-in-a-generation opportunity to provide modern facilities for teachers and students.

Another major focus was health. One of my staffers, Sue Pike, should get credits towards a medical degree given the time she devoted to the complexities of the local healthcare providers. The biggest and potentially most life-changing investment was in securing a $3.5 million PET scanner for Royal North Shore Hospital. It had been on the Liberal 'to do' list for the longest time but it was Health Minister Nicola Roxon who delivered it. Ryde Hospital received $248 million to improve emergency services and, through the disbursement of funds from the Graythwaite Estate, is now building a new state-of-the-art rehabilitation facility.

There was investment in the local TAFE campuses at Ryde and Meadowbank, in community recreation and sports halls in Ryde and Roselea, and in small infrastructure projects, be it the fixing of black spots or stormwater drains. Capital funding for Macquarie University was boosted by just over $56 million. And, not forgetting the original 2007 promise, an early learning centre was built on the site of North Ryde Public School; opened in February 2011, it is run by the Explore & Develop group. Best of all, we secured $3.5 million for the neediest young people in the entire electorate, the seventy-plus students at the Karonga School, who would soon be able to swap their collapsing classrooms for a modern purpose-built facility.

So we built our campaign around: *Maxine – Delivering For Us.* We secured an impressive number of community endorsements, from sports clubs like the Eastwood Ryde Netball Association, from health groups, business operators, childcare centre owners, and from the local Chinese community leaders Hugh Lee, Wilson Fu and Justin Li. It was all printed up in our literature and on our website. I particularly liked the contribution of Frank Murray from Beecroft, who was happy for us to use quotes from a letter he had sent to *The Northern District Times*:

> Whilst I am a diehard Liberal voter, I must offer the highest praise to Maxine McKew. We requested her help re Hornsby Council's Housing Strategy projected rezoning … her intervention played a significant role in the ultimate decision to withdraw the rezoning. I believe she is not getting the credit for the work she does as our Federal MP.

All sounds pretty good, doesn't it? We continued our doorknocking throughout most of 2010. Ministers paid regular visits. John Range and Peter Egan organised the purple army volunteers, and local trade unionists like Neal Swancott from United Voice recruited his own troops to ensure we had a regular presence for early morning rail commuters.

But the Liberals had more. Much more. Alexander offered up some modest promises—funding for a Men's Shed and for CCTV cameras for the carpark at Macquarie University—but he had the most important weapon of all: a clear set of messages and a national campaign that reinforced his local efforts. The Liberals had more money, more people and a sharp focus.

Our weapons? We'd taken the knife to our best asset, Kevin Rudd. His replacement, the *real Julia*, never managed a memorable uplifting idea for the entire campaign. No wonder it left Fairfax journalist Katharine Murphy decrying a 'strange, sullen campaign' that 'forced the candidates into a street fight'.[15] And News Limited's George Megalogenis would write in a *Quarterly Essay* called 'Trivial Pursuit' that he had found the campaign so dispiriting that he felt like writing a resignation letter to his boss: 'Dear Rupert, sorry I can't pretend that this contest is worth reporting. Neither candidate deserves to win. Julia won't talk the country up; Tony keeps talking it down.'[16]

Reporting the campaign was one thing. Being stuck in it as a player was far worse.

In the final week leading up to the 21 August poll, Alexander sent out a hideous little flyer to the entire electorate. In terms of style and negative sentiment, it bore a surprising resemblance to the Sussex Street creation that I'd vetoed. The Liberal effort had big bold declarations in white against a deep-purple background; the text pointed to my monstrous negligence. I was declared BAD. This was printed in two-inch capitals and was the arresting headline that accompanied a compilation of my grievous sins:

> She's DONE NOTHING about our massive debt that is increasing by $100,000,000 every day. She's DONE NOTHING about the home insulation disaster. She's DONE NOTHING on the record levels of illegal boat arrivals and the loss of control of our borders.

Well of course I had done nothing. How could I? I'd been invisible. The wildest claim of all was on the front cover of this extraordinary document: *Maxine McKew—Just Another Cog in the Labor Machine.*

I could have wept. I would have had every other facial orifice not been oozing some sort of liquid; a late winter cold had robbed me of energy and much of my voice.

The real story is that the all-powerful 'Labor Machine' had discarded me as a dysfunctional cog well before the formal start of the campaign. The early refusal to go negative on Alexander, my continued support for Rudd, and an almost indescribably trivial incident involving a young AWU organiser meant that by election day I had virtually no relationship with head office. Or with the trade union movement. It's hard to believe, but in a campaign where every second mattered, the then Secretary of the ACTU, Jeff Lawrence, took up Julia Gillard's time with a charge that I was 'anti-union'. Lawrence confirmed this during a phone conversation I had with him in late July. The offence? Weeks before, I had asked a young AWU volunteer to dress appropriately when we were out door-knocking. It's shocking, I know, but I thought that someone wearing an angry-looking black T-shirt was unlikely to help secure the vote in a conservative part of Eastwood. After the conversation with Lawrence, I took the matter up with Unions NSW boss Paul Lennon. He was equally unhappy with my attitude. It didn't cut any ice when I pointed out that I was the candidate who had beaten the architect of WorkChoices. The result was that Bennelong was removed from the union list of 'target seats', which prioritised resourcing and materials for key marginals. The effort went elsewhere.

The whole thing was confected of course. It was brutally simple. The powerbrokers who had conspired to knock off Rudd were not going to brook anyone who didn't endorse their handiwork. So they cut me off. What they've never understood is that in writing off a seat that the ALP had taken from John Howard, they killed the hopes of Labor supporters right across northern Sydney. I have a very fat file of post-election letters that say exactly that.

One of them quotes the British novelist and poet George Meredith: *We are betrayed by what is false within.*

Chapter 10
BACK TO BENNELONG

T HE INVITATION SAID:
Come family and friends and celebrate Stan's 90th birthday.
Sunday, July 8, 2012.
La Botte Restaurant.
No gifts please.

It's a sunny Sydney morning, and I've flown in from a freezing Melbourne, belted up the M2 to Pennant Hills Road and joined one of my former constituents, Stan Morton, whose family and friends are celebrating a very Australian life.

No longer the member for anything, I walk into the crowded Italian family restaurant to find that a place has been reserved for me at the top table right beside Stan. As he fills my glass, we reminisce about our first meeting at the Ermington Public School fete when John Watkins was introducing me to the locals in the early days of the 2007 campaign. Stan put up my posters outside his house in Eastwood, and together with his daughter Marilyn and son Tony was among the Labor supporters who went a bit crazy when we made history and took Bennelong. Stan has kept the faith—'I've nearly always been Labor'—and recalls, with huge amusement, that on polling day at the last election he told the local Liberals to 'get lost' when he heard their rehearsed denunciations of yours truly.

Today is not a day for politics, but it is a day that reminds me of what I miss about my old job. It's the way it connects you to the stories and lives of Australians. As Stan's guests share plates of pasta and salad, and then move around the room taking photos, I hear snippets of talk: tales of joy and of stress, of struggles and of comebacks. Stan, as buoyant a ninety-year-old as you could ever meet, still misses his wife Beth, who died six years ago. 'She was a young teacher when we met after the war,' he tells me.

Grandson Lachlan has compiled a photo-montage of his grandfather's life and it's played on a large screen in a corner of the restaurant. There's Stan as a young boy growing up in Wagga in the 1920s. There's the eighteen-year-old who joined the navy and served on the minesweeper HMAS *Bendigo* during World War II. Stan and Beth on their wedding day outside St Anne's Church in Ryde in 1948. And black-and-white snaps of a growing family in the post-war years at Eastwood, in the house that Stan still lives in.

It's both ordinary and extraordinary. Stan takes me back further and talks of his dad, George Morton. He was wounded at Villers-Bretonneux in northern France during World War I, came home to Wagga and worked as a linesman. But he lost his job during the Great Depression. The family survived because George had a horse and cart and went around the local orchards collecting discarded fruit.

As I listen, I think of my own grandparents and the pinched times they had in the 1920s and early 1930s. Not for the first time I wonder about the lack of perspective around the current pervasive political mantra that *people are doing it tough.*

Everyone at Stan's birthday party looks like a grown-up. Perhaps if the political class, and my own side in particular, was to call a halt to the phoney wars and the sloganeering and attempt a more truthful story about the country, then who knows? Political leaders might find that they were able to tap the instincts that are there in so many—certainly in Australians like Stan—not just to survive and prosper, but to share and to sacrifice and to feel for others.

But this is a Sunday afternoon fantasy. I take my leave of the partygoers and note Stan's open invitation 'to come for a cuppa anytime at Warrawong Street'.

I've arranged to drop in on some of my former neighbours in Angus Avenue so I head down Carlingford Road. I notice the For Sale signs outside detached bungalows. Bob and I sold our Epping house and moved to his hometown of Melbourne in April 2011, nine months after I lost the seat. I stayed long enough to help two of my younger Labor supporters, Amy Smith and Jerome Laxale, contest the seats of Epping and Ryde at the March 2011 state poll. They both put up a heroic effort but the result was never in doubt. Kristina Keneally was defeated in a landslide, with NSW Labor securing only 25 per cent of the primary vote, and with a reduction to twenty seats in a 93-seat parliament—the worst result for NSW Labor in a century.[1]

I would love to be proved wrong but I made an early judgment that this part of Sydney is likely to be deep conservative blue for the forseeable future. With the ALP doing its best to further reduce its vote—Julia Gillard's suggestion that real Australians live anywhere other than on Sydney's North Shore[2]—it could be quite a while before voters regain their trust in Australia's oldest political party.

I've lived in a lot of places in my life: overseas, in most of Australia's capitals, in the inner city and in the suburbs. And in every place and every corner I've found a mix of ratbags and redeemers. Prejudice sits alongside the poetic and the uplifting. Banality struggles with imagination and the former often wins. But has Labor's leadership become so reduced in ambition that it needs to pick off a part of Sydney for selective mockery and exclusion? Where we need to widen our appeal, we seem determined to keep on reducing it.

I pull up outside Maureen Becker's villa in Angus Avenue. She's been waiting for me, along with her friend Lilian Sheiles. The kettle is on, the best china tea service has been produced, and there are freshly baked carrot cupcakes.

'Where's Bob?' they ask. 'And Louis?'

'Secret men's business, Maureen.' It's called the Melbourne football season, so joint weekend travel is out of the question.

I settle into a comfy armchair and we catch up on each other's news. Now retired and widowed, Maureen ran the family jewellery store in Eastwood for twenty-five years. These days she sings in a choir, looks after an adopted pooch called Maya, and keeps a small but bounteous garden. As does Lilian. When Bob and I left Epping, I gave Lilian most of my orchid pots and she says they're thriving. Both ask about the EO gals, where they're working and how they're faring. Maureen produces an album full of campaign memorabilia and out spill the photos that Trish Hurley took of our Bennelong Bake-off, the cake competition we ran in Eastwood Mall in August 2010. It was Maureen who carried off first prize with her recipe for a knockout macadamia, prune and sour cream cake. Today's carrot cupcakes could easily take off another prize.

I get the news about the locals: the nice doctors who've bought our old place; and a few older couples, now frailer and largely housebound. The area is changing, they tell me. The post-war houses that are bought up are quickly demolished and replaced by boundary-to-boundary megastructures. Empty-nesters are selling up and downsizing. Younger families are moving in, many of them Chinese and Indian Australians.

Politics hardly intrudes, but when it does, both want to know if I will run again. Probably not, I tell them. They follow the news, but while they are both budget conscious, neither is apocalyptic about the carbon tax that has started the previous weekend. Maureen thinks that 'Julia gets a hard time, but then again she shouldn't have knocked off Kevin.' Lilian remains unimpressed by Tony Abbott. She hates his swagger and the too-frequent 'aaah aaah aaahs' that punctuate his speeches. We agree he needs a voice coach.

When I get up to leave I tell them about the book I am writing and that I've come back to Bennelong to talk with some of our supporters. They wish me well and make it clear they want to see Bob and Louis next time. Got it.

I've arranged a final Sunday afternoon catch-up at Eastwood with Justin Li, a young lawyer and an Independent member of Ryde Council.

Justin is waiting for me as I pull up close to the Eastwood Mall. My favourite coffee shop, Rumbles, is closed, so we head down the street to the nursery café. Justin is typical of the many people who found their own political voice during the 2007 Bennelong campaign. As a young, professional Chinese Australian he was constantly sought out by news teams, both local and international, for comment about the David versus Goliath electoral contest. He backed Rudd and he backed me. He tells me: 'Part of the appeal with yourself and Rudd was that you didn't come from a traditional Labor background. But you shared Labor values.'

Justin has thought about what he wants to tell me. And he produces some notes. One of his first comments sets me back: 'The ALP would now kill for the kind of result you got last time. You got 47 per cent of the vote.'

Do I need this much reality on a Sunday afternoon? But I know what he means. He's talking about the difference in 2010 between a recoverable loss and a wipeout.

Two years on, it's not just the strict reading of Newspoll and Nielsen surveys that have barely moved in over a year but the personal soundings that Justin is picking up when he does his own door-knocking for the upcoming Ryde Council elections.

The sentiment for Labor is rock bottom and it's been that way since 2010. The support collapsed after they changed leaders. With the Chinese it was the single biggest factor. When the Labor Party changed from Kevin to Julia, everyone switched. There is a lot of inherent conservatism in the Asian community and, rightly or wrongly, they had difficulty in accepting a woman who was unmarried, and who didn't believe in God. It was there on polling day and it's what the Chinese were saying. I think the whole thing also demotivated a lot of people who helped out and had wanted to see an end to the Howard era. And you know, it's not hard to understand. Most people are decent and don't like to see treachery and backstabbing. Ultimately if Rudd had got it wrong, the people who put him there should have been the ones to take the job away from him. But looking back, I think he would have won comfortably.

Justin has his own ambitions and rightly so. With the 2011 census recording that the Chinese-born numbers in Australia have risen from just over 200,000 in 2006 to 319,000, it brings the overall representation to 1.5 per cent of the population. It means the Chinese are now the third-biggest group behind the British and New Zealanders. Given this percentage, their political aspirations need to be recognised. With Sydney the preferred choice for many Chinese, the NSW branch of the ALP should be rolling out the welcome mat for community candidates with Justin's background. But that's not the case. As Justin points out:

> I don't think they would even look at me. I don't have a background in a trade union or in Young Labor. But I believe in the principles of social justice and opportunity and I wonder now if the Labor Party is the only movement that can deliver on that. I was a member of the ALP but I let my membership lapse. People in this area are not particularly ideological. They are not rusted on either way. But to win the votes of ordinary people around here, you have to talk about the main issues that people care about: education, the economy. Instead Labor is engaging Abbott on asylum seekers. You can never outdo Abbott on this. It's his turf. If you're the government you should be able to shape the debate.

Justin checks his notes and I've only got one other question: 'What will it take for Bennelong to vote Labor again?'

> It's not impossible. The people who vote for me normally vote Liberal. John Watkins held the state seat on respectable margins. So voters do move. It comes down to the amount of effort you put into the area.

I thank Justin for his time and tell him I'll send him a copy of my book.

Lucienne Joy has offered me a bed for the night so I head over the bridge to join her. I'm looking forward to a night of laughs and gossip but I've miscalculated. Luce is in lockdown mode for the big one. The number one man in her life, Roger Federer, is due to face Andy Murray on Centre Court at Wimbledon. Will she stay up all night and watch or won't she? Murray is the crowd favourite, so what if this puts Roger off his game? On and on it goes. The sheer hanky-twisting agony of it. I head off to bed. I have my limits when it comes to tennis players.

*

I've arranged some Monday morning meetings back in Bennelong and my former staffer Trish Hurley joins me. As we battle our way through the Sydney traffic I tell her I've left an exhausted but exhilarated Luce. The world is as it should be: Federer has defied the critics and he's back on top with his seventh Wimbledon in the bag. But good old Aussie gloom is not far away. The only paper I've managed to spot is Sydney's *Daily Telegraph* with a headline that screams: 'DEATH TAX'. News Limited has managed to uncover the first of the carbon tax rip-offs: an attempt to inflate funeral charges that is labelled 'a tax on the dying'.

The story I am interested in will never make the front page of any newspaper. It's the transformation that's underway at Karonga, the special needs school in Epping where builders are finishing work on a new purpose-built facility for seventy-one students who suffer from either severe or moderate disabilities. Trish has arranged a site visit with Principal Sue Dennett; even though she is on a mid-term break, she's keen to show us around. We walk through the four new classrooms, each with its own toilets and utility area. There will be a room for music practice or a 'sensory' room. The design is spacious with a lovely flow from one area to the next and the whole complex has been sited to get maximum sunlight from ceiling skylights. The project is due to be finished by the end of the year and Sue is thrilled with it. As she says, 'It brings us into the twenty-first century and gives a bit of pride to the school. And how do you describe what it's replacing? The dowdy, bleak, unsafe …'

Trish and I first came to Karonga in 2008 and saw the dreadful disrepair of 'F' Block, and words failed us as well. So we took photos. Dozens of them. The leaking roof, the stained walls, the cracked tiles, the flooded walkways and, above all, the narrow doorways to old-fashioned toilets. And then we just annoyed people, state bureaucrats in particular. In the end they came up trumps with $3.5 million in capital funding. It took over two years of lobbying but I consider it among the best investments of my time ever.

When I ask Sue what the Education Revolution means to her, she doesn't miss a beat: 'Usable toilets. My staff won't have to break their backs anymore negotiating large wheelchairs through small spaces.'

David Gonski, the Sydney businessman appointed by Julia Gillard to recommend a new needs-based funding model for Australia's schools, has put a $5 billion price tag on the extra investment he thinks should be directed towards education. He's paid considerable attention to the achievement gap that exists between advantaged and disadvantaged students, as well as to special education. Inequity in Australian education is greatest for the students that Karonga caters to, whether a wheelchair-bound cerebral palsy sufferer or a child at the extreme end of the autism spectrum. In this world success is measured differently. As Sue says: 'With many of our students, a lot of the time is spent just trying to find out how that child communicates. Our aim is to make them as independent as possible. And that could be something as simple as indicating that they want to go to the toilet. As simple and as basic as that.'

The Gonski report is realistic about 'children with complex support needs … where the level of achievement may be more focused on promoting physical and emotional wellbeing'. But tellingly, the report also points out that, as a country, we've yet to determine the scale of what we're dealing with. 'There is currently no nationally consistent data on the number and location of students with disability in schools [or] with their educational needs.'[3]

It's a finding that doesn't surprise Sue. Throughout her entire teaching career, she's seen special education 'tacked on to the rest'. And this time around, with no bipartisanship in sight about either the analysis or the key recommendations of Gonski, Sue is not holding her breath: 'We've had lots of great reports over the years. As for this one? Will it be shelved or funded? I'm not confident.'

The optimist in me is keeping hope alive. Trish takes a few more photos and we thank Sue for her time.

We head off for a very different kind of conversation with Colin Kerr, the editor of the local *Northern District Times*. Newsrooms are quiet places these days and the *NDT*, a News Limited paper, is no different. But Colin still looks like a print journo, or at least the way they used to look before reporters started glitzing up for their next appearance on Sky News. Not quite Hildy Johnson from *The Front Page* but you get the drift. Each Wednesday, he puts out a good punchy paper for local residents: a mix of human interest stories, lifestyle, sport and a good smattering of politics. If anyone can give me a dispassionate read on community sentiment, it's Colin. His paper has reported every twitch in voter volatility for the past five years and there have been some beauties. He never quite produced a headline that said: 'The prime minister, the TV anchor and the tennis player', but he must have been tempted.

Right now, he says that, when it comes to perceptions of our leaders, 'neither Abbott nor Gillard measure up. You often hear that people would prefer Turnbull.' Colin mentions three distinct groups in Bennelong.

> You've got the local business operators who are natural conservatives. Then the Chinese who are pragmatic and want to back the winner every time, and then there is the progressive middle, and that's the group that is very awkward for Labor

right now. I don't think Labor will be able to regain the affection of the middle class for quite a while. The electorate is just not seeing Labor as an evolving, progressive, dynamic party. Instead it is seen as desperate, diminishing, grasping and not to be trusted. Distrust is the big factor.

Colin mentions the issues that have caused grief for Labor throughout 2012: the carbon and mining taxes, asylum seekers and the investigations surrounding the Health Services Union. But regardless of the individual issue, he says it comes back to one thing: the question of trust and the coup of 24 June 2010.

After that there was a lot of disillusionment and voters swung back to the status quo. There's no doubt a lot of people were very annoyed by that. The Chinese in particular saw it as a betrayal. You had Rudd here a lot and they loved him. But I don't detect any particular love for the present PM. With people who are not very political, they say they can't stand her voice. I know that's mean but everybody jokes about it. It shouldn't be the case but it is. The prime ministership does not have the same kind of aura or respect about it as it should.

As we talk more about this Colin concedes that there aren't too many leaders anywhere in the Western world who appear to be able to rule from commanding heights. The political class, whether it's in the United Kingdom, France, the United States or Japan, struggles to explain change and complexity, in particular the way parts of the labour market are being blown apart by rapid advances in technology. Structural adjustment in manufacturing has been a feature for a decade or more, but now other sectors are being hit—aviation, media, energy supply, retail, finance, engineering—and it's well-paid middle-class jobs that are vanishing.

In Colin's own sector, that of media, the landscape is looking scorched. Not surprising then that his comments reflect the fragility of urban professionals. There's a job today, but what about tomorrow?

> What comes through in the community is real concern about the erosion of lifestyle. There's insecurity about employment. People don't know what is going to hit them next. It's very unsettling. In our industry Fairfax will drop nineteen hundred experienced people and News will drop around one thousand. As all this change takes place, I've had two work experience people here who are studying communications. I have told them to change courses as soon as they can. What chance have young people got of getting a job in journalism?

Transformation is the corporate buzzword these days, whether in media or other sectors. For many employees it produces stomach-churning insecurity and is the signal that it's time to start re-inventing yourself. Colin has just put his finger on the human dimension of the change that is squeezing the middle. Our politicians seem to barely grasp this. The right says government is the problem, and the left wants to indulge a nostalgic re-embracing of protectionism and industry assistance. In the case of the ALP, it's selective assistance for union-dominated workplaces, such as the automotive sector.

It leaves the field wide open for a more mature response. A sober analysis of the post-GFC world that goes beyond finger-pointing at the designated villains—international bankers and Wayne Swan's chosen enemies of Gina Rinehart, Andrew Forrest and Clive Palmer—and instead, sets out arguments and policies that point the way to new opportunities.

Malcolm Turnbull had a go in a mid-year address when he talked 'of the loss of jobs [taking] place in big licks' and commented that: 'The major debate that has been sidelined, at least in the Australian political arena, is the one about a flexible economy. It goes much deeper than just industrial relations, let alone the carbon tax. It is all about the ability to change, and change quickly.'[4]

The Labor way is there to be reclaimed. The lesson from Hawke and Keating is that the economic liberalisation that they pioneered, combined with a strong regulatory framework and an evolving social contract, is among the most successful models in the Western world. But as a former journo I'm the first to acknowledge that trying to mount these arguments in a media environment fuelled by high-octane commentary is a dicey proposition.

I've got time for one more stop before heading to the airport. Trish and I find a park on the Oxford Street shopping strip, halfway between Gena Karpf's patisserie, Sweetness, and Banjo's Books. This is the critical part of my research. What's Bennelong reading and what's it eating? You'll be astonished to hear that Banjo's is selling twenty copies a week of E.L. James' *Fifty Shades of Grey*. I have a lightbulb moment. Maybe I should call my own book *Fifty Shades of Political Porn*. Trish thinks not.

Then it's on up the road to Sweetness, the lovely shop that was like a second office for my EO staff. Gena is her usual ebullient self, but as we talk it's evident she is suffering from the stress of success. What she's achieved is astonishing. In the space of two years, a great idea for specialist sweets has turned into a solid business with a busy retail outlet, corporate catering contracts and a constant presence at Sydney's weekend markets. There's now fourteen on staff, many of them trained locally at the excellent TAFEs, but even so, Gena is stretched thin. Revenues are solid but costs are high. In part it's because she's a perfectionist and will never cut corners. She is also determined to run an ecologically sustainable business, so she elects to pay higher rates for 100 per cent green energy use. Discerning and disciplined in her own professional life, she would like to see the same in the political class.

> When I open my mouth as a businesswoman I talk about how special my products are. I don't spend my energy telling you about how some other cupcake that someone else has made is inferior. I don't use my efforts to diminish the work of others. But that's what we have in our politics. And I'm tired of it.

She pauses and then says, 'I just want the bickering to stop.' Hallelujah to that.

Chapter 11

A TORRENT OF TEARS

T HE NUNS AT All Hallows' taught me not to boast but they also told me to stand by what I believe and to call it as I see it. So here it is.

In 2007 I took on a *Liberal* Prime Minister and defeated him in his own seat. In this book I've taken aim at those people who, a bare two-and-a-half years later, brought down a first-term *Labor* Prime Minister. It's never happened before in our party. It was engineered and executed by a small group of people intent on indulging their own political vanities. It had nothing to do with enlarging Labor's vision. If we are a diminished force today it's because of these reckless individuals.

I share my life with someone who has been a member of the Australian Labor Party for fifty-one years. The long hair and the leather jacket have gone but Bob still feels common cause with the progressive 1960s movement that embraced civil liberties: the way that vast public protests led to the abolition of the death penalty in Australia, following the outcry over the hanging of Ronald Ryan in Melbourne's Pentridge Prison in 1967.[1] Bob was also secretary of the Victorian Moratorium Movement when that state staged the biggest of the country's rallies against the war in Vietnam with 100,000 people stretching the length of Bourke Street.

There's still fire inside him about this history, but critically, just like Gough Whitlam, Bob has always understood that protest without power is not worth the candle. The mighty achievement of Whitlam throughout the 1960s was to take on the power-brokers on his own side—those who were content with electoral exile and sectarian conflict—and remake the ALP into a broad-based mass party that wanted to win.

The joke in our household is that Bob, initially, didn't back Whitlam's intervention in Victoria after Labor's near-win in the 1969 federal election. 'I had to hold the left together,' he reminds me in yet another lesson in realpolitik.

'Yeah, yeah,' I tell him. 'You were on the wrong side of history.'

But as Jenny Hocking acknowledges in the first volume of her biography *Gough Whitlam: A Moment in History*, Bob was utterly realistic about what he was dealing with: a Victorian 'Left' that was controlled by a clique of over fifty unions that was 'anti-socialist, anti-youth and anti-intellectual'.[2] Bob went on to fight a lot of battles and eventually, as State Secretary in Victoria, he led the campaign that broke the back of twenty-seven years of conservative rule and saw John Cain become Victorian Premier in 1982. A year later he was working on the personal staff of a victorious Bob Hawke, and by 1988 had taken on the party's pre-eminent organisational role, that of National Secretary. Bob was National Campaign Director when Hawke secured his fourth prime ministerial win, and again when Keating went on to win an unprecedented fifth term for Labor at the 1993 federal election.

It's a proud history but my bloke is not one for nostalgia. Far from it. He was feeling something close to despair when the political editor for *The Age*, Michelle Grattan, called him in February 2012 and asked for comment about the 'leadership crisis'. Gillard was days away from calling a fresh ballot that saw her secure a decisive 71 caucus votes to Rudd's 31. After doing so, Gillard said her victory meant that she 'could be a very forceful advocate of the government's policies'.[3] On the same day, 27 February, Mark Arbib announced his resignation from the Senate and, in an interview with *The Sunday Telegraph*'s Linda Silmalis, said, 'I know it's hard to believe that I'm leaving for my family and to help a political party, but it's the truth.'[4]

The week before, Bob had already come to a more brutal judgment: 'Arbib and Bitar should be entered into the hall of infamy of the Labor Party.' That's what he told Grattan, and for good measure added that 'what started in tears in June 2010 could end in a torrent of tears at the next election'.[5]

We'd both been appalled at the bloodletting and the savaging of Rudd's character by a string of ministers. Nicola Roxon, Tony Burke, Stephen Conroy, Simon Crean—they all got in on the act and spoke of Rudd's deficiencies. Gillard told reporters that Rudd had 'very difficult and chaotic work practices'.[6] But it was Wayne Swan who broke all conventions by claiming that Rudd is someone 'who does not hold Labor values'.[7]

And just to make sure there was no misunderstanding, the Treasurer added: 'The Party has given Kevin Rudd all the opportunities in the world and he wasted them with his dysfunctional decision-making and his deeply demeaning attitude towards other people including our caucus colleagues.'

It is a remarkable statement, most particularly for its breathtaking revisionism. The government only got into serious strife after Rudd's post-Copenhagen ETS planning was leaked to *The Sydney Morning Herald*. The individual responsible for this 'demeaned' every member of the Cabinet by subverting proper process. This was not Rudd's doing. The charge of 'dysfunction' rings hollow given the extreme difficulties Rudd faced when his leadership was further destabilised as a result of this leak in April 2010. It was Swan and Gillard who walked away from the ETS, and in so doing, further 'demeaned' the very voters who believed Labor should honour its 2007 pledge to act on climate change.

On the other issue that led directly to Rudd's removal as leader, the mining tax, it was Swan who had served up a policy that was loathed by the industry, rejected by the key resource state of Western Australia, and largely incomprehensible to the electorate.

Dysfunctional? Demeaning? Rudd, so often accused of being a micro-manager, trusted his Treasurer to craft an acceptable package that could be sold as a key piece of taxation reform.

Nor at any stage did any of Rudd's ministers—not Gillard or Swan, not Conroy or Burke—make any charge about chaotic decision-making before the political ambush of June 2010. No one ever approached him to say, 'Your leadership is in danger.'

Contrast that with events twenty years before when Paul Keating began a campaign to take Bob Hawke's job off him. It came after four election wins, and only then, after what Keating considered to be Hawke's dishonouring of an agreement for a mutually agreed handover. Typical of Keating, it was full frontal. He walked into Hawke's office in Canberra and said to the Prime Minister: 'Bob, I always told you I'd tell you first if ever I were to organise against you. You've broken your word to me, and, from here on, it's on.'[8]

I'm not suggesting for a moment that there's an accepted *etiquette* for dumping a prime minister. These sorts of activities are nearly always accompanied by accusations of *treachery, betrayal* and *bastardry*. These words recur again and again throughout Labor history. But Rudd, at the very least, might have expected a heads-up, a warning. He didn't get it. Not from his deputy, whom he'd supported in all her policy undertakings be they in industrial relations or education. And certainly not from his Treasurer.

Right up until the last twenty-four hours of his prime ministership, Rudd believed he had the support of both Gillard and Swan. In the only comments that Rudd has been prepared to make in response to the many questions put to him about these events, Rudd sent me this:

> Following the 2007 election, I had always said that Julia would be the next Labor PM after myself. I said that because I believed she would make a first-class Prime Minister following a period in office with engagement on the economic and national security agendas. I had also told her and other

Cabinet and Caucus colleagues that she would have my full support in achieving that ambition.

I also said to her in my office in early 2010 that I had no intention of breaking the record book for being the longest serving Labor Prime Minister and that my ambition was to have a seamless transition to her.

So given all of that, I was stunned when the coup occurred. I remember speaking to Julia on the Tuesday night following a robust dinner with the BCA [Business Council of Australia] on Wayne's mining tax.

Wayne had come back to my office afterwards for a drink and had congratulated me on being resolute in defence of the tax. He said nothing about the events that were about to unfold the following day.

I spoke on the telephone later the same evening with Julia as well about the BCA event. Again there was nothing in that conversation that foreshadowed what was about to unfold the following day.

In the case of Wayne, I did not even receive a telephone call advising me he had decided to withdraw his support from me and back Julia as replacement Prime Minister.

I had to telephone him myself.

In response to my question on the Wednesday afternoon when I asked him, 'What's happening?', he replied he would be 'voting for change'. It was only later that I discovered that an arrangement had been put in place to make him Deputy Prime Minister.

But the core point was this: at no stage did either Julia or Wayne say to me that, unless I undertook change x, y or z, there would be a challenge to my leadership, let alone that they would be party to such a challenge.

So did I feel let down and indeed betrayed? Well of course. I am as human as the next person.

Look, I made my fair share of mistakes as Prime Minister, but probably no more than my predecessors during their first terms in office.

The key thing now is to put this whole chapter of ugly political history behind us.

I said to the Caucus in February this year after the leadership ballot that I bore none of them any malice. And I meant it.

I went on to say that if I had offended any of them in my time as Prime Minister then I apologised. And I meant that too.

There is no point in politics or in life ending up bitter and twisted. You pick yourself up, you dust yourself off and you get back into it.

And that's what the party and the government now have to do as well. Learn from all this and focus on the country's future, not on our personal futures.

*

Rudd's earliest Labor hero was Gough Whitlam. But unlike Whitlam's relatively privileged upbringing as the son of a senior member of the Commonwealth Public Service and attendee at Canberra Grammar, Rudd's background was exceptionally modest.

As his close friend, Glyn Davis, now Vice-Chancellor of the University of Melbourne, points out:

Very few modern Australian leaders have come from such a disadvantaged background. But I suspect Kevin Rudd does not think about himself in these terms. He was drawn to Labor values, not by virtue of background, but for philosophical reasons. He is guided by a view of how Australia should be and how Labor can shape that. Keep in mind that growing up in country Queensland meant that he was not part of the Labor tribe. Instead he was the beneficiary of social mobility through education, and this has remained close to his heart—helping people make the best of themselves. It's an aspiration, rather than a belief born of class solidarity. Though

their backgrounds are so very different, the end point is close
to the Gough Whitlam view about what Labor is there to do.
There are strong parallels.

Another close friend, Father Frank Brennan, who teaches law
at the Australian Catholic University, says Rudd is also driven
by his Christian faith, with the important proviso that he is 'not
beholden to any particular Church authority or tradition' but says
that he takes 'radically seriously the idea of Christian vocation'.
Brennan sees this as the key to understanding Rudd.

> He sees himself as called to serve. He wants to work for a more
> just world. In politics he knows this requires a steely resolve,
> cunning and clear purpose. His ambition is thus not severable
> from his sense of vocation. National security and national
> prosperity are for him non-negotiable … but he also wants
> Australia to be the land of the fair go where everyone has
> the opportunity to achieve their full human flourishing with
> just rewards. He wants Australia to punch above its weight as
> a leader in the international community … and above all, he
> wants a tolerant multicultural Australia that is at home with its
> indigenous heritage. That's his dream.

As Prime Minister, Rudd's domestic policy achievements
were grounded in the idea that a Labor government exists to
advance the needs and material interests of Australians through
investment in pensions, a paid parental leave scheme, adequate
superannuation, affordable housing, education, and urban and
regional infrastructure. In foreign policy, he combined realism
with ambition, creating a global role for Australia through the
G20 summit process, and helping to forge a co-ordinated response
to the global economic recession.

It's an approach that is fixed firmly in the modern Labor tradition. And in spite of the personal jihad waged by some in the
caucus, Australians have made up their own minds: Rudd is their
preferred leader. Above Abbott and way above Gillard or any
other contender. Even David Marr, who published an excoriating

attack on Rudd in a *Quarterly Essay* just before Rudd was brought down,[9] has since admitted that: 'Australians warm far more to a man like him than they do to the furious apparatchiks that now lead the government and opposition. We like experts. We like ideas. Thoughtful is appealing. We respect men and women at the top who have some form of interior life.'[10]

We also respect a bit of authenticity. Rudd knows who he is and knows what he wants to do with power, although admittedly he's seemed to struggle with this at times. In part that's because of the almost impossible demands placed on leaders in a world that wants instant judgments, simple solutions to complex problems, and all explained in 140 characters to a million 'friends'. It forces a furious pace and can be inimical to considered policy-making. And woe betide the politician who wants to play it any other way.

But perhaps it's time. Time for something else. An elevated national conversation that treats voters like grown-ups. It's worth a try. We could take a few deep breaths and stop worrying about everything from foreign boats to foreign workers or foreign investment. We could then start to consider the collective challenges *and* the opportunities. How we make our way in the world *after* the peak of the commodities boom and, above all, how a Labor government maintains fairness without inhibiting entrepreneurial spirit. They are the same issues that Rudd addressed in his pitch to voters in 2007. It's been a wild ride since then, but notwithstanding the generous margin of support that the conservatives are now attracting, there is no enthusiasm for Abbott's brand of populism, and his personal ratings reflect this. The field is wide open for the kind of leadership that will leapfrog over the current banalities and give us something better.

Rod Cameron sees the opening. Along with his wife, Margaret Gibbs, Rod was a pioneer of qualitative polling in Australia and from the 1970s worked on successive Labor campaigns. When we spoke during the preparation for this book, he gave me this definition of Labor leadership:

A real Labor leader is someone who can combine the priorities of a progressive party with the values and aspirational outlook of ordinary suburban families and small businesses. Someone who can communicate a vision and inspiration to a sour and (currently) whinging electorate and someone who can successfully translate national goals to individual relevance. This person would restore a level of confidence to an electorate unnecessarily and often irrationally gloomy and despondent. And this person would raise the standard of political discourse and behaviour in order to reconnect with an electorate which is past cynicism and is now disdainful and openly dismissive of the political class. Above all, this person would actually stand for something (anything!) other than a platitude or slogan—something that combines values, ideology and national priorities.

Rod is equally clear about why Labor's support is in the doldrums.

The biggest failure of the Labor government under Gillard and Swan has been its inability to connect with middle Australia. The votes pouring away from Labor are not going to the Greens but straight to the Coalition or to an amorphous group of 'others'. The message is simple. The votes Labor has lost and the additional votes needed for victory will not be won by class warfare, by railing against Sydney's North Shore, or by attacking the super-rich. Nor will they be won by trying to appeal to a fast-disappearing blue-collar, unionised, employee workforce. Labor seems to have forgotten that many skilled blue-collar workers are self-employed and they are feeling particularly neglected. The middle ground—the ordinary outer-suburban working family and the small business owner—is upwardly mobile and does not perceive the Gillard–Swan brand of Labor as appealing in any way.

In order to reclaim this middle ground and deal itself back into the game, Labor has to change the way it talks to the electorate. Plain vanilla language is my suggestion. And how about some principles? Not issues, but principles. So when we talk about refugees, we speak about the *principle* of fair treatment and Labor's historical *principled* recognition of international treaties. How hard is that? But I have an even more radical suggestion. How about embracing the concept that *less is more*? Less media, fewer hand-outs and a total ban on the wearing of hard hats and fluoro vests. Our screens would be transformed and political journalists would be forced to look inside the policy cupboard for stories to fill their programs. Imagine the political leader who only spoke when they had something to say? Perhaps once a fortnight instead of six times a day. It might restore a bit of gravitas. We might think there was something special about it, and pause … and listen. In a world of excess we would start to value what is rare and think about it. Why should leaders play the instant messaging game when everyone from school students to retirees is busy issuing their own daily press releases via Facebook and social media? It makes no sense to compete with this noise and clutter; or worse, to be part of the shout-fest and the mutual abuse game.

Like any bad habit, it will take time to adjust. But surely there's a first-mover advantage for the political leader who embraces technology-free days. Turning off the BlackBerry. Leaving the iPad uncharged. Start with one day a week, then two. A total folly? Not at all. Think of the campaign you could run about the benefits: time to reflect, to reset the brain circuitry. And what an example to the kids! A healthy rebalancing for the digital brain. The possibilities are endless.

As I say, it's worth a try. It might put a bit of heart and humanity back into politics and perhaps some fun as well.

It doesn't have to end in tears for Labor. Sooner or later the question of who 'owns' the Labor Party will have to be addressed. It is surely beyond tolerable that a modern party can have its fortunes determined by half-a-dozen large trade union leaders who see themselves as being more influential than the party's elected parliamentarians. There are plenty of blueprints for party reform, but it will take what it has always taken: an individual or group of individuals with the courage to defy the status quo and the bottle to hang in there when the party's powerbrokers put up the inevitable resistance.

Labor's history is one of renewal. The party that was formed before Federation has survived splits and chronic disunity. And at its best the Labor message has been redefined by a succession of talented, deeply committed leaders: Curtin, Chifley, Whitlam, Hawke and Keating. They still inspire us. It's why progressive people keep the faith. And I'm one of them.

ENDNOTES

Chapter 1: It's a Contest of Ideas

1. In July 2007, Indian doctor Mohamed Haneef was arrested at Brisbane airport in the wake of two terrorist incidents in the United Kingdom. Haneef was alleged to have provided a SIM card to one of the attackers and was detained for almost twelve days before being charged with recklessly providing support to a terrorist organisation. The AFP case against Dr Haneef was dismissed two weeks later.
2. Black, John, 'The Gillard factor makes Labor a pariah', *Australian Financial Review*, 4 May 2012
3. Swan, Wayne, 'The 0.01 per cent: The rising influence of vested interests is threatening Australia's egalitarian social contract', *The Monthly*, March 2012, p. 20
4. Press conference by Julia Gillard, 24 June 2010
5. Crabb, Annabel, *Losing It: The inside story of the Labor Party in opposition*, Picador Australia, 2005, p. 17
6. Quoted in McKew, Maxine, 'Lunch with Maxine McKew', *The Bulletin*, July 2000
7. Megalogenis, George, *The Longest Decade*, Scribe, 2006, p. 9
8. Keating, P.J., *After Words: The post-prime ministerial speeches*, Allen & Unwin, 2011, p. 209
9. ibid., p. 193

Chapter 3: Don't Think You Can Beat a Prime Minister

1. Quoted in Grattan, Michelle, 'Shared fate for Labor and McKew', *The Age*, 27 February 2007
2. Quoted in 'Labor to target more high-profile recruits', *The Sydney Morning Herald*, 26 February 2007
3. Andrew Robb, 'Bennelong seat considered vulnerable', *Lateline*, ABC TV, 26 February 2007

4. Quoted in 'Government says the ALP cocky for recruiting McKew', *The World Today*, ABC Radio, 26 February 2007

5. Quoted in 'Maxine McKew a "blow-in": Abbott', *PM*, ABC Radio, 26 February 2007

6. Hetherington, David and Prior, Dominic, *After the Party—How Australia Spent its Mining Boom Windfall*, Per Capita paper, May 2012

7. Howard, John, *Lazarus Rising: A personal and political autobiography*, HarperCollins, 2010, pp. 619–20

8. Quoted in 'McKew takes on Howard', *The Courier-Mail*, 25 February 2007

9. Mackay, Hugh, 'A stir from slumber: Waking up or just rolling over?', *The Sydney Morning Herald*, 27 January 2007

10. Saville, Margot, *The Battle for Bennelong: The adventures of Maxine McKew, aged 50 something*, Melbourne University Publishing, 2007, pp. 5–57

11. Milne, Glenn, 'PM John Howard faces defeat in his own seat', *The Sunday Telegraph*, 4 November 2007

Chapter 4: Great Expectations

1. MacCallum, Mungo, 'Australian Story, Kevin Rudd and the Lucky Country', *Quarterly Essay 36*, December 2009, p. 66

2. Saville, op. cit., p. 94

3. Bibby, Paul, 'Howard out for final count', *The Sydney Morning Herald*, 13 December 2007

4. Crabb, Annabel, 'Chinese whispers that built to a roar', *The Sydney Morning Herald*, 14 December 2007

Chapter 5: The Grand, the Bad and Everything In Between

1. 'Finally, from 1946 laws and practices which, with the purpose of eliminating Indigenous cultures, promoted the removal of Indigenous children for rearing in non-Indigenous institutions and households were in breach of the international prohibition of genocide. From this period many Indigenous Australians were victims of gross violations of human rights', from National Inquiry into the Separation of Aboriginal and Torres Strait Islander Children from their Families, *Bringing Them Home*, Human Rights and Equal Opportunity Commission, 1997, p. 278

2. ibid., p. 18. In 1995 then Attorney-General Michael Lavarch referred the issue of separating indigenous children from their families, and of compensation, to the Human Rights and Equal Opportunity Commission.

3. Taylor, Lenore and Uren, David, *Shitstorm: Inside Labor's Darkest Days*, Melbourne University Press, 2010, p. 28

4. Appearance on *Q&A*, ABC TV, 12 March 2009

5. Tanner, Lindsay, *Sideshow: Dumbing down democracy*, Scribe, 2011, p. 186
6. Tiernan, Anne and Weller, Patrick, *Learning to be a Minister: Heroic expectations, practical realities*, Melbourne University Press, 2010, p. 152
7. Bachelard, Michael and Gordon, Josh, *Extra*, *The Sunday Age*, 23 November 2008, p. 21

Chapter 6: Not Just Child's Play

1. Federal Budget papers, 2011–12
2. Elliott, Professor Alison, *Early Childhood Education: Pathways to Quality and Equity for All Children*, Australian Education Review, Australian Council for Educational Research, 2006, p. 2
3. Sims, M., Guilfoyle, A. and Parry, T., 'What children's cortisol levels tell us about quality in child care centres', *Australian Journal of Early Childhood*, 30(2), 2005
4. Lally, R., Torres, Y. and Phelps, P., 'Caring for infants and toddlers in groups: Necessary considerations for emotional social and cognitive development,' *Zero to Three*, Vol. 14, No. 5, 1994
5. 'Mem Fox blasts childcare', ABC News Online, 31 August 2008, www.abc.net.au/news/2008-08-31/mem-fox-blasts-childcare/494602
6. *Child Care Update*, Office of Early Childhood Education and Child Care, February 2012, p. 4
7. Schubert, Misha and Topsfield, Jewel, 'Childcare at school, to end the "double drop-off"', *The Age*, 12 May 2006
8. www.gowrie-sydney.com.au
9. Brennan, Deborah, 'Investing in childhood: The progress and the pitfalls', *Inside Story*, August 2011
10. Elliott, op. cit., p. 31, quoted in *Towards a National Quality Framework for Early Childhood Education and Care: Report of the Expert Advisory Panel on Quality Early Childhood Education and Care*, Department of Education, Employment and Workplace Relations, 2009, p. 25

Chapter 7: Pennies from Kevin

1. Dr Ken Henry, *7.30*, ABC TV, 15 May 2012
2. Taylor and Uren, op. cit., p. 220
3. ibid., p. 81
4. Westen, Drew, *The Political Brain: The role of emotion in deciding the fate of the nation*, PublicAffairs, 2007, p. 39
5. Megalogenis, George, *The Australian Moment: How we were made for these times*, Viking, 2012, p. 343
6. Stiglitz, Joseph, 'The crisis down under', *Project Syndicate*, 5 August 2010
7. Appearance by Joseph Stiglitz on *7.30 Report*, ABC TV, 27 July 2010
8. *The Weekend Australian*, editorial, 23 January 2010

9. Quoted in Stewart, Cameron and Uren, David, 'Leadership forged in the financial fire', *The Weekend Australian*, 23 January 2010
10. Statement by Wayne Swan, 22 February 2012

Chapter 8: Ambush

1. Quoted in Cassidy, Barrie, *The Party Thieves: The real story of the 2010 election*, Melbourne University Press, 2010, p. 102
2. Australia's Future Tax System Review Panel, *Australia's Future Tax System: Report to the Treasurer*, (Dr Ken Henry, chairman), Treasury, 2010, Chapter C: 'Land and Resources Taxes', C 1–3 Replacing Current Arrangements with a Resource Rent Tax, Recommendation 45
3. Quoted in Franklin, Matthew and Taylor, Paige, 'Kevin Rudd's take on mining tax backed by Colin Barnett', *The Australian*, March 7 2012
4. Richardson, Chris, 'Economists take issue with RSPT', *The Weekend Financial Review*, 5–6 June 2010
5. Professor Sinclair Davidson, 'RSPT: It's not really about economics', *Catallaxy Files* weblog, May 2010
6. Email dated Sunday, 13 June 2010 from Paul Binsted, Treasury Archive Documents
7. Quoted in Silmalis, Linda, 'Sick of playing the villain, Labor hardman Mark Arbib says his resignation hides "no bombshell, no affair, no execution"', *The Sunday Telegraph*, 4 March 2012

Chapter 9: The 'Traditional Owners' Fight Back

1. Toohey, Paul, 'Staking claim to shifting ground', *Inside Edition*, *The Daily Telegraph*, 26 June 2010
2. Howard, op cit., p. 646
3. Quoted in Howlett, Scott, 'Greens welcome Gillard but Asians "liked Rudd"', *The Northern District Times*, 30 June 2010
4. Stevenson, Andrew, 'A disaster of Labor's own making', *The Sydney Morning Herald*, 4 September 2010
5. Westen, op cit., p. 125
6. *White City Tennis Club Ltd v. John Alexander's Clubs Pty Ltd & Anor* [2009] NSWCA 114
7. Quoted in 'Maxine McKew warns John Alexander not to take Bennelong for granted', *The Sydney Morning Herald*, 17 December 2009
8. Bryant, Nick, 'The Battle for Bennelong: Round Two', *The Monthly*, July 2012
9. Quoted in ibid.
10. Interview, *Saturday Extra*, ABC Radio National, 21 August 2010
11. Quoted in Peatling, Stephanie, 'Maxine McWho', *The Sun Herald*, 15 November 2009

12. Dusevic, Tom, 'Whatever happened to the dragon slayer', *The Weekend Financial Review*, 8–9 August 2009

13. Harvey, Claire, 'Celebrities square up in Battle of Bennelong', *Sunday Agenda, The Sunday Telegraph*, 4 July 2010

14. Quoted in Penberthy, David, 'John's ghost haunts Maxine's voters', *The Daily Telegraph*, 29 July 2010

15. Murphy, Katharine, 'Beautiful speech, free of content', *The Sydney Morning Herald*, 9 August 2010

16. Megalogenis, George, 'Trivial Pursuit: Leadership and the end of the reformers', *Quarterly Essay 40*, Black Inc., 2010

Chapter 10: Back to Bennelong

1. Richardson, G., 'NSW Labor has lost its base, and the plot', *The Australian*, 30 March 2011

2. Transcript of Julia Gillard's interview with David Speers, Sky News, 9 May 2012

3. Gonski, David, *Review of Funding for Schooling, Final Report*, Department of Education, Employment and Workplace Relations, 2011, p. 120

4. Speech by Malcolm Turnbull at the launch of *Asia and the Pacific Policy Studies*, the journal of the Crawford School of Public Policy at the ANU, 20 July 2012

Chapter 11: A Torrent of Tears

1. The hanging of Ronald Ryan, a Pentridge escapee convicted of having shot dead warder George Hodson, marked the last state-sponsored execution in Australia.

2. Mathews, Race, 'Victoria's war against Whitlam', p. 114, quoted in Hocking, Jenny, *Gough Whitlam: A Moment in History*, Melbourne University Press, 2008, p. 357

3. Press conference by Julia Gillard, 27 February 2012

4. Silmalis, op. cit.

5. Quoted in Grattan, Michelle, 'Labor elder warns of torrent of tears', *The Age*, 21 February 2012

6. Quoted in Tingle, Laura, 'Gillard seeks to bury Rudd', *Australian Financial Review*, 24 February 2012

7. Statement by Wayne Swan, 22 February 2012

8. Quoted in Gordon, Michael, 'Two-challenge approach means even bigger risk', *The Age*, 21 February 2012

9. Marr, David, 'Power Trip: The political journey of Kevin Rudd', *Quarterly Essay 38*, Black Inc., 2010

10. Marr, David, 'Resurgent Rudd the man Canberra loves to hate', *The Sydney Morning Herald*, 20 February 2012